The Wave Maker

## *Dedication:*

*This book is dedicated to all the creative risk-takers in the universe.*

*You have made this world fun for the rest of us mortals.*

The Story of Theme Park Pioneer George Millay and the Creation of SeaWorld, Magic Mountain and Wet'n Wild

By **Tim O'Brien**

First Printing
ISBN: 1-893951-08-1
Library of Congress Control Number (LCCN): 2004095585

Editors: Edward Meyer/Anne Millay
Cover Photography: Dominique Brandt
Cover Design: Keith Wright
Text & Page Design: Keith Wright/Tim O'Brien
Flipbook whale artwork: Don Olea

For additional copies of The Wave Maker, see ordering information on Page 352 of this book, or go to: www.ripleys.com

# Acknowledgments

It wasn't hard finding people who wanted to talk about George Millay and to help me, in any way possible, put this project together. Below is a list of those who helped. Please forgive me if I left your name off the list. I'll thank you personally.

For taking time to talk with me about George, many thanks go to: George Becker, Mike Black, Larry Cochran, Gary Daning, Bob Gault, Ron Harper, John Hobbs, Errol McKoy, Anne Millay, Gar Millay, Gavin Millay, Pat Millay, Kym Murphy, Tom Powell, Harrison "Buzz" Price, Rick Root, Jan Schultz, John Seeker, John Shawen, Marty Sklar, Cleveland Smith, Don Stewart, David Tallichet, Marilyn Turner, Tom Vandergriff, Ira West, Stan Wilkes, and Gary Zuercher.

Thanks go out to Gary Slade of *Amusement Today* for the use of his archives, and to Sean Wood, reporter extraordinaire with the *Fort Worth Star-Telegram* for his research assistance.

Through the years, literally hundreds of photographs have been taken of George Millay. Most of the photos I found in the Millay archives and that appear in this book did not have the photographer's name attached. Photographers I could identify are: Ed Culwell, Ted Lau, and John Seeker, the official photographer for SeaWorld and Wet'n Wild for many years. To the rest of you, I apologize for not giving you proper credit. Thanks also go to Gina Lubrano of *The San Diego Union-Tribune* for the permission to use several of the early SeaWorld newspaper clippings.

Thanks to David Powell, for permission to use a George Millay excerpt from his book, "A Fascination for Fish" (University of California Press, 2001), and to Harrison Price for permission to use an excerpt from his book, "Walt's Revolution! By The Numbers" (Ripley Entertainment, 2003). A very special thank you goes out to my wife, Kathleen, my favorite critic, for helping me formulate ideas and for wading through and commenting on the early manuscripts. I couldn't have done it without your insight and support.

And of course, many sincere thanks go out to George Millay. First, for choosing me to be the one to write his wonderful story and secondly for his total cooperation during the often tedious times we spent in collaboration. Thanks George!

# Table of Contents

**Section Two: George's Personal Tributes & Accolades**

PROLOGUE

# Why A Book on George Millay?

It is entirely appropriate to write a book about George Millay and his creations for two very important reasons:

First of all, he was a seminal force in the revolution of attractions started by Walt Disney. George helped establish new concepts for systems-smart operating methods, clean environments, landscaped visitor ambience, environmental sensitivity, and an opportunity for the entire family to play together.

Secondly, he was (is) a very strong personage spiced with original wit and humor. He's something of a latter day, Irish version of Fred Allen, but a bit more caustic.

George believed from the start that he could create a marine park themed to the life forms of the sea in the manner and quality of Disneyland. He successfully did it and by the time he went onto his next dream, his SeaWorld parks were drawing upward of 10 million people annually. George did it with great respect for the mammalian life style.

He illustrated through education and contemporary habitats that mammals could benefit from and enjoy tactile contact with humans. SeaWorld programs showed that man and mammal could respect and learn from each other. It was a new form of entertainment, merging the best of show business and educational instruction.

In due time, after disagreements on construction budgets and constraints at SeaWorld Florida, George walked away from the company he created and took out his frustration by inventing an entirely new attraction form, the world's first interactive waterpark. Wet'n Wild had giant slides, meandering waterways and great wave machines. The world had seen nothing like this. Today, nearly 70 million people visit American waterparks each year.

Two new industry segments were born when others began to copy the SeaWorld and Wet'n Wild concepts. Both segments grew rapidly.

The life experience of George Millay warrants close examination, and that's what this book does. His story teaches us something about creative thinking in the development of new concepts and the application of innate skill in project execution. Both characterized his successful efforts to build new genres of entertainment. His two creations are now a part of the family entertainment landscape of the world.

People like George are not common. He belongs to a special cadre of those who dream, protagonists extraordinary, who have the genius to invent the new idea and make it work. George is in good company. Walt Disney with Disneyland, Angus Wynne with Six Flags, and August Busch with the Busch Gardens parks were all driven by the same creative genius as George. The group built their dreams with an uncompromising perfectionist instinct. They are reminiscent of a certain General named George S. Patton, whose style was expressed by the thought, "I'm coming through. Get out of the way or you're road-kill."

That is the nature of George Millay, the whimsical Irishman with the wry smile. He had an idea and he made it work. He then had another idea and he made that one work as well. Don't bother him, he would signal, unless you can help him do it. This was his method of operation -- and why this book is important. You need to read it to believe it!

***-Harrison "Buzz" Price, semi-retired pioneer consultant of theme park feasibility studies.***

INTRODUCTION

# Why You Need To Know George Millay

As a young college graduate in 1970, I landed a job as staff photographer for SeaWorld San Diego. I found out one thing real fast. Nothing they teach in school prepares you to work for such a dynamic and unusual personality as George Millay, the founder and president of SeaWorld.

I heard hundreds of stories about George during my first several weeks there, but had not met him. Then it happened.

One afternoon, there he was in the flesh, this 220-pound, redheaded Irishman. He stopped me and asked, "What's your name?" I said, "I am John Seeker, the new photographer." He said "Nice to meet you. Now get back to work."

He liked me because I fit the SeaWorld mold. I had a military-style haircut and I had shaved my mustache. I worked hard and long, I had fresh ideas, and I drove an American car.

I ended up working for George Millay longer than anyone else, for more than 25 years. My initial fear of the man turned to respect and admiration. I soon found that behind the rough and brash exterior, there was a deep and thoughtful man that truly cared about people.

He knew how to get the most out of his employees and always seemed to know just how far he could push without us breaking. George was manipulative, but he felt it was for the better of the individual and ultimately the company.

George also knew that to be successful, he needed to surround himself with talented people that he trusted. Lie to him and you might as well kiss your ass goodbye. Tell the truth and you might get a good verbal whipping, but through it all, once you had his trust, you usually kept it.

He was fiercely loyal. If you were honest and hard working, George would do anything for you. To George, you were part of the family. To many of us, he was a father figure.

George was a hard driving entrepreneur who through the

years gave back much more than he ever took. He always saw things differently than the rest of us. He saw the big picture. He was living as much in the future as in the present. Yes, I would call him a visionary.

People always ask me how I could have worked and put up with George for 25 years. The answer is simple. They didn't know the same George as I did. He's like a turtle - hard shell with a tender and vulnerable underside. Penetrate the shell and see the real George.

That's what this book is all about. For the first time ever, a book has penetrated the outer shell and shows the side of George Millay that few of us have been honored to know. Everyday I thank God that I was lucky enough to work for and learn from him. I am a better person because of him. He is one in a million! Thanks, Chief!

***-John Seeker, a George Millay Veteran, is now with MARC USA Advertising, Dallas.***

FOREWORD

# Writing the Book on George Millay

I've been eager to write the story of George Millay for nearly a decade. I felt his was a story that needed telling. Here's a man who created two magnificent, totally different genres of outdoor recreation over a 40 year period, but he would never sit down and talk about those experiences beyond a cursory glance.

Whenever we would talk about me writing his biography, he would say he wasn't ready to tell the whole story. He didn't want this book to be written until he was prepared to bare everything and tell the complete, unabridged story.

In October 2003, George called and said he was ready to talk. Boy, did we talk. Countless hours in person, countless hours by phone. What a wonderfully candid story he told. I approached this project with a guarantee from him that he would hold nothing back. I wanted him to talk about anything and everything as it pertained to his life and career. He appears to have kept his word. Not a question went unanswered.

We talked about his incredible successes and about his family. We delved into subjects ranging from his life-long prejudices to the actions that caused his fall from grace at SeaWorld and the events that led up to his resignation. We talked about his unique management-by-intimidation style and about how disappointed he would become when his employees didn't live up to their potentials.

From a historical and business perspective, most of what he reveals here has never been in print before. He openly speaks of revenue and attendance figures; he recalls bringing home his first million-dollar check; and he talks about the capital-raising challenges of every project in which he has been associated, topics he has never openly discussed with anyone but his closest confidants.

George spoke candidly of his home life, of his parents, of his emotions and feelings. He spoke of his bouts with cancer that have caused the right side of his face to be disfigured. Speaking with George is a joy. He is bright, articulate and has the vocabulary and style of a voracious reader, which he is.

In researching this book, I spoke with dozens of those who have worked for him. What fun, first-hand color they provided to this story! They related tales of George's loyalty, of his generosity, of his brash and most often politically incorrect actions. Most importantly, they spoke of their love and respect for the man, once their initial fear of him subsided. They spoke of his ability to lose anything and everything, and of his love for classical music.

I read practically every story ever written about him. Days were spent perusing box after box of clippings, photos, and memorabilia from his 40 years of SeaWorld and Wet'n Wild experiences.

Those who have known and worked for him will undoubtedly be pleasantly surprised to discover new things about the man. His wife Anne, upon reading the manuscript told me she learned a couple new things about her husband of more than 40 years.

I don't think I could have lasted 15 minutes working for the "old" George. I appreciate his new, mellowed state. His earlier style was certainly not one I would have tolerated. But to be fair, with my penchant for long hair, I don't think he would have hired me in the first place. His loathing of long hair and alternative life styles is notorious. We joked many times during the past year how ironic it was that after years of not allowing anyone with less than a military style haircut to even talk to him, that he would end up with a pony-tailed, ear-ringed writer as his biographer.

I think I can speak for both of us when I say this has been a fun, rewarding experience. After working together all these months on his story, I can truly say I am lucky, one of a few to really get to know and love this mellowed, but far from worn out, man who claims to be George Millay.

### *About this Book*

What started out to be a biography of George Millay turned into a much larger project. The "Wave Maker" is not only the official story of George, but it's the first book to chronicle, in-depth, the early history of SeaWorld, Magic Mountain and Wet'n Wild.

The "Wave Maker" goes way beyond George. It includes the people, the events, the challenges and the successes that went along with creating the first of their genre of attractions. George Millay was the force behind the creations; but those who worked for him were pioneers in their own right.

It's important to remember that this was all new ground these professionals treaded upon. The sales and marketing, the operations, the ticketing, the marine trainers, and the ride builders - they were all doing something that had never been done before. They had no roadmaps. They were trailblazers who set many of the standards still in use today.

Many of those early pioneers were interviewed for this book, and George spoke of the important roles each played during his career. They were instrumental in the creation and the early growth of the parks and deserve a rightful mention in any history of their industry.

***-Tim O'Brien, author, is VP Publishing & Communications, Ripley Entertainment, Inc.***

You hold in your hands an
interactive biography! Turn the book sideways,
flip the pages and watch Shamu jump!

- CHAPTER 1 -

# The Early Years

It was a typical, balmy Hawaiian morning. The sun was rising slowly above the mountains to the east and all seemed to be at peace. Twelve-year-old George Millay, walking along a promontory overlooking Pearl Harbor and Battleship Row, was on his way to set up an altar for Sunday Mass at Block Arena. Suddenly he heard strange booms. He saw smoke rising from Hickman Field and saw unfamiliar planes flying low. It was 7:25 a.m. on December 7, 1941.

George was witness to the USS Arizona blowing up. He saw the USS Oklahoma get hit by a torpedo and roll over and he watched as the dry-docked USS Pennsylvania went up in flames. The confused and frightened young man rushed home.

William Paul Millay, his father, a career Navy man, had already reported to his battle station by the time George reached home. That night, fear gripped the Naval housing complex in which he lived. He slept under a mattress up against a concrete block wall with his loaded BB-gun by his side. The attack and the days immediately following are the most vivid, the most significant memories of George's life.

Nearly 65 years later, George claims, "The bombing instilled a deep sense of mistrust, even hatred, for the Japanese. That mistrust has mellowed over the years and I've gained an admiration for their culture and organizational skills."

George and his family survived Pearl Harbor unscathed, and following high school, he would follow in his father's footsteps and serve in the U.S. Navy. He graduated from UCLA and later made his first million dollars in the restaurant business. In 1964, he created the SeaWorld marine park chain and in 1977 conceived Wet'n Wild, the world's first waterpark.

Through the years, he had many successful business dealings with the Japanese and spent a great deal of time in that country.

### *Little George Joins the Party*

George Daniel Millay was born in San Diego on July 4, 1929 at 11 p.m., a true Yankee Doodle Dandy by anybody's standards. His mother, Elizabeth Anna Brannigan, was an Irish immigrant from County Monaghan who had come to the U.S. in 1924 with her family to become a housemaid for a wealthy San Diego family.

William Paul Millay, his father was born in Columbus, Ohio and was a World War I Navy veteran. He was a first class petty officer stationed in San Diego when little George was born.

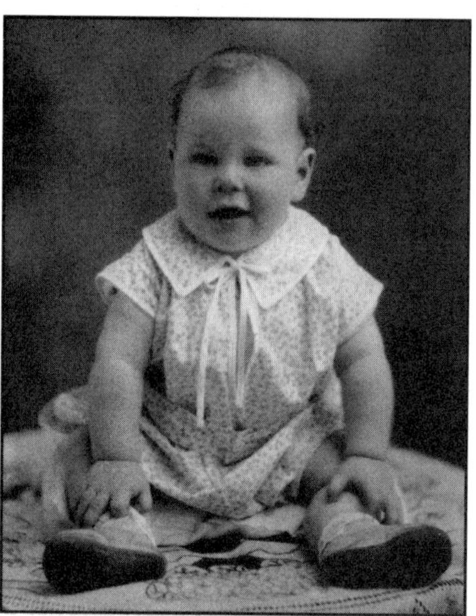
*George Millay, 1930*

"I think I caused everyone to miss the fireworks that night," George laughs. He was born at Mercy Hospital, where many years later, all four of his own children would be born.

At the time of George's birth, his father was stationed on a military personnel ship. He had been a fireman on a wooden minesweeper in the North Sea during World War I and following the war stayed in the Navy.

In San Diego, the Millay family lived at 2115 Eber Street in Ocean Beach, a house that still stands. He went to kindergarten and the first grade at Ocean Beach Grammar School. Given that his father was at sea so much, his mother decided in 1935 to move the family to San Francisco to be closer to her family. At first they stayed with his grandmother but soon moved into their own rental in the Richmond District. George and his brother Bud went to St. Monica's Grammar School, a predominantly Irish-Italian school, run by Irish-American nuns, a group of women who George describes as "fantastic, dedicated women."

George claims he was a "very average student, kind of a livewire, wild hair, a red-headed Irishman." His middle name is Daniel and his immediate family called him Dan. He was Red to most of his friends.

His mother was "the tough one of the family, " he recalls.

"She was a little toughie. I was afraid of her until the day I walked out of her house to marry Anne in 1963. I was 33 and making $125,000 a year. I wouldn't turn my back to her when she was really, really pissed. She would whack me with anything she had in her hand but she had a heart of gold."

His father was an easygoing kind of a guy. According to George, the worst his dad ever said to him was, "Mend your ways, boy. Mend your ways. Dan, I don't necessarily want to be happy in this world; I just don't want to be unhappy and Dan, right now you're making me unhappy." George recalls his father as a man with "quite a sense of humor who could tell a good story."

**George On God**
*Sometimes I wonder why God loves mankind so much - mankind doesn't show too much promise to me. But far be it for any human to question God's will.*
*- George Millay*

Religion played a major part in his upbringing and he became a true believer. "Life doesn't make much sense if you can't subscribe to the existence of a higher being. A being that loves you and has asked you to live according to His wishes. Catholicism was drilled into me by my devout mother and by many Jesuits during my elementary and high school days. For many years, it was a belief totally out of fear. Now it is one of both love and fear," George says, adding that he strongly believes in the teaching that the "fear of the Lord is the first step toward wisdom."

Throughout his illustrious career, many of those who worked for George might modify that expression to "Fear of George is the first step toward job security."

George thinks the biggest puzzle in his faith is not the trinity or transubstantiation but the answer to "why the Father would ask the Son to come to earth, take human form and suffer excruciating pain, humiliation, and crucifixion for mankind? That's the mystery to me." George still laughs at Bill Buckley's statement made a few years ago on TV. Buckley was confronted with the statement from an adversary that, "Christianity is a failure." Buckley retorted, "How can you say that when nobody has ever tried it."

## *Danger: No Lifeguard on Duty*

The sea played an important part in the early life of the little boy who would grow up to make millions of dollars from water-related attractions. George was a self-proclaimed "dare devil" around water, always pushing the boundaries. One of his earliest treks to the beach was nearly a disastrous one. He came close to drowning in San Diego's Mission Bay when he was five years old.

"I couldn't swim and I'd tiptoe out until the water came up to my nose. One day I went too far and got knocked off my feet. Luckily the wave pushed me to shallow water and I was able to get back on my feet. My mother didn't even know. She was on the beach talking to some girls and I damn near drowned." He doesn't recall much about the actual incident but knows that it "obviously didn't make me wary of water."

George's love affair with the ocean began at China Beach, near the Golden Gate Bridge in San Francisco. The historical beach area received its name when it served as a landing area and campsite for Chinese fisherman and railroad workers during the mid-19th century. "That's where I learned how to swim in cold, rough water. It was the place where all the local kids went to go swimming."

*The Millay family is seen enjoying their Pearl Harbor home, eight months before the 1941 bombings. From left, are Bud, Anna, Paul, and George.*

In 1938, after serving for 21 years, William retired from the Navy as a chief petty officer and went to work for Bethlehem Steel Company building ships at the shipyards in San Francisco. Things were going well for the Millay family. Father wasn't traveling and had a good-paying job along with a Navy pension.

In mid-1940, he was called back into the Navy and shipped off to Pearl Harbor.

His family went with him and they lived on the base in military housing until February 1942, three months after the Japanese attack.

George recalls December 7. "My grandmother had just arrived the day before from San Francisco to spend some time with us. She had never been to Hawaii and was excited to see the Islands and be with her family. She and my mother were both terrified during and after the attack, but pitched in to help in any way possible. For about a week some of the wounded were taken to Block Arena because all the hospitals were crowded. We went down and did anything we could do to make the young guys comfortable. I had plenty of time, because there was no school until after Christmas."

### *The Blacked Robe Jebbies*

In February 1942, families of naval personnel were sent back to the United States. George recalls the trip. "We came back in a big convoy. There were 10 or 12 transports and there were a couple of destroyers and a big cruiser escorting us. We returned to San Diego and then went back to San Francisco by train."

Several months after he and his family returned to San Francisco, George and Bud were accepted into St. Ignatius High School, an all-boys Jesuit institution. He had every intention of becoming a star on the football team. He knew he couldn't excel at the sport, but wanted to play anyway. The curriculum at the school was classical and George fared well at Latin and reasonably well at trigonometry, solid geometry and history and not very well at chemistry and physics.

Despite his lack of ability, George played first-string football and first-string baseball at St Ignatius. He turned out to be a better baseball player than football player. "I wasn't coachable in football. I was a scatterbrain and a wise ass and wasn't disciplined enough to blend in with the team. I was a good defensive back because they can roam around back there and play with a gut instinct. I was probably the best tackler on the team because I liked to hit people, but overall, I wasn't a good football player." He recalls that he once tackled Ollie Matson, a running back who went on to play in the National Football League for 14 years, "and almost broke my ribs."

Sports and "goofing around" were his two favorite pastimes while in high school. On the other hand, he was a bust with girls, having only two or three dates while in school. "No one in our crowd was a ladies' men. We all had to scrounge around for a date."

His brother Bud, 13 months younger than George, was the social sibling. They went to the same high school but Bud ran with a different, "much cooler" crowd than George did. "Now, there was a ladies' man! He had women coming out his ears," the older brother bragged.

*William Paul and Elizabeth Anna Millay with sons George, left, and Bud, at home in San Francisco, 1944.*

The two were friendly but never close until later in life. "We became closer as the years went by. We never ran in the same crowd even when we were in the same fraternity at UCLA. He went into the Navy a year after I did."

While in high school, George didn't fare very well at a couple of part time jobs. "I got a job at a food processing plant and my duty was to disembowel dead chickens. I spent two days there and couldn't take any more." Another short-lived career was his clerking job at a military store. "The chief petty officer I reported to didn't give a damn about my religious beliefs. The store sold condoms and I kept telling him it wasn't proper to be selling them. I kept harping on the issue until he eventually kicked my butt out of there."

George didn't know what he wanted to do after he graduated from high school but realized that he wasn't emotionally or psychologically ready for college. Even though his father was a career Navy man, he never pushed George or Bud to join the Navy. The spring George graduated from high school, his dad was in the hospital recovering from a heart attack.

"I visited the hospital to see him with my mother and told him that since I didn't know what to do, I was thinking of joining the Marine Corp. He said, 'No, you're not. I want you to join the Navy.' So I joined the Navy."

### *The Sailor Boy*

George enlisted during mid-July 1947 and went to San Diego for boot camp. From there, he was sent to aviation school in Jacksonville, Florida. During the 10-week course there, he was taught the rudiments of aviation and the broad scope of naval aviation. All the recruits took an aptitude test and the smartest of the lot, including George, were weeded out and sent either to a control tower operator school or naval aerographer school, a weather academy, in Lakehurst, New Jersey. Lakehurst was famous for the

*George Millay, standing fifth from right, on the deck of the USS Bairoko, 1949.*

Hindenburg airship tragedy that killed 36 people, 10 years before George arrived.

After completing the four-month course at Lakehurst, George was sent back to San Diego to Fleet Weather Central, which covered the entire Eastern Pacific and where he soon made third-class petty officer. In 1949 he transferred to the USS Bairoko, a CVE-115 anti-submarine warfare carrier as part of the weather detachment.

George recalls a funny story that took place on the Bairoko. "Every morning when I was on duty I'd take the weather forecast up to the old man. He'd be in his quarters having breakfast and he was quite a character. He would say, 'Oh, here's the weather guesser today.' He'd grab it out of my hand, crumble it up and throw it in the wastepaper basket. 'That's what I think of you weather guessers.' He had a little Filipino mess boy who I became friendly with. His name was Malabana and he was a fun little guy. The old man would chew Malabana's ass off and constantly complain about everything. Malabana used to get mad and he'd run back to where he prepared the meals. He'd grab the captain's soup and he'd spit in it and then he'd bring it out to the captain with a big smile and he'd say, 'Here's your soup, captain sir.' It was very funny."

Even though he was accustomed to being around water and had spent a great deal of time on ships and boats as a child, George would get seasick every time the ship would hit rough weather, "which was about a third of the time," he recalls. "I was totally seasick. When I was on duty I was vomiting all over the place. Nobody cared how sick you were, and you were expected to man your duty station sick or not. Fortunately, I was only on that ship about seven or eight months and then she went out of commission."

He then transferred to Whidbey Island, at the tip of Puget Sound in Washington and from there he was discharged on May 20, 1950. President Truman was cutting costs and anyone who wanted to get out of the Navy three months early could. George applied and was accepted.

His discharge came three weeks before the Korean War started. "I had every intention of joining the reserves to earn extra money to help pay for college, but of course when the war broke out, I decided against it."

- CHAPTER 2 -

# George Becomes a Bruin & Gets His First Job

George came home from the Navy knowing it was time to commit to college and focus on a career. His creation of SeaWorld and Wet'n Wild was still more than a decade away.

"I started wising up while I was in the Navy. It didn't take long to realize that the guys who had the best quarters, the best food, the best uniforms, could come and go when they pleased, and worked the least, were the officers. The guys who had the worst food, the worst pay and the worst quarters were the enlisted men. What's the difference between the enlisted men and the officers? A college education," mulled George. "Even for a dummy, I got it!"

*George Millay, center, and two of his UCLA fraternity brothers ham it up during the Moonshiners Brawl, fall 1952.*

When he was at Fleet Weather Central in San Diego, he thought highly of a couple officers who were aerologists, both well-educated gentlemen. "I thought I'd like to be like them. They had gone through the Naval School of Aerology in Monterey, California. I decided when I got out I'd go to college and study to be a weatherman. I liked being a meteorologist in the Navy. It was a good job."

George decided to attend UCLA because it was the only university on the West Coast that offered a degree in meteorology. Upon returning to San Francisco after his Naval stint, he was determined to get his collegiate feet wet as soon as possible and enrolled for the summer session at San Francisco City College, a junior college. He stayed there for a year and matriculated to UCLA in early 1952 from which he graduated in 1955 with a degree in meteorology.

### *Hard to Forecast*

Things went well academically, but he ran into a last minute snag concerning his curriculum. During his senior year he realized he didn't want to be a meteorologist. He couldn't decide what he wanted to do, but he was sure he didn't want to change majors and start all over again, so he continued on the same track and received his degree in meteorology.

During college, he was the UCLA intramural handball champion and was a light heavyweight on the UCLA boxing team in 1953 when he won five bouts and lost just one. The school dropped the sport in 1954, "Lucky for me," he says. He joined the Phi Kappa Sigma fraternity.

He occasionally looks back at those fraternity years and while he says they were important, formative years for him, they were also "very detrimental" to his studies. "I did reasonably well academically until I pledged the fraternity and then my grades started to decline because it was one big circus in the fraternity," he admitted. "It was great fun and there were unlimited supplies of booze, broads, and horseplay."

Even before he decided against being a weatherman, George had questions concerning what he wanted out of life. "You don't have any money during college but you don't care. You can do without cash when you're 22 and still be happy. I was going through life on a lark and having a good time in school. I played a great deal of handball," he said.

He worked three different jobs during college. His parents paid a portion of his tuition and helped him financially, but he earned his own spending money. He missed being eligible for the GI Bill that would have paid his tuition, by two weeks.

George's first college part-time job was in Santa Monica

at Hoover Electric, where he worked in the stockroom at night for 18 months. He calls his next job an unexpected gift. It was on campus with the Air Pollution Foundation of Los Angeles studying air currents and the Los Angeles climatology. "We'd draw maps and trace where smog began, where it ended, where it went." It was good job and he was paid $3 an hour, lucrative part-time money for those days. That job lasted for little more than a year until funding ran out.

***The Trucker Boy***

His entrepreneurial spirit came alive for the first time when he ventured into the dump truck business during his senior year at UCLA. He met a guy who was selling a dump truck and with a loan from his father, bought it for $300. The truck owner said, "Red, you're gonna make loads of money." His name was Cooley. "He was a crazy bastard. He said if I bought the truck, he'd get me some work." Based on that promise, Red Millay went into the trucking business, picking up trash from construction and demolition sites around Los Angeles.

George learned the business of trucking, but knew little when it came to maintaining old trucks. He discovered that his fraternity brother, Dick Tatus, was a good mechanic and George partnered with him to form Miltate Dump Truck Company. George marketed the business and hired the help and Tatus kept the trucks running. If Tatus needed a few extra bucks, he would

*The vehicle that put George Millay into the dump truck business, 1955.*

work a few job sites, in addition to his mechanic duties.

Tatus recalls one of the earlier jobs in which he and George decided to work themselves. It shows George's budding management savvy. "It was hotter than hell. My partner (George) is standing on top and I'm on the ground tossing old cement bags and trash into the truck," Tatus said, adding that he soon asked George for a bit of help on the ground.

"How about helping me toss up some of this stuff?" Tatus yelled. "Dick, I have to be up here to redirect the trash to fill the truck better and I have to pack the load," replied George. "I'm heavier than you and I pack the load better."

They were getting $50 for the job, and Tatus was expecting $25. "You don't mind if we split the take differently today, do you? I need some extra money for a big date tonight," asked George, as he handed Tatus $5. "Yes, I was surprised, but looking back, I probably was lucky he didn't keep it all," laughed Tatus.

Business was going well, and it just so happened that Cooley had a second truck he wanted to sell, and George took it off his hands. He hired fraternity brothers and paid them $20 to clean up a site, while he was charging the customer $100 to $150 for the job. "I did very well. The last year of college I had lots of money in my pocket. I was Mr. Big Time and I actually considered staying in the trucking business."

### *Meet Uncle Miltie*

Little could he know that it was during those years at UCLA that he would meet the three men who would later change and in many ways, shape his entire career path. They became partners with him in the creation of SeaWorld, the world's first modern, themed marine park, and the success of that park served as the impetus for his other successful creation, Wet'n Wild, the world's first waterpark.

One of those men was the fraternity's advisor, Milton Shedd. He was in his late 30's and was a fairly successful stockbroker at Dempsey-Tegler, a major west coast over-the-counter stock house. He and George became friendly and would often talk when Shedd visited the fraternity house each month to advise the brothers.

One day Shedd told George he should think about going into the securities business when he graduated. "Hell, I didn't know a stock from a municipal bond from a mutual fund to a warrant. He told me I was a good salesman, that I was presentable and that I could make a good living in the securities business." Nothing else was said about that career path until several months later.

George graduated and spent the summer of 1955 raking in good money from his trucking business. "I was bringing in a couple hundred dollars a day which was great money then."

He holds the distinction of being the first true entrepreneur in the Millay clan, but he didn't set out to be his own boss. After graduation, he was faced with the monumental question once again. "Now, what am I going to do?" He did some soul-searching and gave up his trucking business. George sold his two trucks and Tatus went off to law school.

Toward the end of that post-college summer, George called Shedd and told him he wanted to take him up on his offer. Shedd put him in touch with Lou Whitney, one of the partners of the company. At first Whitney shunned George, but after a dozen or so phone calls, Whitney was convinced that George was serious and hired him. But plans changed.

"He called me a couple of days before I was to start and said he had another job for me, one that I would like better." He introduced George to a man named Rufus Carter, the West Coast representative of National Securities and Research Corporation, a successful mutual fund company. "He hired me for $700 a month and I didn't know what a mutual fund was. I was to cover the West Coast trying to entice brokers to use our funds."

It didn't take long before reports started getting back to headquarters that George didn't know what he was talking about and that he was a little too aggressive. "When a guy wouldn't buy

GEORGE D. MILLAY

PAINE, WEBBER, JACKSON & CURTIS
FOUNDED 1879
MEMBERS NEW YORK STOCK EXCHANGE

LOCUST AT FOURTH
LONG BEACH 12, CALIFORNIA
HEMLOCK 2-4401

our funds, I would get pissed and challenge him and I guess I was a little too overpowering."

George was sent to New York for more training. "I was there three days and they called up Rufus and told him to get rid of this clown. These brokers had been in business for 25 or 30 years and I was just out of college. It was plain that I wasn't going to pull any wool over their eyes and they knew 50 billion times more about the fund than I did."

They fired him and sent him back to Los Angeles, saying he shouldn't have been hired in the first place. "I went in to see Rufus and God love him, he handed me a check for $1,400, which was two months' salary, and apologized for the entire thing. It was my first job out of college and I got fired and I was crushed."

Lou Whitney heard about it and offered him the job he had intended for George in the first place. He went to work immediately for Dempsey-Tegler. "I went to Long Beach in 1956 and started from scratch being a stockbroker. I had no customers, no clients. I didn't know my ass from third base about the stock and bond business but I soon found that most of the guys there didn't know anything either. As long as you're one step ahead of the customer, you're doing all right. I was moderately successful."

**Presidential Choices**
*James K. Polk has been our best president; Bill Clinton, the worst.*
*- George Millay*

### *A Meeting with Dame Fortune*

It was another routine day of cold calling, when George called David Tallichet, the person who he refers to as his mentor; the person instrumental in helping him make his first million. That million however, didn't come from the stock market. It came from the restaurant business.

Tallichet was the young manager of the Conrad Hilton-owned Lafayette Hotel in Long Beach, one of the two principal hotels in the city at the time. "I called him cold and we started talking and I tried to sell him some securities." Tallichet told him, "I don't have any money right now, George. I'm up to here in debt." But he told George to keep in touch and to call if "anything really good" came along.

The Miss Universe pageant was held in Long Beach at the

time, and Tallichet's hotel was host to the contest. Several months after that first call to Tallichet, the girls came to town and George had gotten a glimpse of Miss Colorado on television and wanted to meet her. He called Tallichet who arranged for him to sit next to her during a luncheon. From then on, George and Tallichet were friends. George doesn't recall what happened with Miss Colorado. At least, he's not admitting to anything.

The 35-year old Tallichet had never been married and George was single and 28. The two found they had much in common. Meanwhile, George had switched firms and was working for Paine Webber and doing fairly well.

*George Millay, 1963.*

At a beach party about a year later, Tallichet confided to George that he was tired of working for Mr. Hilton and wanted to go out on his own, but he didn't have the money to do it. George assured him that money could always be raised for a good project, but nothing more was said at that time. That short conversation, however, sowed the seeds for Specialty Restaurant Corporation, a highly successful restaurant chain that lasted into the 1980s. It's also interesting to note that if it weren't for his successful relationship with Tallichet, SeaWorld and Wet'n Wild would probably never have been built.

***Let's Just do it!***

Tallichet remembers the day they decided to get into the restaurant business. "We started realizing that neither one of us was going to get very far with our current business careers and that we ought to go into business for ourselves. George was a stockbroker and that's about all he knew and all I knew was from the hotel business - rooms, food, and beverage. We figured we couldn't get enough money to buy a hotel so we decided we'd try to build a restaurant," Tallichet said.

George recalls how he got the ball rolling in early 1957

for what was to be the Reef Restaurant. One Sunday afternoon three months after the two had that conversation; George called Tallichet and suggested they go look for a restaurant site. "We crossed the bridge over the Los Angeles River to Terminal Island. I wanted to head north toward L.A. but Dave made a left turn and we headed into the Port of Long Beach. We wound up out on a point at the edge of the harbor looking back on Long Beach. It's a magnificent view of the city and we were both awestruck. I told him if he could get a lease for that land, I'd get the money."

Tallichet knew Charles Vickers, the port manager and had no problem negotiating a lease. George raised the $135,000 needed and the 4,000 square-foot, Hawaiian-themed Reef Restaurant opened on that spot in August 1958. Tallichet notes the Island atmosphere kept them alive "until we finally got around to serving good food." George speculates it would cost $2 million today to build a restaurant of that size and scope.

"I told George later in life that if I had not associated with him at that moment I probably would have never gone into business for myself. I might have just worked for Hilton the rest of my life," Tallichet observed. "I was fortunate to get involved with a guy who pushed me and shared my desire to do something. His enthusiasm and his ability to turn ideas into reality made a huge difference in my life."

Raising money to develop the Reef Restaurant was George's first personal crusade to raise funds for a dream. Neither George nor Tallichet had any money. George sold two of his best customers, Nevan Von Rohr and John Czinger, on the deal and they put in $35,000 each. Tallichet recruited Red Ellison, a third investor, who was

**Conservative Thinker**

*I really don't recall if I was ever a bonified member of the John Birch Society, but I subscribed to most of their thinking and financially supported the organization from time to time. I have never been much of a joiner. I stupidly quit the San Diego Downtown Rotary after three months and I never joined any church organizations. I was too busy with all my various enterprises around the Western Hemisphere. I chose to spend all my free time with my wife, sons, and daughter.*

*- George Millay*

West Coast VP of the Hilton Hotel Corporation. Tallichet also brought a contractor, Ed Simpkins into the deal. When the Reef opened, there were six owners: George's two clients, Von Rohr and Czinger owned 45% between them, and Ed Simpkins and Red Ellison each owned 10%. For putting the deal together, Tallichet got 25% and George received 10%.

Now known for his amazing vision and creative innovation, George says the building of the Reef Restaurant was the first true test of those skills. "I truly feel that helping in the planning of that restaurant was the kindergarten of a life of creativity," he waxes. "To this day, I think meeting Dave Tallichet was the luckiest thing that has ever happened to me in business."

### *Sweet Smell of Success*

The Reef was a success from the day it opened. "I was a big man for the first time in my life. The restaurant was cranking out great salaries and huge profits for more than 12 years. I took a $25,000 salary and didn't do a thing. Tallichet took a $35,000 salary and didn't do a thing except watch over the manager. Ellison took a $12,000 salary."

Neither George nor Tallichet quit their day jobs and Tallichet began almost immediately to hunt for another restaurant site, which created a problem among ownership. It wasn't

**George the Maitre d'**

*A year or so after the Reef opened I got it into my head that I wanted to be a maitre d'. I went to Dave (Tallichet) and I said Dave, let me be the maitre d' on Friday and Saturday nights. I don't want any more money, I just want to do it. He says OK. I went out and bought a beautiful white suit and white shoes and I showed up the first night ready to roll. I screwed up that restaurant so bad the hostess started crying and wanted to quit. The chef was pissed and several customers complained of long waits. On Monday, the manager called Tallichet to complain. Tallichet then called me and told me that he could hire a dozen maitres d' that afternoon because they were a dime a dozen. He told me I should stick with what I know and to go out and put a deal together and make some money. So I did.*

*- George Millay*

long before Von Rohr and Czinger got upset with Tallichet for not paying enough attention to the running of the business, even though it remained a goldmine for those investors. The two, who owned a collective 45% visited George and asked for support and a proxy for his 10% of stock, which, when combined with theirs, would be enough to vote Tallichet out of the business.

"The restaurant was doing just fine, but I felt I had a moral obligation to these two guys. I had brought them in and they trusted me." George signed a proxy agreement giving them his deciding vote and in essence, control of the entire company. "As we kept chatting, I realized I had made a rash move and told them so," George notes. To appease his apprehension, Czinger hand wrote at the bottom of the proxy that it was revocable on 60 days written notice. He signed his name to the addendum.

***Turbulence at the Reef***

Tallichet was voted out and within a few months the profits at the Reef began to slip without him overseeing the operation. Needless to say, the relationship between Tallichet and George became quite cold. It wasn't long before Von Rohr called George and offered $10,000 for his 10%. At that point, George realized he was in the catbird seat with the deciding vote and that he had better keep a close eye on Von Rohr and Czinger.

Three months later, George went back to Tallichet, who still owned 25% of the business, expressed his concerns and started the movement to get Tallichet back in as president of the company. "When I went back, he was quite cold toward me, but of course he warmed up damn fast when I told him I was going to get him back in, which I did at the next board meeting. We've been friends ever since."

A month after reinstating Tallichet, George read in the morning newspaper that Czinger and Von Rohr were suing him for reneging on a deal and for forging Czinger's signature on the proxy. They weren't just suing George; they also had included Paine Webber in the $800,000 lawsuit.

George hired Fred Mahl, a Los Angeles attorney to represent him and investigative due diligence began. Czinger's main case was that George had signed the option and had forged Czinger's signature on the cancellation agreement. "I had forgotten all about that addendum and then remembered that he signed a disclaimer on that option at my request."

The document was presented as evidence at the first hearing and Czinger claimed it was a forgery. George recalls the predicament. "I was caught between the devil and the deep blue sea. My job at Paine Webber was in jeopardy, the restaurant was in jeopardy, and I was being accused of forgery." His attorneys took the document to the same handwriting expert who had cracked the Lindbergh case in 1933 and they proved that it was not a forgery. The lawsuit was dropped.

Shortly thereafter, George and Tallichet bought Czinger and Von Rohr out for $100,000 each. Simpkins was bought out as well. The Reef was then owned by George with 35%, Tallichet with 45%, and Ellison with 20%.

Tallichet recalls that George has three qualities that always set him apart from the others. "George associated with smart people. He hired smart people and he was smart enough to hire top-notch consultants when he realized he needed additional input. He combined his natural smarts with huge ambition and on top of all that, he was a creative thinker. He did very well for himself and for whoever he associated with," Tallichet said. "Those things not only helped us create the Reef, but they served him well for the rest of his career."

### *Meet George's Dream Girl*

Anne Reul began dating George on a casual basis in early 1958 as he was putting the finishing touches on the Reef Restaurant. She remembers planting a few palm trees outside the restaurant and showing up at the opening in her Polynesian outfit.

While they were dating, but before moving permanently to San Diego to work on SeaWorld, George would drive down from Long Beach, sometimes several times a week. He was still working for Paine Webber and was still involved in the Reef Restaurant.

On one of those trips, he invited Anne to ride along. "On the way home, we started talking about the park and that he would soon be moving to San Diego. That meant we would have a long distance relationship," Anne said. "Neither of us wanted that, so we decided we would get married. I would end my teaching career and we would move to San Diego together." They married in 1963, a year before SeaWorld opened.

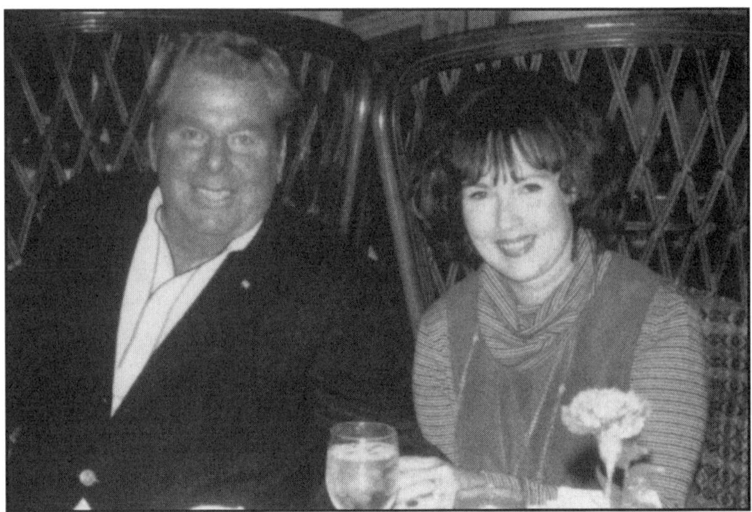

*George Millay and Anne Reul are seen enjoying their date at the Coconut Grove, in Los Angeles, 1961.*

### *Tallichet University*

The Tallichet era served as graduate school for George and prepared him nicely for the SeaWorld journey. He began to hone his business acumen and learn skills that would lead him to success throughout his life. "During the time I spent with Dave, I learned the skills needed to approach bankers and to make a deal. He taught me how to work with city managers and commissioners and he taught me the skills of being a promoter and developer."

In 1963, by the time George started severing ties with Tallichet, there were 12 restaurants in the Specialty Restaurants family, but George only had a piece of four of them.

"I was always a number two man to Dave, but he was smarter and mentally tougher than I was, and I just had to get away from him," George said. "Although I admired and respected him, I wanted to be on my own and I knew at Specialty Restaurants that would never happen. It wasn't anything personal; I just didn't want to spend my life shadowing Dave Tallichet, even though he was a close friend. Dave is one of a kind."

When George left Tallichet's tutelage to build SeaWorld, he was the second largest stockholder in the restaurant company. He remained so until Specialty Restaurants went public in 1968. George sold his stock for approximately $3.2 million, and after taxes, he was able to stick $1.8 million in his pockets.

- CHAPTER 3 -

# George's First Really Big Pay Day

SeaWorld opened in 1964, and George kept his stock in Specialty Restaurants until 1968 when he officially became a millionaire for the first time.

"My first big score in life came from Specialty Restaurants' initial offering. I brought home a check for nearly $2 million. We closed at the headquarters of Bank of California and I couldn't believe my good fortune. Flying back to San Diego that night I kept pulling out the check and staring at it."

He rushed home from the airport and showed Anne the check. She was shocked and could only gasp four words: "Nice going, Big Red!" She took a picture of him holding the check and they toasted to their good fortunes.

With more than ample money for the first time in his life, George reveals that he still didn't think he had it made. "No one truly has it made. Life may be a little more comfortable but all the more reason to just keep punching and doing what you do best."

*George Millay holds up a $1.8 million check. His first million dollar check, 1968.*

He received that big payoff early in 1968, several months before SeaWorld's first public offering took place. He took home a handsome seven-digit paycheck from that offering as well. George and Anne designed and built the Riviera West Apartments and their spacious penthouse home overlooking Mission Bay, in which they still live, with the proceeds from the SeaWorld and Specialty Restaurants offerings.

- CHAPTER 4 -

# The SeaWorld Idea Gets Roots

In early 1961, while George was still very involved in the Reef Restaurant, he started thinking about building a submarine bar at the restaurant. A person would walk out on the patio of the restaurant, get on an escalator, ride through an acrylic tunnel under water and come out into a submerged capsule, which was anchored to the ocean floor. People would sit there, look out through the large windows and watch fish as they swam around, trapped by a system of nets. Basically, it would have been an underwater aquarium at the bottom of the bay.

George went to Tallichet with the idea. "I think he thought I was nuts, but he humored me by giving me a $2,000 budget to investigate it, and I still think I was lucky to even get that much."

George met with Moffatt & Nichol engineers, who later became stockholders in SeaWorld, and he started putting a team together. He consulted with Kenny Norris, then curator of both fish and mammals at Marineland in Palos Verdes, north of Los Angeles. Following testing, they found visibility so poor in the Port of Long Beach, that once people got down there, they wouldn't have been able to see anything. They tried to flood light it, but the more light they threw on it, the worse it got. They had no choice but to abandon the project.

He invited Kenny Norris to the restaurant one night to tell him he had decided to kill the project. Norris told George. "Well, don't feel too badly because I have always wanted to build a little marine park down on Mission Bay." George asked Norris why he hadn't done it. "He told me he was a zoologist not a developer," George recalls.

That piqued George's interest and it led to his questioning Norris about the marine park business, but he told George he didn't know much about the business side of things. George asked him if he could get some financial information on

**The Underwater Bar Test**

*When George wanted to build an underwater bar at the Reef Restaurant in 1961, he hired Moffatt & Nichol, a big West Coast marine engineering company, to help in the design and fabrication and attaching of the underwater chamber to pilings. John Moffatt and Frank Nichol themselves visited the site to discuss their participation.*

*"As we glanced across the water viewing downtown Long Beach, I thought I would test their engineering skills," said George. "I asked, if you had a transit and stood here and could move back from the spot another 1,000 feet, how could you determine the height of the buildings across the water? It was, of course, the application of the sine and the co-sine functions." Frank Nichol gave George an understanding paternal grin and said, "Look sonny, I didn't come out here to solve questions found on the US Naval Academy Freshman entrance examination. I came out here to investigate an underwater bar. Where do you want to put it?"*

*George was surprised. "I didn't know Frank had been a professor of mathematics at Oregon and was chief engineer for Guy F. Atkinson Co. during the war." Thus began an association with Moffatt and Nichol that has lasted nearly 50 years. Young Bob Nichol put the first pencil to the SeaWorld engineering plans. Moffatt and Nichol became stockholders and John Moffatt served on the SeaWorld board. Bob and Jack Nichol, Frank's sons, became Wet'n Wild stockholders.*

Marineland, and Norris thought for a second and said, "You know, one of my trainers goes around with the assistant bookkeeper, let me see what I can get."

### *One Call Starts it All*

A bit of marine park corporate espionage took place and about three weeks later in the mail, George received a package with raggedy, crumpled up copies of statements which revealed Marineland's numbers, and those numbers showed that

Marineland was a goldmine.

George was excited and called Norris and asked him if he still wanted to build a park in San Diego and when he said he did, George said, "OK, let's build one!"

That's how SeaWorld came to be.

After deciding to move forward with the idea, George discovered that the city of San Diego had been making initial overtures to several developers to build something like he had in mind. Within six months of George and Norris deciding to pursue the concept, the city had come out with an official RFP, a request for proposal.

Realizing he needed help in financing and projecting cash needs, George asked Milt Shedd to become a partner and help him raise the capital and secure the debt necessary to accomplish their goals. Against Shedd's advice he brought Dave DeMotte, another fraternity brother into the deal as secretary-treasurer and numbers man.

The three put together a proposal and were one of three groups to make a bid. They won the competition and the Mission Bay Commission and city council voted unanimously in favor of granting the lease to SeaWorld's parent company, Marine Park Corp. In doing so, they were given one of the first commercial land leases on Mission Bay, in a city park on the southern end of the bay.

*George talks business, 1965.*

The deal for the 21 acres called for a lease payment of $35,900 for the first year; $39,800 for the second; and $43,800 a year for the third year and beyond. In addition, Marine Park Corp. would pay the city 2.5% on all gross admission revenues, 3% on all food and beverage sales, and 7% on all other revenues.

### *The Other Bidders*

"The other two competitors for the project were San Diego based and well-known," said Anne, who was still dating George during the bidding process. "George's small group was labeled the L.A. Syndicate. You know, those outsiders from the big city."

Most of the barbs thrown at George during the early days weren't personal. Most were thrown at the project, which of course was his baby, and that definitely hurt, but he didn't take the criticism personally. Clint McKinnon, an influential congressman who controlled several local newspapers threw one of the early barbs. In his column, he used George as a metaphor for the guys from the big city who were coming to San Diego to take over. He called George a shark and predicted that the shark would soon gobble up the locals.

*George helps fill the tanks in the new Shamu Stadium, at SeaWorld San Diego, 1971.*

George took McKinnon to lunch and presented himself as a professional, non-shark type of guy. He explained his plans and what SeaWorld wanted to do and assured him he had no plans to gobble up anybody or anything. McKinnon was on SeaWorld's side from then on.

Over the years, George has overlooked most of the vitriolic comments written or spoken about him or his dreams because he didn't think his response would be worth the time and in the end, wouldn't solve anything. However, if he felt the comments could do damage to him or the park, he would take them by the horns and would usually win them over in a diplomatic way.

Anne laughs when people think "Diplomatic George" is an oxymoron. "Sure, George comes on strong and rules by intimidation, but he can purr like a kitten when he wants. He has an incredible power to win people over."

### *They Liked Us!*

To this day, George feels Kenny Norris was the main reason the lease was given to his group. Les Ernest, the director of parks, took a liking to Norris, to George's success as a restauranteur and to George as a person who could make things happen. "We made a damn good proposal and Kenny Norris was an excellent public speaker and it didn't hurt that he was curator of Marineland, the most successful ocean park in the world," George remembers.

Shedd was eventually responsible for raising half the equity. Within two months after winning the right to build the park, George left Paine Webber to devote his full time efforts to SeaWorld. Financially, he was doing OK and was still getting nearly $130,000 a year out of the Reef Restaurant, enough of a cushion that he didn't have to worry. If the Reef hadn't been successful, George would not have been able to leave his job at Paine Webber and devote money and time to his SeaWorld dreams.

Originally, George took up offices with Chadwick and Buchanan, a marine construction company. They were brokerage customers of his and he had gotten to know John Buchanan quite well. They were a medium-sized construction company that specialized in heavy marine engineering and building.

The SeaWorld deal was not the first time Demotte and George had teamed up. They and another fraternity brother had been partners in a couple of real estate ventures in the desert. The partnership, known as Strathmore Associates was named after the street on which the fraternity house was located in Westwood, California. The partnership purchased desert real estate in big chunks for as low as 25-cents a square foot, and would turn around and sell it for 40 to 50-cents per square foot. The company made money, but it was a slow process. Even then, he wanted to see quick results in return for his hard work and creativity.

### *John Moffatt Hits a Homer*

The architects at Moffatt and Nichol were initially utilized to help George create a vision for the park. Norris impressed George by coming up with several unique ideas on what he thought should be the next generation in marine mammal and fish entertainment. However, no one idea jumped out as the best, and the team had a hard time focusing on any one direction.

They went down a number of paths with some of the Moffatt and Nichol staff. At first, Bob Nichol, Norris and George thought SeaWorld would be a boat tour with guests riding in 50-passenger boats, going from one exhibit to another. A person would get off and stay at an exhibit for as long as he wanted, then get back on a boat and go to the next one. The team initially

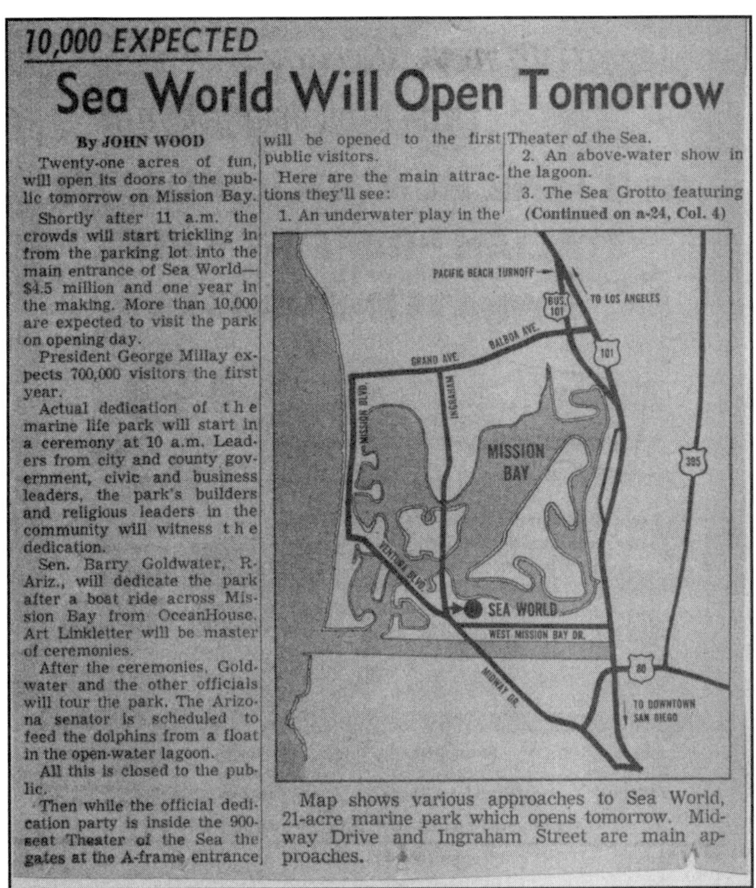

10,000 EXPECTED

**Sea World Will Open Tomorrow**

By JOHN WOOD

Twenty-one acres of fun, will open its doors to the public tomorrow on Mission Bay.

Shortly after 11 a.m. the crowds will start trickling in from the parking lot into the main entrance of Sea World—$4.5 million and one year in the making. More than 10,000 are expected to visit the park on opening day.

President George Millay expects 700,000 visitors the first year.

Actual dedication of the marine life park will start in a ceremony at 10 a.m. Leaders from city and county government, civic and business leaders, the park's builders and religious leaders in the community will witness the dedication.

Sen. Barry Goldwater, R-Ariz., will dedicate the park after a boat ride across Mission Bay from OceanHouse. Art Linkletter will be master of ceremonies.

After the ceremonies, Goldwater and the other officials will tour the park. The Arizona senator is scheduled to feed the dolphins from a float in the open-water lagoon.

All this is closed to the public.

Then while the official dedication party is inside the 900-seat Theater of the Sea the gates at the A-frame entrance will be opened to the first public visitors.

Here are the main attractions they'll see:

1. An underwater play in the Theater of the Sea.

2. An above-water show in the lagoon.

3. The Sea Grotto featuring

(Continued on a-24, Col. 4)



Map shows various approaches to Sea World, 21-acre marine park which opens tomorrow. Midway Drive and Ingraham Street are main approaches.

*Big news in San Diego, March 20, 1964. Reprinted with permission from* The San Diego Union-Tribune.

thought that four or five stops would be needed to see everything.

As planning on that concept continued, it became clear that it would be nothing short of a logistics nightmare. Moving crowds, the size needed to make the park viable, would be non-manageable on boats.

During this time, George used Anne as a sounding board for many of his ideas. Anne would pull no punches when telling him what she thought. If anything she over analyzed things. She's a ying to his yang. "It took awhile for SeaWorld to fall into place," she said. "In the beginning, I didn't think he had thought it through enough. To me, it was a kind of an impulsive, creative thing that I could not visualize as he did. Only during the third year of operation did I appreciate the full impact of the project."

Anne said he never got angry with her for expressing doubts or her personal opinions. "No, he was always quite the gentleman. He would let me roll until his interest flagged and he had already gone quickly onto the next subject, which of course happened all the time."

### *Time for an Architect*

John Moffatt, a senior partner with the firm, became very interested in the project and saw the team floundering. He called George into his office and said, "George, this project has too much potential and we don't have the creative talent here to do it justice, we're engineers. You don't want an engineering firm. You've got to get some architectural flair in here." He introduced George to Ben Southland, the senior partner and senior planner for Victor Gruen Associates, the second largest architectural firm in the world at that time.

Southland was headquartered in Beverly Hills, which George saw as an immediate benefit to the SeaWorld team. By this time, Norris had left Marineland and was a professor at UCLA. It was getting increasingly more difficult for him to get away and attend design meetings in Long Beach. Ben Southland took on the project and his firm was given the task of designing the park. George was still funding the entire project at that time and a man of Southland's reputation didn't come cheap.

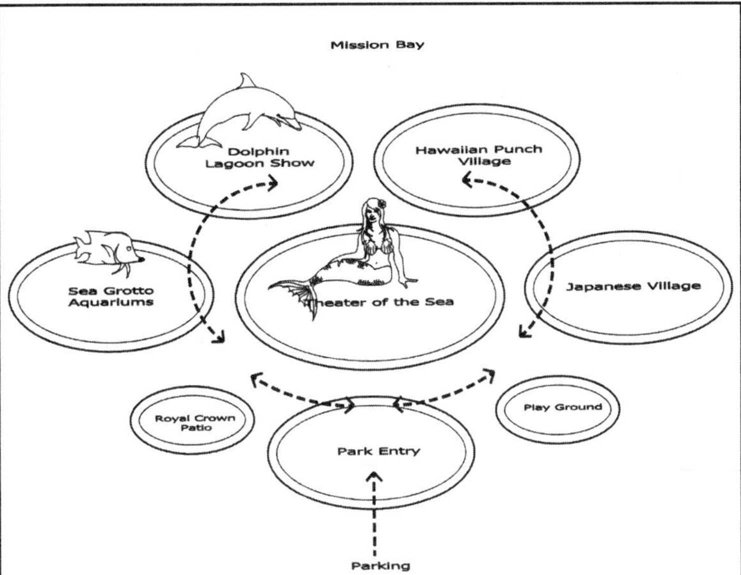


## The Classic SeaWorld Layout

The original SeaWorld San Diego layout was a triple barbell configuration with spokes running out from each center, with walkways around the exterior perimeter.

The layout took advantage of the beauty of the adjacent Mission Bay and had continuous flow from show to show. Guest movement at SeaWorld San Diego has always been excellent, and still works well today, which is quite an accomplishment for a pioneering design created more than 40 years ago. Credit for that efficient layout goes to Ben Southland, of Victor Gruen Architects.

Because of a long narrow and hilly lakeside parcel, the San Diego design was not usable for SeaWorld Ohio. Instead, the backbone of the layout was a 1,500 foot-long main street running parallel to Geauga Lake, from the front gate to the Japanese Village. Off that street, major walkways dead-ended into Shamu Stadium, the seal and penguin exhibit, and the water ski stadium. Because of the huge Ohio crowds the design was troublesome and never worked as well as the layout of the other SeaWorld parks.

When designing SeaWorld Florida George Walsh followed the San Diego layout with a few modifications. The Florida park was larger and more attention had to be given to cool and shady areas, such as air-conditioned stadiums, shade structures and covered outdoor eating areas.

### *Not a Big Fan of Architects*

George says finding Ben Southland was a lucky happening. "He's one of the few architects I have liked in my life. Maybe out of 100 architects I've known, I've gotten along with five or six of them, and in general, I'm not a big fan of architects."

Another park pioneer who didn't think much of architects was Walt Disney, who, while visiting George a few years later in 1966 at SeaWorld, expressed that same feeling.

Walt visited the park with Tommy Walker, the director of productions at Disneyland, to see the Shamu show. Following the presentation, as they were walking away, Walt said to George. "That's a great show you have there, but don't you think you should get the whale in a bigger pool, in a bigger stadium?" George said he completely agreed with him and noted that he had architects working on the plans for a new stadium at that very minute. Walt stopped, grabbed George's arm and while squeezing it looked directly at George and told him. "Remember one thing, there's nothing more dangerous in this world than an unsupervised architect. Stick your nose in and keep it in there."

*George Millay checks out the progress of porpoise training in late 1963, eight months before SeaWorld San Diego opens to the public.*

- CHAPTER 5 -

# SeaWorld Takes Shape

Slowly but surely, Ben Southland started coming up with the design, consisting of acres of gardens and strategically placed, unique buildings that would house the shows and exhibits that Norris had created.

George is quick to give credit for most of the original design ideas to Norris and Southland, including the ponds, the flowing rivers, waterfalls, and rockwork - the elements for which SeaWorld San Diego is famous.

By the time Shedd joined the team, George had already invested nearly $70,000 of his own money. He had been paying DeMotte $500 per month to crunch numbers and was also paying for the services of Ben Southland. Shedd came in and said he would match George dollar for dollar on expenses. The two started in earnest to raise the capital for SeaWorld.

Through a fellow brokerage friend, Shedd introduced George and DeMotte to Paul Hughes, the founder of Hawaiian Punch. The two then proceeded to sell Hughes on the idea of building, what was to be the $170,000 Hawaiian Punch Pavilion at the park. Hughes eventually became a big stockholder in SeaWorld. The fact that George already had created two highly successful Hawaiian-themed restaurants, the Reef and the Castaway, was crucial in Hawaiian Punch's decision to invest in SeaWorld. They knew they had someone who understood the Hawaiian culture and would stay true to its authenticity.

Milt Shedd was in the picture mostly for his expertise in financing and didn't have too much to do with the design, although he would stick his head into the meetings at times. At that time, an inkling of things to come that eventually would lead to George's downfall within the company, surfaced.

"Right from the start, Milt wanted to be the boss, and I said no, this is going to be my project. If you want to come along, you'll be a stockholder, and he agreed. We finally got it down to where I was the president and CEO, and he was the chairman of the board, which was mostly an honorary position. He had no duties, he drew no salary, but he came to all the board meetings and that's about it."

In retrospect, George says, "Milt Shedd was a pain in the ass at SeaWorld from the day he came in, but he played a very prominent position in getting the crucial, original financing. He would open doors to his contacts and Dave (DeMotte) and I would move in. With youth, enthusiasm and organizational skills, we'd close the deal. Milt was extremely important in those early stages. I would say he probably raised or was responsible for at least half of the original capital."

### *Great, But Where's the Money?*

In the beginning, raising money was tough, but between Shedd and George, they had raised about a million dollars of equity before they hit a wall. "We just weren't getting any additional equity for the company that would allow us to proceed. We had signed an option to lease with the City of San Diego, and we were supposed to be starting construction in a year, but we didn't have enough money. Our approved loans were all dependent on getting a specific amount of equity and we didn't have it. We had come to a dead stop and I was worried. Shedd was tapped out and I really didn't know what to do."

Once again, the Gods smiled on George. Marineland went public, and out came a prospectus showing that the park was a goldmine. Armed with that information, the SeaWorld team went back to Boston Capital, who had turned them down the first time, and within days they came up with the rest of the needed money.

After Marineland's golden prospectus came out, everything went together within 30 to 45 days. If Marineland had not gone public, there is doubt in George's mind that he would have ever gotten the money. Ironically, Marineland going public made it possible for SeaWorld to be built and become a major competitor and ultimately its downfall.

When Boston Capital changed its mind about investing in SeaWorld, it did so in a big way and came in with a 20% stake in the park, the largest single stockholder. At the same time, Shedd brought in fishing buddy Herb Bell, the founder of Packard Bell Corporation. Having come in as an early investor, Bell's was a great name to use in obtaining additional monies. Those three, Boston Capital, Hawaiian Punch, and Herb Bell, were Milt's three big contributions. George's biggest catches were Moffatt and Nichol and Chadwick and Buchanan who each put in $250,000. Dave Tallichet, George's former partner in Specialty Restaurants put in $50,000 and Ben Southland, a partner of Victor Gruen, put $35,000 of his own money into the deal.

Most of the money came in (relatively) small increments. When the park opened, there were 21 shareholders, who had invested $1.5 million between them. The park received a $2 million first mortgage from Home Federal Savings and Loan and acquired a $250,000 chattel mortgage from Associates Discount Corporation, with the park's equipment as chattel.

SeaWorld was built and opened for approximately $3.5 million and the first year was a fiasco, both operationally and financially. A pre-opening feasibility study projected first year attendance at 400,000 with an admission price of $2.50 per person. Actual attendance for that first year was 200,000 and the company lost $400,000. The nearby San Diego Zoo at that time was bringing in approximately 1.5 million visitors a year with an admission price of $1.

### *Water Problems*

The operations side had myriad problems that first year. The park had a sophisticated filtration plant that took care of primary water, mammal water, fresh water, chilled water, heated water, and recycled water. Moffatt and Nichol's mechanical engineers had problems understanding how to operate the system. They were able to design and install it but needed more input from the supplier on how to run it. Adding to the problem, a series of red tides hit Mission Bay in 1964 and two or three times during the first season, those tides came in and clogged the filter systems.

Red tide, so called because of the presence of millions of tiny red microorganisms, destroys water clarity and suffocates the fish. The re-circulation system needed to occasionally bring bay water into the primary system and during that time couldn't adequately filter out the red tide, thus causing poor water clarity in certain shows, especially in the Theatre of the Sea, and the dolphin and sea mammal shows.

Many who remember that bout with red tide recall seeing George out there all night, with his sleeves rolled up, helping clean the filtration system. Everyone worked hard cleaning filter bags and George was in the trenches with the rest of the crew.

Water clarity was horrible on opening day and for most of the first season, even when the red tides weren't affecting it. "We went through three superintendents of maintenance before I found the right man that could give us good water," George said. "John Rognlie came from General Dynamics and knew his stuff. He built a great maintenance department in about two years, and then staffed our Ohio and Florida parks with well trained professionals."

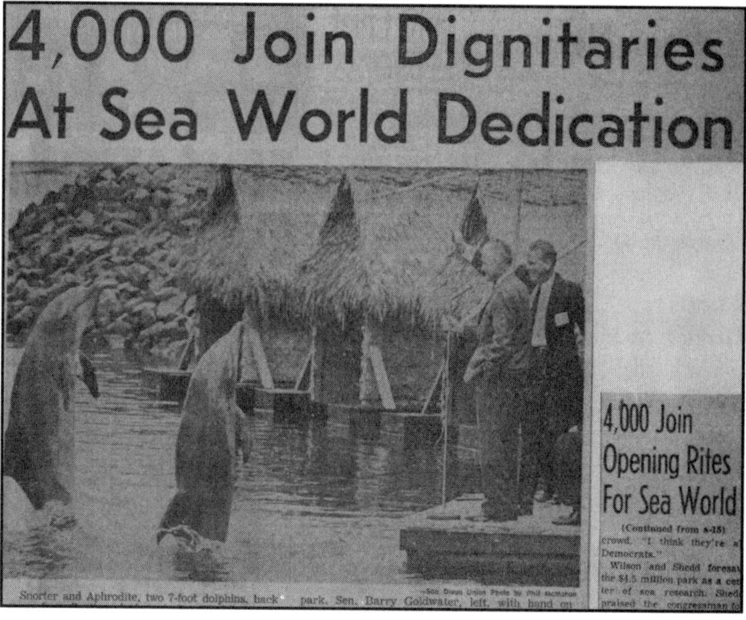

4,000 Join Dignitaries
At Sea World Dedication

4,000 Join
Opening Rites
For Sea World

(Continued from A-15)
crowd. "I think they're a[ll]
Democrats."
Wilson and Shedd foresa[w]
the $4.5 million park as a cen-
ter of sea research. Shed[d]
praised the congressman fo[r]

Snorter and Aphrodite, two 7-foot dolphins, back park. Sen. Barry Goldwater, left, with hand on

—San Diego Union Photo by Phil McMahon

*Front page news on March 22, 1964. George Millay and Barry Goldwater are seen at right. Reprinted with permission from* The San Diego Union-Tribune.

### *Don't Mess with the Teamsters*

Most are unaware that SeaWorld had a picket line around it on opening day and for at least two years afterward. Art Linkletter, Barry Goldwater, and Bishop Furry of San Diego were among the guest celebrities who were invited to the park on opening day. To avoid any negative publicity that crossing a picket line might produce, the guests arrived by boat, on the Bahai Bell Paddleboat. The picket line was mostly ineffective and became a joke to management as the months passed.

"Twenty-five or so young people in the operations

*Barry Goldwater, left, greets Kirk Nonaka, president of Murada Pearl and Mrs. Murada, following the opening ceremony at SeaWorld San Diego, March 21, 1964. George Millay, right, strikes a Secret Service agent pose.*

department were not happy and under urging from two or three suspected ring leaders, signed a request to be represented by the union, complaining of long hours and $1.25 an hour," George said. "We were flabbergasted."

DeMotte called in a labor counsel who urged management to get to the bottom of the problems immediately. Make no threats but find out their grievances and try to dispel them was his advice to DeMotte. The suspected ringleaders were called in and with DeMotte present, they expounded at length on their grievances. At the same time they admitted, "The union move was our last resort." Park officials moved quickly to erase their grievances. First they placed Lee Roberts, then manager of food and beverage and a popular manager with the kids, into the operations director's position. Ten cent an hour pay raises were then announced. At that point, "the revolt by the young Turks collapsed," notes George.

Following the official opening ceremony, George walked Art Linkletter around the park. He remembers taking Linkletter to see the underwater Sea Maids show. The water clarity was terrible and visibility was nil. Linkletter looked in, smiled and said,

Walt Disney visits SeaWorld, December 1964.

"Look George, I'll come back some other time. Let's don't look at the show today. I'll come back."

***The Park on Opening Day***

The beauty of the park on opening day was not lost on George. "It was a pretty little park and was beautifully done. (Ben) Southland had assigned a landscape architect by the name of Bill Dreiss to head up the landscaping design team. He was a good detail man, in placing rocks, waterfalls and sidewalks into the landscape," George recalls. "We were okay in our fish department and had good exhibits, but from a standpoint of good shows, we were a disaster. We didn't know how to control our water quality and as the first season proved, our marketing was poor."

He had anticipated some of those problems. Three or four months prior to the March 1964 opening, George started becoming increasingly concerned about the lack of progress that the dolphin and pilot whale trainers were making. There was no script prepared and no behaviors had been taught, and according to George, "All the animals were doing was eating us out of house and home. They were real socialists, both the trainers and animals."

Fortunately for the park, Fred Lowe, a merchandising manager whom George had hired from Marineland, was also con-

## Sea World Is a Wonderland

SAN DIEGO's wonderful world of spectator attractions has been expanded tremendously by the addition of Sea World, the multi-million-dollar extravaganza in Mission Bay Park.

Sea World is a wonderland as fascinating as that visited by the fictional Alice. We can make statements such as that without feeling they are tinged by San Diego partisanship. Newsmen from all sections of the state who attended a preview of Sea World's wonders, said, in effect, "greatest show about the sea on earth."

Sea World complements San Diego's other great attractions such as the zoo, beaches, fishing opportunities, and dozens of historical points.

The shows exhibited there, even when they were initially revealed, were examples of what can be accomplished by skilled, professional direction.

Sea World, we predict, is destined to become one of the nation's outstanding attractions. We welcome its opening, and we are sure those from around the world will join us.

*Editorial praising SeaWorld San Diego, March 22, 1964. Reprinted with permission from* The San Diego Union-Tribune.

cerned. Kenny Norris was in Honolulu helping build Sea Life Park and to most, he seemed unconcerned with the SeaWorld situation. Lowe told George of a private animal trainer who had come to Marineland once a year to help trainers sharpen up their skills and training methods. He said the park had tried to hire Kent Burgess several times but he didn't like the Marineland setup. George called Burgess and sent him a plane ticket to San Diego. Following a walk-through of the park, George offered the job to Burgess on the spot, and he accepted.

### *A Promise of Good Shows*

Finding Kent Burgess was another stroke of good fortune for George. After surveying the situation, he told George he could have "an adequate" show program for opening day, a "good" show program in six months and in one year he would have the best trained staff and the best marine mammal shows in the world. George said Burgess "more than" fulfilled that promise and in doing so, produced a half-dozen or more professional animal trainers who brought even greater creativity to the SeaWorld shows, not only in California, but later in Ohio and Florida as well.

During that first year, the shows were at best mediocre but in general, people like animals no matter what they do, and the park got away with much more then than it could today. Professionalism in the shows was yet to be developed but with Kent Burgess on board, the trainers soon realized they had the makings of a quality product and with a bit more effort and direction, could easily take the shows up several levels.

In addition to being a superb trainer, Burgess knew how to answer George's questions. One day George asked him how long it took to train a dolphin for a show. Burgess reflected a moment and then offered, "If you have a smart trainer and a smart dolphin, a couple of months. If you have a dumb trainer and a dumb dolphin, never."

Another time George queried as to how Burgess knew which animals could and couldn't be trained. With a cocky smirk on his face he calmly stated, "If it eats it can be trained. I could train you George."

Burgess did not develop the themes for the shows. Phil Roberts and two or three other writers created and wrote the story lines to the early productions. Burgess would give them a list of the behaviors that each animal could accomplish and shows centering on those behaviors would be developed. Tommy Walker of Disneyland and Bob Shipstad of the Ice Follies were both free-lance producers at SeaWorld during those early years and Jack Nagle and Larry Sands, both independent producers created the shows in later years.

Of all the people George and his staff hired that first year, Kent Burgess still stands out from the rest today for George. "Kent is one of the five men I credit for creating the fine marine parks now enjoyed by more than 10 million guests each year. He was the watershed in the company's success story," George claims.

***Fate and Timing Helps Again***

Looking back, George said he was fortunate to have had two "hard-working, powerful, honest, top-notch contractors on the job." The firm of Chadwick and Buchanan, whose owners were both stockholders, organized the construction and were the general contractors on the job. The firm's Fred Chadwick went full-time on the project, moved to San Diego and became head superintendent. Chadwick brought in San Diego's Nielsen Construction Company, a reputable group known for quality work, as the biggest sub-contractor who would eventually do all the SeaWorld work. Falck Nielsen, the company owner, later became a sizeable stockholder and director in Wet'n Wild, George's later claim to fame. To this day, the families remain close friends.

Bob Gault, one of the early hires at the park, was destined to become a well-known park executive throughout the SeaWorld chain, as well as the Universal collection of parks. He started his long and successful career in the industry at SeaWorld a few months after the park opened in 1964 as a ticket taker, butt sweeper and parking attendant.

Gault started while a college student in San Diego, and remembers seeing George around the park many times before actually meeting him, face to face.

"He was this big, redheaded Irishman with a straw hat and zinc oxide on his nose and face to keep from getting sunburned. He always had that white nose as he walked around the park helping us keep the place clean and helping us provide good hospitality," recalls Gault. "I saw him as very intimidating. I was

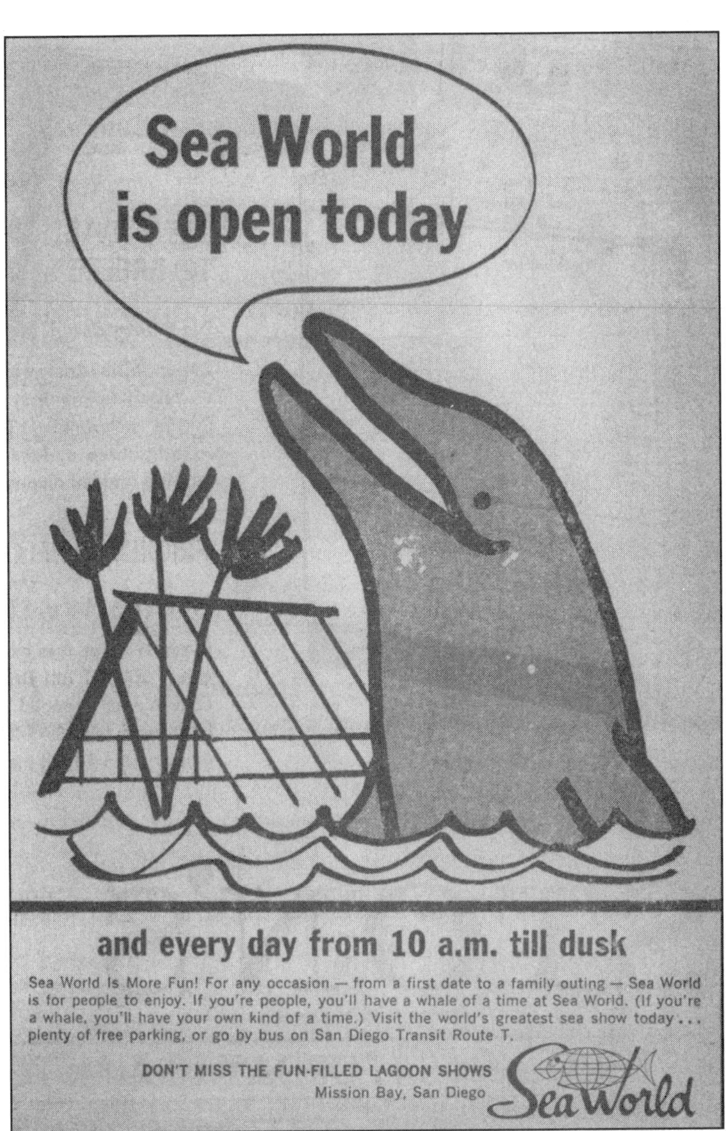
Sea World
is open today
and every day from 10 a.m. till dusk
Sea World Is More Fun! For any occasion — from a first date to a family outing — Sea World is for people to enjoy. If you're people, you'll have a whale of a time at Sea World. (If you're a whale, you'll have your own kind of a time.) Visit the world's greatest sea show today... plenty of free parking, or go by bus on San Diego Transit Route T.
DON'T MISS THE FUN-FILLED LAGOON SHOWS
Mission Bay, San Diego
Sea World

20 and he had a very strong, aggressive personality. To me, he was a scary guy. He had quite a temper in those days and you always knew where he stood on things. He was very direct."

Gault said it was obvious that George was very concerned about the quality of the operation. "He wanted everything to be as perfect as possible and he wanted the employees looking good, the place clean, the shows well run, and the landscaping beautiful. He paid a tremendous amount of attention to detail and showed a great sense of urgency to get it done right and get it done now. Business was very, very tenuous in those days. Many times he couldn't make payroll and had to pull it out of his own pocket."

George took no salary from SeaWorld during its construction or the first year of its operation. He depended on his checks from the Reef Restaurant for support.

Gault was soon promoted to supervisor in the operations department. One day, he was going through security and George was coming the opposite direction. "I said, hello, Mr. Millay, and kept right on walking." He hadn't gotten far when he heard George call him by name. "He had me come back and he grabbed my arm and pulled me off to the side and he put his hand on my shoulder. He looked me right in the eye, nose to nose, and asked when was the last time I had fired someone. I was shaking in my boots and I said, to tell you the truth, I haven't fired anybody lately. George looked at me and told me to go out there and get rid of someone who wasn't doing their job and do it now," Gault remembers.

George's charge was not wasted on Gault. "His point was are you disciplining enough? Are you counseling them? There was a message in there someplace that I needed to balance my style with the need to be a good manager. I needed to make tough decisions and really look closely at my people and get rid of the ones that weren't carrying their share of the load."

### *Blame it on the Marketing*

George put a good deal of the blame for a bad first year on inadequate advertising. The park had retained Barnes-Chase, a San Diego ad firm, and George didn't think it had produced for the park. Mike Downs, SeaWorld's VP of marketing, suggested that the park needed to increase its exposure in the Los Angeles market. The old agency was fired and the Beverly Hills office of

J. Walter Thompson Company was retained to represent SeaWorld.

At the time, it was the largest agency in the world but George said they "treated us as if we were a General Motors account. They really cared about us." The key players handling the SeaWorld account were Ron Ziegler and Bob Haldeman. Ziegler was just out of USC graduate school and SeaWorld was his first account. He and Mike Downs worked well together, but

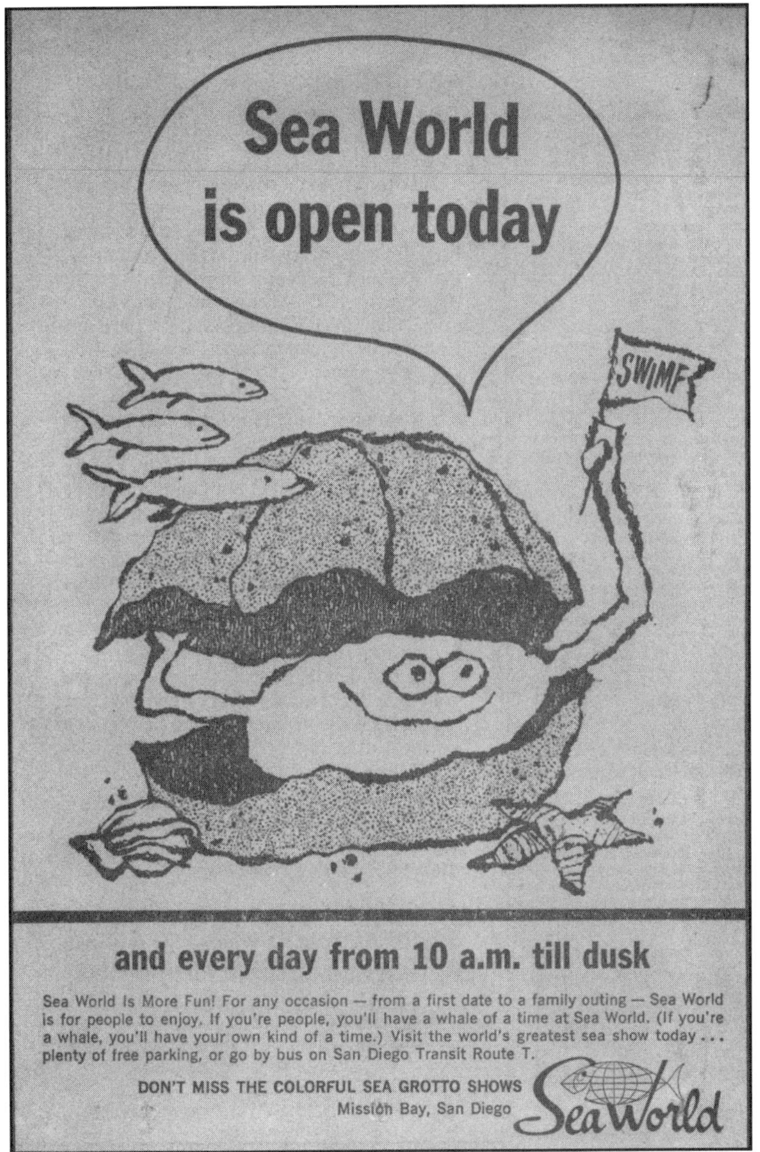

Ziegler "was terrified of me for some reason," George recalls.

They produced a 30-second TV commercial called the "Adventures of Bobby." It featured a young lad dreaming of all the things he would be doing next week at SeaWorld - seeing dolphins, fishes, mermaids, and riding a hydrofoil. The park ran the commercial at 400 gross rating points for two months starting mid-May 1965. "Bingo," George said. "Attendance on Memorial Day topped 7,000 and we were off to the races." Seven years later, both Ziegler and Haldeman were working in the White House.

- CHAPTER 6 -

# The Lovely Sea Maids

One of George's all-time favorite show concepts made its debut on opening day, March 21, 1964. The Theatre of the Sea was centrally located in the park and architecturally unique. It seated 1,200 people facing into a large 4-sided glass tank. The pool was 15 feet deep and had a series of 12 foot by 6 foot laminated glass viewing portals. The show was by far the most difficult to produce at the time as it was entirely underwater and was viewed from all four sides.

The production starred four Sea Maids, two dolphins, and one seal. The Sea Maids were a unique group of young ladies who performed with the animals in a scripted underwater scenario including animal behaviors, theatrical lighting and sound, intricate staging and an underwater ballet. The show was a hit right from the start, especially once the water quality issue was cleared up and the audience could see them.

***Cool Job!***

Being a Sea Maid was one of the choice jobs for young ladies at SeaWorld San Diego for the first 15 years of the park. Each day from four to 10 times, depending on the crowds, the girls entertained guests from inside the large tank.

The theater was usually packed as guests crowded in to watch up to four girls perform underwater with trained mammals. Unlike the mermaids at Weeki Wachee Springs in Florida, the only other location where an act like this was performed, the Sea Maids wore masks and had small air tanks attached to their waists. The show was 22-minutes long. During the winter months, when the water got quite cold, the girls were outfitted in form-fitting wet suits.

Jantzen Swimwear was a promotional partner and provided the suits and the clothing for the girls while the other sponsor, U.S. Divers, supplied the masks and air tanks.

To this day, George thinks the Sea Maids Show in the Theatre of the Sea was one of the most original shows SeaWorld

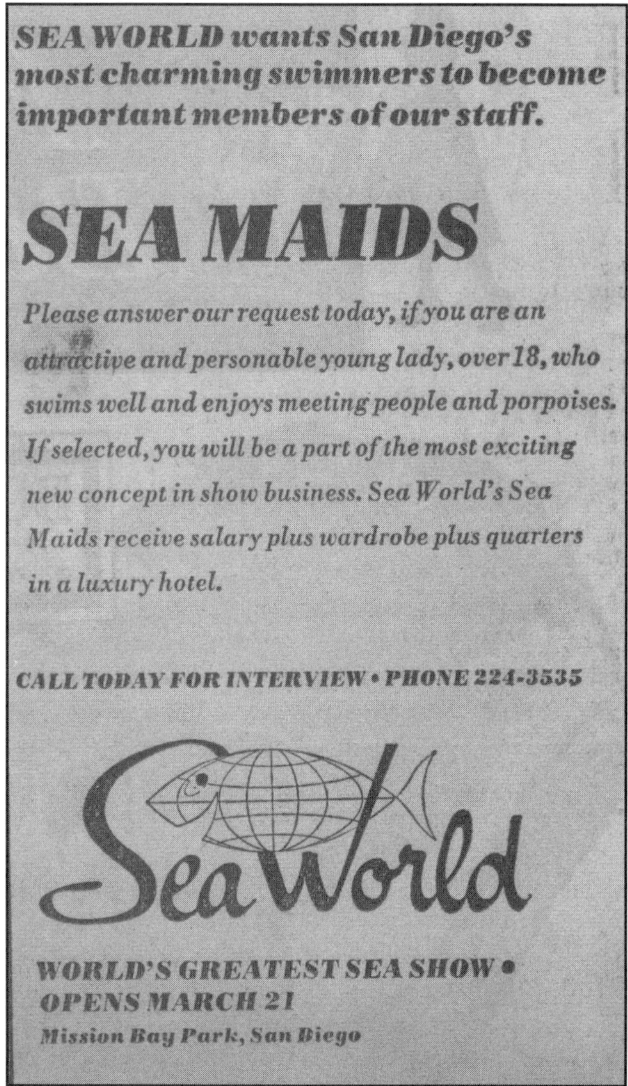


ever presented. Once again, his creative innovation took the concept up several levels. The Weeki Wachee mermaids use a hose for air, which can be distracting at times. They don't wear masks and they don't interact with any fish or mammals. In Florida, the girls swim in an open spring outside, while the audience sits inside a darkened theater looking out. George presented his entire show inside, where the water quality and the lighting could be controlled at all times. The Weeki Wachee production still exists. Unfortunately, all the SeaWorld Sea Maid shows were discontinued in the late 1970s. "Too much work for the production staff," George adds sarcastically.

The shows were heavily scripted and had excellent music. Several first class producers through the years, including Bob Shipstad of the Ice Follies, independent producer Larry Sands, and Jack Nagle of Miami who had also written several scripts for the Weeki Wachee mermaids, created them.

### *Mickey Becomes a Sea Maid*

Mickey Baltes joined the park as a Sea Maid on her 19th birthday, February 13, 1965, less than a year after the park first opened.

"SeaWorld changed my life, just as it did for thousands of other young people," she said. She was a student at San Diego State University and was looking for a part-time job. She saw the ad in the San Diego Union newspaper. It read that SeaWorld was looking for a specific type of person to be a Sea Maid. "If you are an attractive and personable young lady, over 18, who swims well and enjoys meeting people and porpoises. If selected, you will be a part of the most exciting new concept in show business." Baltes asks, "How could I refuse to answer an ad like that?"

She was one of 300 girls who showed up trying for one of the two available openings. She recalls that day. "We were interviewed by Phil Roberts, the department head and the head Sea Maid, Jerri Watmore, and then were asked to put on bathing suits. One at a time, we were told to get into a tank, feed a hand full of dead squid to the fish, swim underwater, listen to instructions over the underwater speakers and attempt to perform different stunts. It was exciting and terrifying at the same time."

She was offered a full time job and took it, earning $1.25 per hour and she says there wasn't one girl there who "wouldn't have done what we were doing for free." With that salary, she points out, none of them could eat well, but the friendly folks running the nearby snack stands, kept the girls fed with the leftover hot dogs at the end of the day.

"The work was physically exhausting and emotionally exhilarating. We were an extremely close-knit group of young women. We were proud of ourselves and of what we were doing, and we were part of the most wonderful organization we would ever be privileged to have a hand in building."

### *Learning to Scuba*

Once hired, the girls had to be certified in scuba diving before learning the specific performance routines. "My first impression of being in the tank for the first time was that it was very, very cold," Baltes recalls. "That was before they started heating the water. It could get as low as 53-degrees at times. I was also impressed with how big it looked from the inside out. The dolphins were lovable, gentle and fun."

*The Sea Maids performed in the underwater Theatre of the Sea at SeaWorld San Diego, 1965.*

In the early days, the Sea Maids performed two different shows. In the Theatre of the Sea, they would perform the choreographed productions, and in the Sea Grotto they would feed the fish by hand and interact with the guests as they walked by the tanks.

One of the first shows in the Theatre of the Sea was the Zeke show. It started off with a ballad by Burl Ives. The music for the entire show was soft and mystical and when combined with the underwater ballet of the Sea Maids, it created a dreamy, soothing effect. The dolphins, Homer, Sugar, Sally and Dolly, usually upstaged the girls and were the true stars of the show, Baltes points out. The animals' antics and interaction with the Zeke character and their graceful playfulness with the Sea Maids mesmerized the audiences, most of whom had never seen anything like this before Baltes said she performed in several shows after the Zeke Show, but she felt none had its charm.

### *Sea Maids as Ambassadors*

The popularity of the athletically fit Sea Maids and their dexterity in the water soon had them performing other duties in the park. They performed the role of the Polynesian girl in the lagoon show and were towed in an outrigger by a dolphin. They did a hula dance with the dolphins, and when the tide pool exhibit was built they began the job of narrating the exhibit and interacting with the guests. Shortly after Shamu arrived in 1965, it was the Sea Maids who were chosen to be the first to ride the killer whale as part of the show.

"We also used them as ambassadors for the park," George said. "We would send them out for special appearances, which always drew large crowds. We often used them in our TV commercials." Baltes liked the PR work, except for the fact they always had to wear swimsuits to the events, many times feeling very out of place while everyone else was wearing formal wear.

The Sea Maids evolved into trainers' assistants. "It sounded like fun at first, but would usually involve hours and hours in the cold water doing something pretty boring," Baltes notes. "Because we were around the animals so much, we were often bitten by them. Dave Kenney, our veterinarian, acted as our first aid kit. He even sewed up our wounds a couple of times."

Baltes and another Sea Maid, Christine Snell, were assigned the job of keeping an eye on Shamu the night she arrived at the park. "I remember the thrill of that night. There were photographers, veterinarians, trainers and executives everywhere. It was an exciting night for us."

### *Ailments Go with the Job*

Cold water swimming caused a great deal of health problems for the Sea Maids. "We were constantly battling ear infections, sinus infections, colds, skin problems, and wounds," she said. "It was funny because we all loved what we were doing so much, we didn't much care, and SeaWorld was very generous with sick day allotment. We were allowed two a month, and if we didn't use them, we would get paid for those hours or they would be added to our vacation time."

Baltes became head Sea Maid within two years of joining the team and stayed in that position for the rest of her Sea Maid career. There were seven Sea Maids when she started in 1965. When she left in 1970, there were 23.

# Buy Your Sea World Annual Pass Now!

**Make it easy on yourself to entertain all the guests you'll have in San Diego this year . . .**

## Only \$4.25

*THE SEA WORLD GOLD PASS COSTS ONLY \$4.25. It's good for a full year of unlimited admissions PLUS a \$1.00 discount for an adult guest each time you visit. (Regular one-time adult admission is \$2.25.) It's a great gift item, too, for birthdays and all special occasions.*

**ANNUAL PASS ORDER FORM**

U-2/2

SeaWorld 1720 So. Shores Rd., San Diego, Calif. 92109

**Please send me ___ Sea World Gold Passes at \$4.25. My check is enclosed.**

NAME

ADDRESS

CITY STATE

**FOR SEA WORLD INFORMATION CALL 224-3535**

Even the Sea Maids felt the wrath of George on occasion. Baltes specifically recalls George being "distinctly unhappy" when she began driving a small motorcycle to save on gas. Her friend, Christine Snell, liked the idea and bought one as well and the two of them tooled around town having fun. George noticed them one morning in the parking lot. "He saw us, chased us down and delivered a talk on the imprudence of (girls) being seen on motorcycles. Plus, SeaWorld had invested a great deal in us and they didn't want to see their investment all scarred up or worse. Fortunately that phase of my life only lasted until it got cold."

SeaWorld worked with young people and gave them opportunities and encouraged them to succeed and grow, according to Baltes. "As we grew and as we learned, SeaWorld rewarded us. Many of these young people took what they learned here and went on to become very successful in both related as well as non-related fields. SeaWorld has been a positive and integral part of the lives of thousands of people, including me."

### *Sea Maid Graduates*

Most of the Sea Maids went on to successful and happy lives. Some chose to be successful parents and homemakers, some chose to enter the corporate world. A couple of biographies stand out from the rest:

Kathy Kassebaum became a Sea Maid in 1974. While working at the park, she met Jim Gillcrist, a young trainer apprentice, began dating and soon married. Today Gillcrist is a Navy captain and air officer on the USS. Peleliu and he and Kathy have nine children. She home schools their children and both she and her husband visit SeaWorld often and love to share their memories with the children.

A Point Loma high school girl named Sharon Patrick was one of the original Sea Maids. She then matriculated to Stanford and onto Harvard Business School. While climbing Mt. Kilimanjaro in Kenya she met Martha Stewart and soon joined her company. Patrick was COO of that NYSE company for nearly 20 years and was recently elected CEO by the board. George is proud to point out that, "In the business world, Sharon Patrick is by far the most visible of all Sea Maid alumni."

*Howard Cosell and Don Meredith interview SeaWorld's Chimp on national TV during a Monday Night Football game featuring the San Diego Chargers, above. Off camera, Chimp bit Cosell. Debbie Reynolds meets Shamu, below.*

- CHAPTER 7 -

# SeaWorld Opens & The Fine Tuning Begins

Once the initial rush to get SeaWorld opened was over, George started fine-tuning various elements within the park. One of his main concerns right from the beginning was that the park needed a bit more pizzazz in its fish exhibits. He had been told that the Steinhart Aquarium in San Francisco did a good job in every area, including display. Hoping to pick up a few ideas on how to improve his park, he visited the aquarium. He picked up much more than an idea. He landed the best fish guy in the world.

"I went up there and was very impressed. The way the tanks were decorated, the selection of fish, the lighting, the graphics, all the things that make an aquarium successful were there in great evidence." He was excited about what he saw, wondered who was responsible for it and started looking around for someone to talk with about the facility. He saw an open door, walked through it and asked a man working back there who ran the place. The guy looked up and said, "I do, and my name is Dave Powell." That was the start of a long, successful relationship between Powell, George, and SeaWorld.

George introduced himself and suggested the two have breakfast the following morning and George offered him a job on the spot. In his autobiography, "A Fascination for Fish - Adventures of an Underwater Pioneer," Powell recalls meeting George.

*"George knew little about marine life, but he knew enough to know that the fish and invertebrate exhibits could be better than they were (at SeaWorld) and he wanted SeaWorld to have the best.*

*"I'd heard disturbing stories about the hiring and firing of more than one of SeaWorld's managers. I worried about leaving a financially secure, if frustrating, position at Steinhart and once again uprooting my wife and our young daughters to take a job that might be*

*much less secure. Jobs for marine biologists who wanted to work in aquariums were few and far between. If this didn't work out and I ended up with no job, our family would be in a real fix. So I asked Millay for a two-year contract. He agreed, but I needn't have worried. I ended up staying at SeaWorld for nine rewarding years. George Millay wasn't afraid to try something new, and I admired him for that."*

"REMEMBER, ALBERT... WATCH EVERYTHING THE TRAINERS DO SO YOU'LL KNOW EXACTLY WHAT TO DO WITH THE GOLD FISH I GAVE YOU."

George says, without question, that Powell was the number one aquarist and one of the top fish collectors in the world. "We used to send out expeditions to collect fish and the junior guys would come back and tell me never to send them out with Powell again, that he worked them too hard. Dave could do more dives per day at deeper depths than guys 20 years his junior. He was modest and quiet, but you didn't step on him, or he'd quietly tell you exactly where to go."

Powell, according to George, was very straight-laced and strictly lived by the code of do unto others, as you would have others do unto you. "I remember when the curator of fish at a California oceanarium was caught by federal agents smuggling fish into the country, Dave was incensed that he would break the law and break that code of ethics of the sea and of his profession." Today, Powell is credited as being the creative driving force of the Monterey Bay (California) Aquarium.

- CHAPTER 8 -

# SeaWorld Receives a Name & Other Early Happenings

The name SeaWorld was born at the Disneyland Hotel in Anaheim, California, but George is quick to point out that the SeaWorld concept was born in the minds of Ken Norris, Ben Southland, and George Millay.

It was a Disneyland official who originally gave George the idea to call the park SeaWorld. Before construction began in early 1963, George was visiting with one of his consultants, Disney's Ed Ettinger, Disneyland's marketing director at the Disneyland Hotel, across the street from Disneyland. "We compiled a list of possible names for the planned park and Ed mentioned he thought SeaWorld would be most descriptive and very easy to recognize and remember. I liked it and we jumped on it, applying for federal and state registration immediately and developing our first logo."

During those early days, many of George's basic ideas came from the Disneyland organization and many of his early consultants came from the Disney group as well. Card Walker, then president of the Walt Disney Co. gave his blessings to the SeaWorld project and personally approved of the use of some of his key staff to help George and his team.

Tommy Walker, Disneyland's head of show production, Ettinger, and Disney attorney Bob Foster, were all on George's list of regular consultants. He could pick up the phone and talk with them; or they would visit him at the park for a couple of hours. Jack Sayers, Disney's institutional director was also helpful in the early days introducing George to potential park sponsors, including Richfield Oil, Murata Pearl, Foremost Dairies, Sparkletts Water and Pepsi Cola.

### *Pearls & Ama Girls*

It was Jack Sayers who came to George one day and said,

**Shortest-Lived Attraction**

*One of our original attractions at SeaWorld San Diego was a tank filled with yellowtail fish. Guests could fish for them and we used rubber hooks because we didn't want to hurt the fish. It was strictly catch and release. The rubber hook would come out easily as we had planned, but it would rip the fish's mouth more than we expected. By the time they were caught twice, there was nothing left of their mouth and they were dying. There was so much blood in the water that you couldn't see into the tank after one day. It turned out to be a lousy idea and after about a week that attraction was closed and elephant seals were brought in to fill the tank. It later became the first home to Shamu when she first arrived at the park.*

*- George Millay*

"There's a Japanese company that's been knocking at our door trying to get into Disneyland to build a Japanese Village, but Walt doesn't like it. I think it's a hell of an idea and you should go see him." That's how George got in the door and signed a deal with Murata Pearl Company. The group built the authentically themed Japanese Village, an expansive and popular attraction at SeaWorld.

Murata Pearl Company spent $2 million to build the Japanese Village attraction and in return, they were allowed to sell pearls and originally they were allowed to charge extra for people to come into the village. One of the draws was the authentic Ama Divers the company brought from Japan to dive at the attraction.

People would pay admission to SeaWorld, go through the turnstiles, turn right, and immediately run into Murata Pearl's gate. This additional charge didn't go over too well with guests who had already purchased one ticket at the front gate. Mike Downs, VP of marketing, kept urging George to get rid of that additional gate charge. DeMotte negotiated with Kirk Nonaka, general manager of Murata Pearl and in return for lifting the admission, gave them a small percentage of the SeaWorld paid gate. It worked well and Murata Pearl became a big part "of our concept and our early success," said George.

### *Riding with Richfield*

George had visited a hydrofoil operation on New York's Hudson River in 1962 and was determined to bring this "exciting and cutting edge sea vehicle" to SeaWorld. When the park opened in 1964, the hydrofoils at SeaWorld were the first commercial hydrofoil operation on the West Coast. Three boats were designed and built at Sprague Engineering in Los Angeles. Bob Sprague, one of the park's founding stockholders, was a "boat building genius," according to George. Each boat was built for approximately $50,000 and carried 30 passengers. The hydrofoil operation became immensely popular and carried an extra charge of 50-cents during the first year. The ride lasted about 10 minutes and there were always people in queue.

Disneyland's Sayers introduced George to Fred Jordan, director of advertising for Richfield Oil Co. and Jordan quickly agreed to name the boats "The Richfield Hydrofoils" and paid SeaWorld $50,000 a year for institutional advertising rights and brand name identification fees.

Richfield purchased billboards throughout the San Diego area for three years after the park opened, promoting their boat rides at SeaWorld, which helped promote the entire park in the process.

George says Richfield's biggest contribution was to come during the winter following the first lackluster summer season. "We were broke and although the stockholders had anteed up an additional $400,000, we were short of cash going into our second spring," George recalls. He called Richfield's Jordan and told him of the precarious financial predicament and asked him to lend the park $50,000.

**Walt Visits George**

*Walt Disney liked everybody and everybody liked Walt Disney and when he visited us at SeaWorld (San Diego) he was mobbed by people. He came down twice; once to see Shamu and the park and another time he visited us while he was in San Diego for another meeting. The last time he was here, he came over to the house for dinner. My little son, Patrick was in his highchair and spilled stuff on Walt and Walt just laughed and had a great time with Pat. What a humble man he was.*

*- George Millay.*

**Saturday and Sunday**
**You're invited to Sea World's**
**1st Birthday Party!**

**See** King Neptune and his beautiful Sea Maids in a 3-act stage play in the underwater Theater of the Sea.

Free Balloons

**See** an authentic Japanese Village with a pagoda covered in 14-karat gold.

**Free** RC Cola for everyone!

**See** a dolphin leap 18 feet high in the big Sea World Lagoon Stadium.

**Free** rides on Richfield hydrofoil boat for all kids.

Free Candy

**Free** 100 genuine pearls given away each day!

**See** a performing whale who brushes after every meal.

**Free** birthday cake!

**Sea World on San Diego's Mission Bay**
**Now open 7 days a week.** 22 acres of continuous entertainment!

There was silence on the phone, and then Jordan stated, "George I can't do it." More silence and after what seemed to George an eternity, Jordan said, "But I can prepay next year's advertising fees a few months early. Send me a bill and we will pay the $50,000 in a week."

Hawaiian Punch joined Murata Pearl Company and Richfield Oil as one of the first major corporate sponsors of the park. The Hawaiian Punch Pavilion was a Hawaiian-themed indoor lounge that served non-alcoholic Hawaiian Punch mixed drinks, complete with umbrellas and a cherry on top. Light snacks were also available. "It was a place for people to sit down and relax in comfort," George said. "I got the idea that to help entertain the guests in that pavilion, we should show South Sea travelogue films on a big screen. We approached Los Angeles TV travel personality Bill Burrud to put together the tapes and to be the personality on them."

Burrud was well known in the Southern California market and starred in his own top rated weekly travel show. He liked SeaWorld and became a stockholder as well as a board member of the fledgling company. Burrud plugged the park every chance he could, giving SeaWorld valuable exposure in the Los Angeles market.

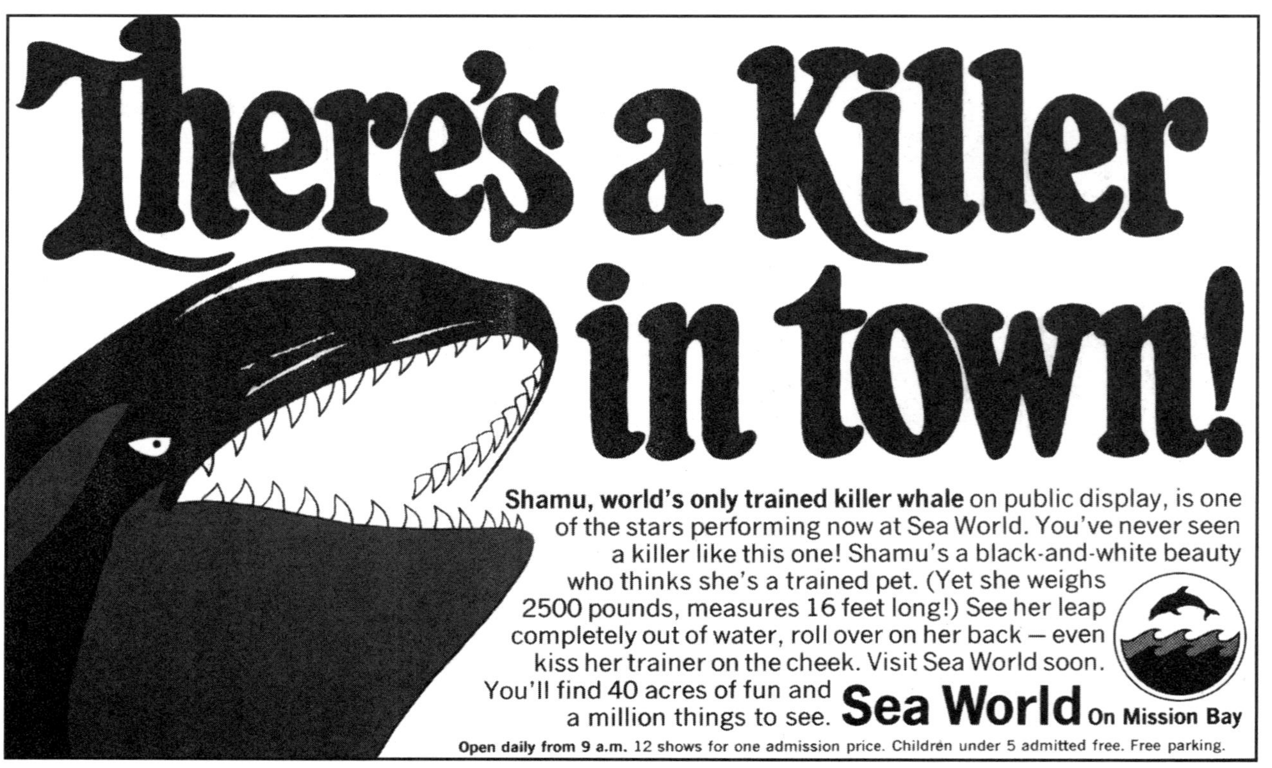
There's a Killer
in town!
Shamu, world's only trained killer whale on public display, is one
of the stars performing now at Sea World. You've never seen
a killer like this one! Shamu's a black-and-white beauty
who thinks she's a trained pet. (Yet she weighs
2500 pounds, measures 16 feet long!) See her leap
completely out of water, roll over on her back — even
kiss her trainer on the cheek. Visit Sea World soon.
You'll find 40 acres of fun and
a million things to see.
Sea World On Mission Bay
Open daily from 9 a.m. 12 shows for one admission price. Children under 5 admitted free. Free parking.

- CHAPTER 9 -

# The Arrival of Shamu

Shamu quickly became the iconic leader of the SeaWorld organization and was to SeaWorld what Mickey Mouse was, and is, to Disney parks. Shamu today remains a powerful image.

The phone call that would change the face and image of not only SeaWorld, but of every marine park in the world to this day, was made to George one Sunday afternoon in early 1965.

"I was at the park and I came home around 2:30 and Anne said I had missed a ship-to-shore call from a fellow named Ted Griffin," George recalls, noting that he had never heard of him. Griffin told Anne he would return the call later and mentioned he had a whale in tow up in the Puget Sound. "He's on his boat and he wants to talk to you," Anne told George.

Griffin called back about a half hour later, identified himself and said that he and Don Goldsberry had captured two killer whales in the Puget Sound, 40 miles north of Seattle near Whidbey Island. One was a big male, too big to introduce into captivity and one was a little female, about 13 feet long, weighing about 1,500 pounds that would be ideal for a marine park.

SeaWorld had pilot whales that were popular with the guests, and George and his team had talked about killer whales in the past. "I asked him if he had offered the whale to Bill Monahan, the manager of Marineland, and he said he had but that Monahan turned him down, saying it was too dangerous to keep killer whales in captivity." Griffin asked George, "Do you want her?" and George, without hesitation, said he did.

A deal was struck that would give Griffin $25,000 on delivery and another $10,000 if the whale lived for a year. George sent the park's veterinarian, Dave Kenney and chief trainer Kent Burgess to Seattle to examine the whale. Even if she was healthy, the challenge remained of how to transport her. Flying made the most sense, but at the time no whale had ever been flown and it had to be determined if it was possible.

### *She's Beautiful, Let's Keep Her*

Dave Kenney called back to George and said, "She's a beautiful healthy animal. I will be back tomorrow to start preparing for the move." Kenney, Kent Burgess, and operations manager and jack-of-all-trades Bob Gault, began preparing for the first transportation by air of any whale. Mike Downs lined up a charter flight and everyone chipped in and started building harnesses and transportation equipment for one whale of a whale move. The final product looked like a big coffin full of water with filters and nets and a hammock-like stretcher. They went up to Seattle, picked up the killer whale, flew her back to San Diego and as George loves to say, "the rest is history."

Kent Burgess and his staff named the young female Shamu, and today most killer whales in captivity are named after towns along Vancouver Island and Puget Sound.

When Shamu moved to SeaWorld, she took up residence in an existing tank. There were no seats or stands around the tank and there was no show. People would stand three or four deep around the tank watching Shamu as a trainer worked with her. She spent the first five months of her new life getting acclimated and meeting the public in that manner.

During that time, the trainers started playing around in the tank and became acquainted with her and her mannerisms. They developed a first of a kind killer whale show and named it "Shamu Goes to the Doctor."

### *Big Time & Bright Lights*

That original show took place in the old make shift stadium, a far cry from the massive stadium that was built in 1971. In 1987, an even larger stadium was built and that one still features the Shamu show today. To open the new stadium in 1971, the biggest whale show ever created, "Shamu Goes Hollywood," was presented.

To publicize the debut of the cutting-edge show, park officials pulled out all the stops. John Campbell and show producer Larry Sands brought in a load of Hollywood celebrities to welcome Shamu into the elite circle. Debbie Reynolds was the ringleader. She brought along Steve Allen, Jayne Meadows, Caesar Romero, Ruta Lee, Victoria Principal, Tim Conway, Vincent Price, Robert Wagner, Tina Sinatra, Jean Simmons, Jack Haley Jr., and Nelson Riddle and his entire orchestra.

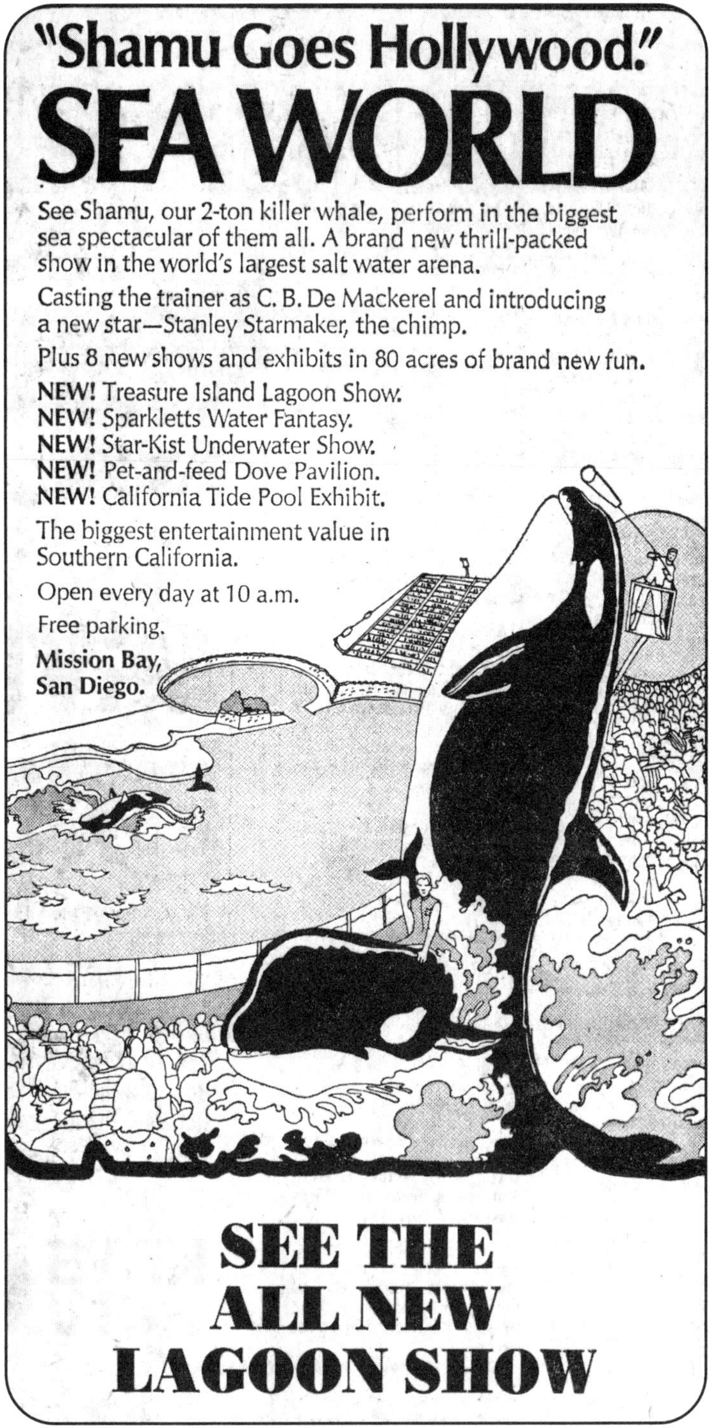
"Shamu Goes Hollywood."
SEA WORLD
See Shamu, our 2-ton killer whale, perform in the biggest sea spectacular of them all. A brand new thrill-packed show in the world's largest salt water arena.
Casting the trainer as C. B. De Mackerel and introducing a new star—Stanley Starmaker, the chimp.
Plus 8 new shows and exhibits in 80 acres of brand new fun.
NEW! Treasure Island Lagoon Show.
NEW! Sparkletts Water Fantasy.
NEW! Star-Kist Underwater Show.
NEW! Pet-and-feed Dove Pavilion.
NEW! California Tide Pool Exhibit.
The biggest entertainment value in Southern California.
Open every day at 10 a.m.
Free parking.
Mission Bay, San Diego.
SEE THE ALL NEW LAGOON SHOW

San Diego Mayor Pete Wilson, Debbie Reynolds, and George were to be introduced by a young San Diego talent named Regis Philbin but at show time, 8 p.m., there was no Regis. They waited and waited and were about to start without him when Philbin appeared all disheveled with his pants torn. "Where the hell have you been?" George asked amusedly. "Your damn security locked the front gate and wouldn't let me in," Philbin replied. "So I drove my car over to the back fence and climbed over." That's how Shamu was introduced to the world by Pete Wilson, future two-term governor of California and Regis Philbin, soon to be one of the most successful and admired TV hosts in America. "I never saw Regis again. The world was to be his oyster," George said.

*Hollywood stars line-up for a photo shoot following the "Shamu Goes Hollywood" premiere. From left, are Jack Haley Jr., Victoria Principal, Jayne Meadows, George Millay, Debbie Reynolds, Anne Millay, and Steve Allen, 1971.*

### SeaWorld Without Shamu?

Compared to Mickey Mouse, Shamu was not heavily commercialized until the late 1980s and early 1990s. "In the early years, we never merchandised her because we just didn't have that expertise," George said.

Surprisingly, George doesn't feel Shamu was omnipotent. Shamu sparked the excitement about SeaWorld, he admits, but feels the park could have done, "Just fine without Shamu because by that time, we had started several other very good shows. The Japanese Village, the Sea Maids show, and the pearl diving were very popular. Shamu certainly sparked it, I will give her that credit."

George said the dolphin show, starring Aphrodite, "was by far the best dolphin show in the world." The seal and penguin shows were also big crowd pleasers, he points out.

### *SeaWorld Starts a Collecting Program*

Following the success of Shamu, the first trained Orca to live for more than a year in captivity, the SeaWorld team started its own whale-collecting program. Kent Burgess and Dave Kenney headed one of the first park-sponsored expeditions. They led a group to Scammon's Lagoon in Baja, where they captured a little gray whale, the first in captivity. Her name was Gigi and she was approximately 14 feet long. She was brought back and put into a quarantined holding pool. George recalls the fiasco that followed.

"We never opened her to public viewing and the young whale started growing like crazy and she would eat up to 12 buckets of clams a day and about 50 quarts of cream. Foremost Dairies, a park sponsor, supplied us with all the cream. They loved all the publicity," added George. "It started costing us $400 to $500 a day to keep her. Dave (DeMotte, chief financial officer) kept telling me we had to get rid of that damn whale." By the time she was released six months after capture, she was 23 feet long and had gained about 3,000 pounds. "Every time she took a crap, she'd close out our whole filter system," chuckles George.

On the day of Gigi's release, a barge was pulled into Mission Bay to transport her out into the ocean. For publicity purposes, Lloyd Bridges, the actor who starred in the Sea Hunt television series, was invited to join them on the release. George, Bridges, and SeaWorld's VP of Productions John Campbell, followed the barge in George's personal boat, a Bertram 31.

It was quite a media event, with several TV crews and helicopters following the barge. "There were the three of us in my boat and the water got real rough but we kept going. I looked over at Lloyd and saw him getting sick and it wasn't long before he was barfing over the side. Here's a guy who made his reputation on an ocean diving adventure show, and he became deathly seasick. He was quite embarrassed but while there was a great deal of silent snickering going on, no media saw him get sick. Lloyd was a class guy and his help in our early years was invaluable," George said.

- CHAPTER 10 -

# Fine Dining, Whales On Wheels & Mrs. Millay

By the third season, business was booming and the 750,000-attendance barrier had been crossed. One of the most pleasurable vistas in the park for George was from the Hawaiian Punch Pavilion patio. He would sit there viewing the bay with its array of marine recreational activities and dream up ideas. From this vantage point he could look directly west and see a point of land about a half-mile from the center of the park. The property was located across Perez Cove and featured an even better view. It was also adjacent to the main thoroughfare through Mission Bay.

George figured it would make an excellent restaurant site, but the lease to the eight-acre site was under option and was not contiguous to the SeaWorld site. "I called Les Earnest, an old friend at the City Parks and Recreation Department, and he told me that the Perez Cove option was soon to expire, and to just lay low and we could probably assume the lease in a short time. We did and were rewarded within six months with the lease," George said.

### *The City Loved Atlantis*

When the city saw George's plans for the marine-themed Atlantis restaurant, including massive aquariums and a Von Roll sky ride across the bay connecting the park to the restaurant, they were ecstatic and he had no trouble getting the permit to build. George had long admired the architecture of the Canlis restaurant chain that operated on the West Coast and in Hawaii and retained Roland Terry, the Canlis architect, to work with SeaWorld on the design of the new restaurant. Terry, along with Dave Powell, curator of fish, and Al Vollenweider, the chef-manager, fashioned the Atlantis.

The sky ride was an immediate success attracting hundreds of thousands of riders both from within and outside the park. The Atlantis and sky ride opened in late 1967.

"We spent $2 million and built the most beautiful restaurant in the world," George notes. "It had a great view of the bay and was gorgeous inside, with browns and yellows." The interior was classic Mediterranean with unique light fixtures, wall sconces, fountains, waterfalls, live plants, two major aquariums and several smaller ones. Dave Powell created the tank habitats and the Sea Maids swam in the major habitat during the evening. The building's exterior was driftwood rock and dark brown barn wood salvaged from a Montana farm. Clear ponds and lush gardens surrounded the restaurant.

The Atlantis went downhill, according to George, after he left the company in 1974. Jan Schultz was president of SeaWorld

San Diego during the later Harcourt Brace Jovanovich years and was ordered to shut the restaurant down in 1987, with hopes that it might reopen. When Busch Entertainment purchased the parks in 1989, it was closed down completely and turned into the Hubbs SeaWorld Research Foundation.

George is disgusted that "his" restaurant was abused and closed down. "Busch turned the most beautiful restaurant in the world into a research foundation. The most ideal location in San Diego for a restaurant is now home to those bureaucratic fish chasers who should be working out of trailers down the street."

According to George, the city has lost millions of dollars in rent and taxes over the years because it allowed the restaurant, which sits on city land, to close its doors. He feels the city should have insisted that Busch sell its leasehold interests in the building and business to a qualified buyer who would have kept the restaurant open.

### Whales on Wheels

Among George's eclectic ideas, once the park opened, was the creation of a child's stroller in the shape and color of a killer whale. Avis came on board as a sponsor, and soon, the Avis Rent-a-Whale program was in full swing and getting an abundance of media attention. SeaWorld was the first to commercialize rental strollers to that extent.

Ron Harper, now president of Harper Construction Company in San Diego became infected with the Millay Madness when he accepted the development director's position at SeaWorld in 1968.

"I had been working one week and George said he was sending me to Japan," Harper recalls. "He wanted to build a sky tower and at the time, I had no idea what a sky tower was. He sent me anyway. We bought it and in April 1969 we had it up and in operation in San Diego."

Harper was not only an important element in the expansion of SeaWorld San Diego, he also proved invaluable during the creation of the Ohio and Florida marine parks as well as a couple of the Wet'n Wild parks. However, Harper is quick to point out that George "was the creator and the entrepreneur. He had the concepts and he used me to help him fulfill those ideas."

Pacific Southwest Airlines (PSA) became a corporate sponsor for the sky tower, which was named the PSA Sky Tower, affording a 360-degree view of the park and the Mission Bay area. PSA was an intra-state air carrier known mostly for its young, beautiful and provocatively dressed flight attendants. Although PSA sponsored the sky tower ride, all ride attendants were SeaWorld employees.

**GEORGE D. MILLAY** President
1720 South Shores Road, San Diego, Calif. Phone 224-3535

Tim Brown was responsible for hiring sky tower attendants that first year and was told to "stay with the current PSA image." He instructed the human resources manager, Anne Hodges, to only forward the resumes of women, 17 to 21 years of age. No men were considered for the job, something that Brown admits wouldn't fly in today's work environment. Brown hired approximately 20 "very attractive" women that year, and said one of the best workers, and one of the "best lookers" was a young lady named Fabienne.

What makes this ride stand out from the other SeaWorld attractions is that those 20 women were required to wear PSA flight attendant (stewardesses at the time) uniforms supplied by PSA that screamed "dress code violation!" The SeaWorld employee manual had a grooming section that showed a female employee with a very conservative uniform, including high button blouse and skirt hem within four inches of the knee. The PSA crew was clearly a departure from that standard.

The PSA Sky Tower ladies were outfitted with form fitting uniforms, hot pink hot pants and mini-skirts. Brown said, "Everyone was shocked to see these gorgeous women strutting around the park like real PSA flight attendants, which everyone thought they were. They were more shocked when they learned they were SeaWorld employees."

Brown recalls that the single men in the park would always route themselves by the ride to check out the "talent." Terry Hanks, an operations manager, was a sky tower regular and got lucky. He ultimately married Fabienne.

### A Drive Named SeaWorld

By 1966 SeaWorld had made a mark as one of the most successful tourist attractions in Southern California. The crowds were growing each year but the main entrance to the park was still a one-way asphalt road off I-5. George felt the park needed better identification along the interstate and came up with the idea of renaming South Mission Bay Drive, the road that led to the park, SeaWorld Drive. The park applied to the city manager's office and a date was set for a council appearance.

A seven-minute video was produced that expounded the virtues of SeaWorld and the impact on business and family entertainment in the area. It suggested the name change made "good sense" and hinted that if any city council member didn't vote for it, that member didn't have good sense. Whatever the reason it worked and SeaWorld Drive went up on five state highway direc-

*George Millay welcomes invited guests to the May 28, 1966 opening of SeaWorld San Diego's new Royal Crown Seal and Penguin Arena.*

tional boards giving the park great name recognition and at the same time, substance to the passing traveler.

It was an early coup for the park and Anne and George drove the route for a week thrilled at the achievement. "We were the first major recreational attraction in California to be so favored and honored, and from what we learned in San Diego, we did even better in Florida when it came to naming roads," he adds.

### *Mrs. Millay: The Lady & the Man*

Anne would show up at openings and go to parties and events with George, but she says she was there mostly for support. "Support is a good word. With him, business came first and family came second. I knew that going in, but we had many, many fun times. We still do. We agreed very early that he would take care of the business and I would take care of the home and manage the apartment house that we built," Anne said. "I was on the outside, yet on the inside, meaning that officially those were the lines and that is the way that we progressed successfully together for all of these years. I was the boss' wife with everything that entails."

However, Anne always made it a point to know what was going on. "I would do my research, meaning I would listen to everything he had to say and read the *San Diego Business Journal*, the *Wall Street Journal* and the *San Diego Union and Tribune* every day. I knew a lot more about the business side of things than anyone ever thought I knew and exercised some influence in myriad ways. Let's put it that way," she smiled.

### *Time to Lose a Few Pounds*

By the mid-1960s, thanks to all the good living, George had put on a few extra pounds that he couldn't get off by jogging to work. He went to a doctor who prescribed a regimen of diet pills.

In the fall of 1967, Chip Muglia, a young stockbroker for Francis I. Dupont & Company of San Diego, was asked by his company to conduct research on the park, in conjunction with its upcoming public offering.

"I was sitting across from him at his desk and saw a series of diet supplements of the current fad variety," said Muglia. "Although I was starting out a new career in finance, I held a degree in pharmacology."

As the two discussed business, Muglia's eyes lingered over the bottles again, George saw what he was looking at and explained they were diet pills. Muglia asked if he could read the labels and George said he could.

"As I read the labels, he sensed a bit of disapproval in my expression. I should have kept my mouth shut, but when he asked what was wrong, I told him I wouldn't take those pills if I were him," Muglia recalls.

George looked at him and asked, "Why not, what the hell do you know?" Muglia started squirming and figured this important meeting was coming to an abrupt end. "I briefly explained my background and then told him the pharmacology of each prescribed tablet. When he heard the words thyroid and diuretic, he stood up, grabbed all the bottles, walked across to his private lavatory, and flushed them all down the toilet."

He walked back to the desk, picked up Muglia's card and shook his hand. "Chip Muglia, you know I started out in business myself as a stockbroker. Let me give you a tour of the park." They have been friends ever since.

### *Down at Ernie's Place*

Tim Brown, operations manager, recalls that many after-work discussions during those early years took place in Ernie's Bar, on Midway Drive across from the Sports Arena, about two miles from SeaWorld. While most of the SeaWorld "suits" frequented the upper-scale Atlantis restaurant, directly across from SeaWorld, Ernie's was a popular hangout for the maintenance men, aquarists, operations people and trainers. It was a place the line workers could relax out of the SeaWorld spotlight.

"Ernie's was a casual sanctuary for us to relax, share camaraderie and vent about the day's challenges. Starting at 4:30 until 11 p.m., there were always 10 to 25 off-duty (well, mostly off-duty) employees kicking back," Brown remembers.

Ernie's was a victim of commercial sprawl in 1973 and on the final night of operation, the owner threw a party for his SeaWorld friends. "The place was packed and could hardly accommodate the massive crowd, many who just wanted to be part of the end of an era," Brown said. As things started to clear out around 11 p.m. a loud voice yelled, "Clear the way," followed by a sharp, loud, buzzing sound. It was John Ronglie, director of park maintenance with a chain saw. He walked up to the bar and cut it in pieces.

"The next day, many of Ernie's regulars bragged that they took home a piece of history and many said they saw John dragging out a large piece of the bar and loading it on his truck," said Brown.

Chances are it was an American made truck, notes John Seeker, a park photographer at the time. "George has always been very pro-American. One day, he found out some of the employees were driving foreign cars, which of course he didn't like. So he changed the car allowance policy to cover only American made cars. You could drive a foreign car if you wanted, but you could not be reimbursed for its usage. Naturally, I expressed my love for American cars and financially thought it was a good idea to drive one."

George still decries the loss of American jobs to overseas competitors.

### *Inadvertently, Politicians Lend a Hand*

When a House Committee first discussed the Marine Mammal Act in early 1972, George and his SeaWorld crew received the news with great apprehension, but were slow to act. Confused on what the act really meant to SeaWorld and totally inexperienced in national political workings, the executives began assembling a plan of action to help protect SeaWorld's interests.

The company hired the L.A, law firm of Bob Fitch, a former Lt. Governor of California, a prominent California Republican and long time friend of Richard Nixon. "All Fitch did was hire a Washington D.C. lobbyist and set up a meeting with Ron Ziegler. He made two phone calls and a sent us a bill for $25,000," George recalls. He met with Ron Ziegler and Bob Haldeman, who had both worked on the SeaWorld advertising account several years earlier, at the White House.

"They were sympathetic but as it turned out had far bigger problems, a situation called Watergate," said George. "We entered the fray too late to have any impact on the legislation itself. It was popular in both houses and had abundant support in the scientific community. It cleared both houses and became law immediately."

SeaWorld had been collecting and training dolphins and

# Lloyd Bridges' SeaWorld

Hollywood's underwater pro, Lloyd Bridges takes you under the sea and around the world as he hosts 13 entertaining specials filmed in the deep salt water tanks of SeaWorld and the oceans of the Earth.

Why are SeaWorld oceanariums always packed with families? Because SeaWorld is based on two imaginative concepts – marine animals in spectacular shows, and a center for quality family entertainment.

Wrap this notion into 13 thrilling specials hosted by Sea Hunt's Lloyd Bridges and you've a package of shows that'll delight and charm.

In or out of a wet suit, Bridges is known to viewers as 'A good man to have along for an evening of adventure programming.' He appears in the 13 specials as host and narrator. He'll tell how dolphins communicate, show techniques of teaching tricks to Shamu, and other marine mammals. Adding to the enjoyment will be his personal tour backstage where you'll discover the workaday world SeaWorld visitors miss.

What goes on back here is just as fascinating as the show out front! Bridges explains it all as he expertly guides you through your evening at SeaWorld.

-Promotional material promoting the 1972 syndicated television series.

*Lloyd Bridges enjoys a kiss from Shamu, above, and gets instructions from SeaWorld trainer Mike Rowe on how to work with Rocky, the performing sea lion, below.*

killer whales for several years and had a good population of both for its three parks but George realized that times had changed and SeaWorld might have complications in the future collecting animals. "We were spooked," he admits.

The act established a moratorium on the collection and importing of marine mammals, their parts and products. It protected polar bears, sea otters, walruses, dugongs, manatees, whales, porpoises, seals, and sea lions. It prohibited the collecting of those mammals in U.S. waters and it prohibited importing them from outside U.S. territorial waters.

The new law was frustrating and difficult for those who operated before its existence, but SeaWorld broke through many of the obstacles by helping the federal bureaucracy codify rules of collecting, design of animal enclosures, and how to initiate successful breeding programs, among other things.

As it turns out and by a strange quirk of fate, the Marine Mammal Act was a bonanza for SeaWorld. Although not its intent, the law helped the SeaWorld parks become a monopoly. It made it practically impossible for anyone to initiate competition against the parks and forced upon potential competitors costly specifications in design and construction of new facilities for marine mammals. It also put severe restrictions on collecting.

By default, SeaWorld became the only major marine entertainment center that had the know-how, the existing facilities and in-hand capital to subsist and expand under the harsh bureaucratic regulations of the law, according to George, adding that SeaWorld "became the only game in the U.S."

The legislation led to the development of the world-famous breeding programs at SeaWorld because at the time officials feared they would have problems getting additional marine mammals in the future.

- CHAPTER 11 -

# Short Hair: Keep Cutting

George admired the look and feel of Disneyland and a big part of that admiration came from the fact that everyone who worked there was well groomed, looked good in the various styles of uniforms, and had been trained well to interact with the guests.

From day one, SeaWorld had a strict employee grooming policy. The employee manual featured a photo of traffic department employee, Bob Kenniston. He was pictured in his neatly pressed white shirt, pressed slacks, SeaWorld-issued tie and the approved tapered haircut, both front and side view, with side burns no lower than mid-ear. Additionally, there was a picture in the lobby of the administration building showing "poster boy" Kenniston's short haircut. Under it were the words: "Don't bother to apply for a job if your hair doesn't look like this."

By 1970, the traffic department was staffed primarily with high school and college-aged employees, aged 16-21, working as parking lot attendants, ticket sellers, and information specialists. They were also among those most guilty of dress code violations.

Tim Brown, operations manager at the time, said when it came to employee grooming, there were few issues with the female employees but his real challenge came with the young men who were opposed to the strict hair length standards. Those were the days when the Beatles and the Rolling Stones were the teenage role models.

### *Long Hair Takes Longer to Cut*

"We would often send those in violation out to go get a haircut which would generally take them away from their jobs for an hour or more," Brown said. "Frustrated by consistently having people absent from their jobs for that long, I was asked by George to open a SeaWorld barbershop to expedite the process of getting the violators trimmed and back to work faster."

With a modest budget, Brown went to a barber supply

November 25, 1969

Sea World
1720 Southshores Road
San Diego, Ca 92109

Gentlemen:

I read in Neil Morgan's column about your not wanting to waste your time if applicants had long hair, sideburns or a mustache.

More power to you. I think it is a spendid idea and you are to be congratulated. I have heard of but one other company that apparently feels the same way and that is IBM. They insist that their employees have suits, white shirts and short hair.

It is most disgusting to see all the male youths with such slovenliness. Most adults look ridiculous too. Long hair and sideburns ages them. I feel if the persons on TV got back to haircuts and trimmed sideburns most adults would follow suit, and parents could and would do something about their children. Many parents today are trying to follow suit and dress like their children instead of having their children conform to decent standards of dress and appearance.

Most Sincerely,

Norma M. Batchelder

Norma M. Batchelder

shop and purchased a barber chair and the traditional barbershop signage. John Rognlie, director of maintenance for the park, built a 150-sq. ft. barbershop close to the employee lounge.

The real challenge for Brown was finding a barber who would work four days a week with a mandatory Saturday and Sunday schedule. Brown was in the Marine Corps Reserves and conducted his duty work at Camp Elliott across from Miramar Air Station. "The Marine Corps. was the only organization stricter than SeaWorld when it came to grooming," Brown pointed out. "In my early days, my approved SeaWorld haircut often did not pass military inspection and I was sent to Miramar to get a haircut. That's where I met and ultimately hired, the first SeaWorld barber."

That barber became known as "Nick" because he was well into his 70's, had shaky hands and the lack of consistency of his work left something to be desired. Once Nick was hired, the park had a strange and potent grooming motivator. "When the young men would arrive to their jobs and were in need of a haircut, we would not allow them to leave the park to go to their own barber, but instead, we would send them to Nick," Brown recalls, adding that "employees were not happy with Nick's work and compliance with SeaWorld grooming policies greatly increased." Haircuts initially were free, but ultimately cost $1 to help cover costs. Once Nick retired and a younger, more contemporary barber was hired, business increased at the park.

### *Employees Weren't the Stars*

"George didn't want the employees to stand out or be the star of the show," said Bob Gault. "He wanted Shamu to be the star and he wanted the animals in the shows to be the stars. He wanted employees to be uniformed and to blend in, not stand out with fancy hairdos or colorful clothing. He often said he wanted guests to look at the beautiful landscaping, not the moustache or sideburns on that employee standing over there."

George hated long hair, but had nothing against moustaches except that they weren't appropriate for the park environment. During the early construction of SeaWorld, George had a full moustache that he loved and that his wife hated. He ended up cutting it for her, not because of his own dress code standards. "I'm taking her down to Mercy Hospital to have our first born in 1963, while the park was under construction. We get her checked in, and comfortable in bed and she's in labor. She looked at me and she says, 'George, when I wake up honey, I don't want to see that mustache, please.' I said, honey, it'll be gone. I went home that night and shaved the mustache." Their first son, Patrick, was born the following morning at sunrise.

### *Long Haired Hippie Freak*

George, an active hawk on the Vietnam War attached long hair to all the chaos that was happening in the country. "I associated long hair as symptomatic and ancillary to the anti-war movement, the anti-establishment movement, and what was happening on college campuses. I associated all that with long hair. I hated it because I thought it was symbolic of our nation's defeat in Vietnam, which pissed me off," George stated.

He still doesn't particularly like long hair but now, he can at least tolerate it. "I know it just reflects the personality of the person and not necessarily his philosophy or his political ideas. I would probably wear a ponytail today if I could," George readily admits.

No one at SeaWorld was immune to George's hair wrath, even his favorites. After a long collecting trip, Dave Powell came back with a beard. Powell was one of George's boys and had gotten a great deal of latitude from George through the years on many things. He had heard that Powell had come back from this trip with a beard, and George didn't think much about it.

A day goes by, two days goes by, a week goes by, and Powell still had the beard and finally George couldn't take it any longer and pulled Powell into his office to remind him that beards weren't allowed and told him he had to shave it off. Powell stood his ground. "No, I'm not going to cut it off. I like this beard and my wife likes it," he said to George.

"You know damn well I can't let you have a beard. Everyone else would have a beard in five minutes around here," responded George, informing Powell that if he didn't shave it off by the next day, he would be fired. "As much as I like you, I'm going to can you. I don't want to, but I will," George said. The next day Powell came to work clean-shaven.

### *Buzz has a Buzz*

George's fear of long locks continued into the early 1970s when he had several confrontations with his outsourced number cruncher, Harrison "Buzz" Price. In his book "Walt's Revolution! By the Numbers," Price addressed George's aversion to long hair.

*"During our early work (on SeaWorld Florida), George was the central protagonist and it was always fun to spar with him. Our argument on the subject of hair is a typical pungent interchange, one of many. At the time, hair length was a metaphor for the then current intense generational clash of cultures. Short meant conservative.*

*"Long meant liberal. Each side was deeply offended and even threatened by the hair length of the other. George would roam around our downtown fifth floor office and tell me what he thought about the hair length of our staff in acid metaphor, usually ending with a general challenge like 'what is this, a bunch of left wing sodomites?'*

*"It came to a head when George Chalmers, generally thought by our female staff to be one of our most handsome men, was assigned to the Florida project. George Millay was not very gentle, so I decided to deal with this festering crisis. I wrote him in August 1970."*

Written eloquently, the letter was totally tongue in cheek:

*"Dear George, Your comments about our staff have been considered with interest. As an addicted researcher, I immediately went around the office gathering data pertaining to your stated objectives. Some conclusions from the investigation:*

*1. We do have a wide variety of hair lengths and styles, ranging from the quarter inch average of Jim McCarthy (an Irishman like yourself) to one full beard (coupled with very short hair) and two rather questionable coiffures in the mod style that we recognize as something of a problem.*

*2. As to the men we have sent on your jobs, Bob Shedlock and Chuck Belotte are almost bald. I am right behind him although sometimes too busy to get to the barbershop. I assume, therefore that your concern is directed to George Chalmers and Doug Hinchliffe, both of whom are blessed with luxuriant growth.*

*3. I examined both men carefully this morning and found them to be extremely well-groomed, devoid of upturned curls and generally impeccable. I cannot classify them as a hair problem. I did notice that Doug needs to trim the hair in his ears and George could use a little bit of nostril snipping. As to George's moustache, bare in mind that it would be identical to the style of our late leader whom you admire so much, Walt Disney, were it not for the slightly sinister turndown at the corners."*

Price continued with more of the same, then closed by saying:

*"Don't think for a minute that I am unaware of the significance of hair as a political and social symbol in these troubled times. I have fought the problem on the beaches, in my home and in the office. The attached corporate policy memo on the subject will show you that my heart is in the right place. As to the future of our relationship with you, I believe that it will be entirely possible for me to combine reasonable hair and creative ability in the same man.*

*"We are delighted to have this project and will proceed forthwith to find you the best-damned site in the state of Florida."*

As promised, Price proceeded to send out a memo to his staff pointing out that "hair as a symbol of philosophical position is irrelevant to the client relationship."

Don Stewart, of Economic Consulting Services, worked for Buzz Price during that period. "I was sent to work with George on a SeaWorld expansion analysis. I had been a Marine officer and had worked at Mobil Oil Company and had the haircut that most closely fit the Millay profile," Stewart recalls with a laugh. "While I was waiting in his reception area waiting to see him, a male college student with a ponytail came in and was waiting to pick up a package he was to deliver. George came out and I introduced myself."

Then George looked at the pony-tailed delivery guy. "What are you doing in my office," George bellowed. The young man tried to explain but was cut off by George. "Get out and don't even think about returning until you get a hair cut." Stewart remembers that the young man looked at George like he was crazy and promptly left.

### *Wrath Beyond Associates*

Millay and DeMotte, as well as the other top executives were all clean cut and could have passed as Marines, says Jan Schultz, who joined George in 1971 as a marketing executive. He points out that George's aversion to long hair was not confined only to his employees or associates. George would avoid going through sections of town where he knew he would most likely see longhaired guys, but he wasn't shy about reacting whenever he saw one.

If he was driving down the street and saw one, he would roll down the window and yell something like "hey you commie pinko left wing pervert, go get your hair cut." If he was walking down the street and would see one walking toward him, he would stop them and go face to face with them with similar remarks. Schultz was with him during many of these confrontations. "He would start badmouthing the guy and I would say, oh shit, here we go. I can't tell you how many fights we nearly got into because of that, but I don't remember ever coming to blows with anyone."

Schultz said the advertising agencies he dealt with at the time, and all the other creative people, including musicians, had to pass muster and pass the SeaWorld dress code. There was one musical group coming in to audition and Schultz had a picture of them on his desk and George saw it. "What are you doing with these guys?" he asked. Schultz said that he was looking at the possibility of bringing them in to do some entertainment. "Not in my park," he said.

"George relax, maybe we can get them to cut their hair," Schultz replied, half jokingly. The group was asked to come in anyway and Schultz had them set for a time when George would normally not be around. They were out in the lobby early one evening and George spotted them. "He comes charging back into my office and tells me I have to get them out of his reception room. Then he asks me what I'm going to do and I tell him that I plan to tell them to cut their hair if they ever want to play at SeaWorld. He tells me to tell them to get their hair cut before they'll ever be allowed to sit in the SeaWorld reception room," Schultz said.

"C'MON OUT, HENRY! THAT WASN'T MR. MILLAY... BESIDES... YOUR HAIR'S NOT THAT LONG!"

***Overnight Haircut***

John Seeker, who worked at the time in the marketing department as a photographer, was in the office late one night. George was still there and was in a bad mood. The two ran into each other in the hall and Seeker knew he was in for trouble. His hair was "a tad too long" and he hadn't had time to get it cut. "He looked at me and just went nuts and started screaming at me. How dare you! I want you in my office at 8:30 in the morning with a haircut!"

The young Seeker was petrified. The SeaWorld barber had already left, but he was able to find a Navy barber who gave him a real hack job. "It was the worst haircut I've ever had. He only knew one way to cut, the Navy way. One sideburn was up and the other was down and it was very short."

He said he didn't sleep much that night worrying about losing his job and the next morning he got to work early and paced until he heard George arrive. "He had jogged from home to the office and by the time I got to his office, he was already in the shower. I hung around outside his door and he finally came out, wearing nothing but a bathrobe. I knocked on the door jam and he asked me what I needed. He had forgotten about the haircut and I had to remind him."

George stood up, and motioned to Seeker, "Come over here" and he proceeded to look closely at the haircut. "That's a damn good haircut. Does your wife like it," George said. Seeker replied, "No sir, she'd like to have it longer." George looked at him and said "Tough shit; she doesn't sign your check."

***Hide, Here Comes George!***

When George would leave his office to go out into the park, his secretary, DeEtta Sharp would call the operations department and tell them where George was headed. A flurry of activity would follow that call, and if supervisors saw someone who needed a haircut or wasn't up to snuff on the dress code, they would be hidden or quickly reassigned to another area.

George's path would be walked ahead of him, out of sight, to make sure there was no trash on the ground. "It was like a CIA operation. They would clear the area between where he was coming from and his final destination. It was a well-kept secret that we were doing that," Seeker said. "I still don't think he realized that we had always been warned."

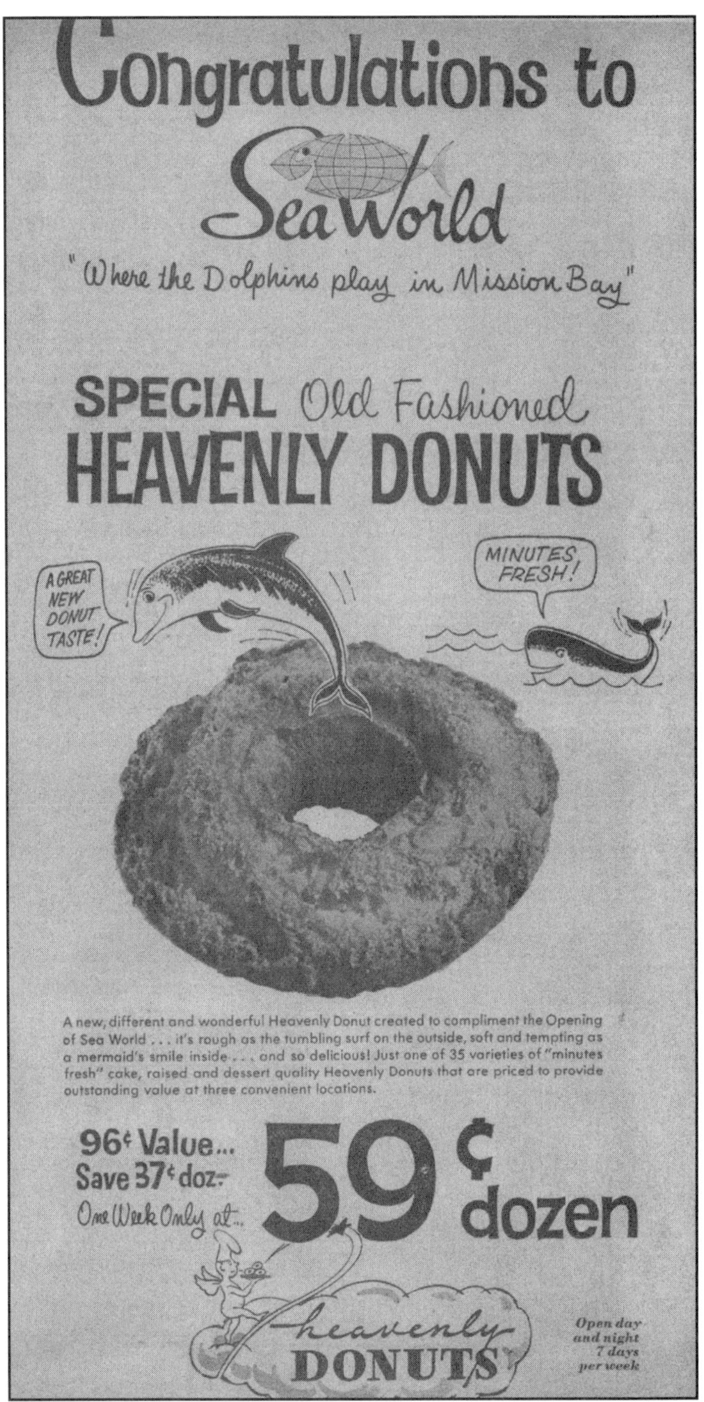


*A Heavenly Donut created especially for the opening of SeaWorld San Diego, 1964.*

- CHAPTER 12 -

# Creating Unique Entertainment

In early 1969 George received a call from George Whitney, the well-known general manager of the CBS television affiliate in San Diego. He told George that John Campbell, a good friend of ABC President Elton Rule, was looking for a job and said that George should talk with him. Campbell had just resigned as president of ABC's owned and operated television stations.

"He and I hit if off immediately and I hired John, put him in charge of show production and he started glamorizing the shows right from the start," George said. Campbell came in and took SeaWorld shows to another level. After he left SeaWorld, Campbell would show up again several times to play important roles in the George Millay story.

While at SeaWorld, Campbell introduced George to Larry Sands, who created two or three of what George considers the best shows ever produced at SeaWorld. "It was obvious right from the start that John got it and knew what we needed."

### *The Importance of New*

In the recreation business, the two essential ingredients of success are the concept and location, and if you've got a good concept and good location, you usually have a winner unless the financing is onerous or the management is sub-par. George likes to quote the old saying about the classic American business failure, "It was mismanaged, under-financed and over-built."

SeaWorld officials learned quickly that "we had a good location and a good concept, but if we wanted return business year in, year out, we needed to come up with something new and appealing at regular intervals that would also fit into our theme," George notes. "You can't randomly add things or have a radical departure like putting bumper cars around Shamu Stadium. If you don't have a clear picture of who you are, you start becoming a hodgepodge and an amalgamation of various activities, and you lose your identity."

Ever cognizant of that, officials were cautious whenever they wanted to enhance the existing park. During the years, using creativity and a knowledge of what would work for their audience, SeaWorld officials were able to come up with activities and shows that lent themselves to both the marine park and to the marine environment.

One of the first departures from the fish exhibits and mammal shows was the Water Fantasy Fountain show. The show's prototype had been developed by Rain Jet Corporation of

*Carlo Mosca, SeaWorld's first director of education, enjoys a sled ride during Snow World at SeaWorld, 1972.*

Burbank and offered to Disneyland first. After they turned it down, Disney's Jack Sayers called and told George that he ought to take a look at it. He did and was sold on the idea immediately.

The concept was to stage the show indoors and Ben Southland designed a unique structure that seated 1,000 people in the round with the fountain in the center. Independent producer Larry Sands was hired to script the show and prepare the score. The 15-minute light, music, and fountain production, presented in a dark, comfortably air-conditioned auditorium, was an instant hit vaulting to the top 10% of all park activities in visitor surveys.

***Bring Along Your Friends, Burt***

George said he had a fun time selling the fountain show sponsorship to Sparklett's Water Company and its "flamboyant" president, Burt Arnds. "We were getting good at attracting commercial sponsors and Burt bought the idea in a heartbeat. He loved his fountain show and constantly dragged guests down to San Diego to view 'his' show, for free of course."

The success of the Sparklett's Water Fantasy Fountain Show proved to George that various other forms of quality water-oriented entertainment could be integrated into SeaWorld's show lineup while the park retained its elite status in the marine park industry. Later, George found that he could diversify in the same manner at his Wet'n Wild waterparks.

Jan Schultz brought many of the ideas to the table for diverse programming and entertainment to the park. "How many marine mammal exhibits and water shows can you continue to build if you're trying to stick to the pure form of a marine park," Schultz said. "George, I would say, we're in the entertainment business and on years that we don't have major capital improvements, we've still got to give people the feeling that there's something new and different happening."

That attitude forced creative thinking. "The creativity and the ability to take a risk was something I really liked about working for George. Being allowed to bring in non-water or animal related entertainment and trying things that most people would set aside and say no to, spurred me on a great deal," Schultz noted.

The park started promoting Country Days and Nights at SeaWorld and to the surprise of most everyone, Schultz hit pay dirt with his Snow World at SeaWorld promotion. "Everybody thought I was nuts. Here we are in the middle of San Diego and I wanted to create a snow mountain. I found that it would cost too much to actually build a mountain so we went to an area of the park that had a 14-foot tall berm and we brought in 400-tons of snow every day. We sold hot cider and created an entire winter environment.

"I felt people were laughing at me around the park until they went out there on opening day and saw kids lined up for literally a mile wearing their stocking caps, gloves and their mittens. We had a success and it doubled December's attendance in 10 days," Schultz said proudly. It became a yearly tradition at SeaWorld for more than a decade.

Based on Snow Mountain's success, Schultz and his crew were allowed to keep trying things and the park started moving from a "pure" marine park, to a diverse marine park that presented eclectic entertainment.

### *A Kite Daredevil*

During the early 1970s, Air Devil Jim Rusing was one of the first Delta Kite Flyers in the country. George and Schultz had seen him entertain in San Francisco and hired him on the spot to perform during the summer seasons at SeaWorld San Diego. Hanging under a large kite, Rusing would be pulled into the air by a boat, cut loose and would glide over Shamu Stadium, circle around and land in an open field just prior to each of Shamu's scheduled shows.

Well, he was supposed to land in an open field. "He'd actually land in the parking lot, he'd land in the stands, he'd land in the water, but most of the time, he'd land on that field," said Schultz, laughing as he reminisced. One day, George summoned Rusing and Schultz into his office and proposed a major, new stunt for Rusing to perform. After hearing the details, Rusing sensed that it was unsafe, but assured George he would try to figure out a way to do it.

It was designed to be a more intimate act, closer to the crowds, and more visually exciting. After George walked everyone through the stunt, even Rusing, caught up in the boss' enthusiasm, was convinced it could be done. Rusing said yes, he would be willing to do it, pointing out that it could do great things for his reputation.

The next morning Schultz got to his office early and Rusing was there, sitting on the floor outside his door. It turned out Rusing hadn't slept the night before, having stayed up working out the stunt on paper. He showed Schultz the calculations he had made. "It won't work, I'm going to kill myself, it won't work, I can't do it," the shaking Rusing told Schultz who agreed with the daredevil. They went into George's office, showed him the calculations and Schultz reiterated that Rusing stood a good chance of killing himself if he tried it. George looked at him and said, "Damn it, Rusing, I agree with you. I don't mind breaking your damn leg, but I'm not going to kill you."

The stunt wasn't done and Rusing went back to doing his original act three or four times a day around Shamu Stadium. As Easter approached, Schultz had another, less dangerous change in routine in mind for the daredevil. "I wanted him to fly in over the stadium dressed as the Easter Bunny," Schultz said. "Here's this big, rugged, tough son-of-a-bitch who has had every bone in his body broken at least once, and he looked at the costume and told me he couldn't wear it. I said, Jim, not only do you have to wear it, we're going to film it for commercials. Several days later, we had the film crew out and Jim is landing everywhere, he's landing in the parking lot, he's landing back in the bay, I mean he could never hit the target, but we got the film we needed and we made the commercial."

### *Bad Luck, Lot's of Press*

One day John Campbell set up a publicity TV shoot with a young lady riding on Shamu's back with CBS crews doing the coverage. Evidently the lights or the strange new rider spooked the whale and Shamu grabbed the girl, Anne Eckes, and pulled her to the bottom of the tank. Shamu then breached two or three times with Eckes' legs in her mouth and the rest of her body hanging limply across the nose of the whale. Eckes was screaming, "Help me, help me," all the time the TV cameras were churning. The trainer and Campbell got a long pole in Shamu's mouth and finally Eckes was released.

George couldn't figure out why Eckes, a secretary, was permitted to be on the whale in the first place. He called around and found that George Becker, then part of the marketing team, had chosen her to be the one to be featured for the filming. He thought she would represent the park well on national TV. "Are you sure that's the real reason?" George queried Becker.

On the news that night Walter Cronkite led off with the footage of Shamu breaching with a girl dangling from her mouth.

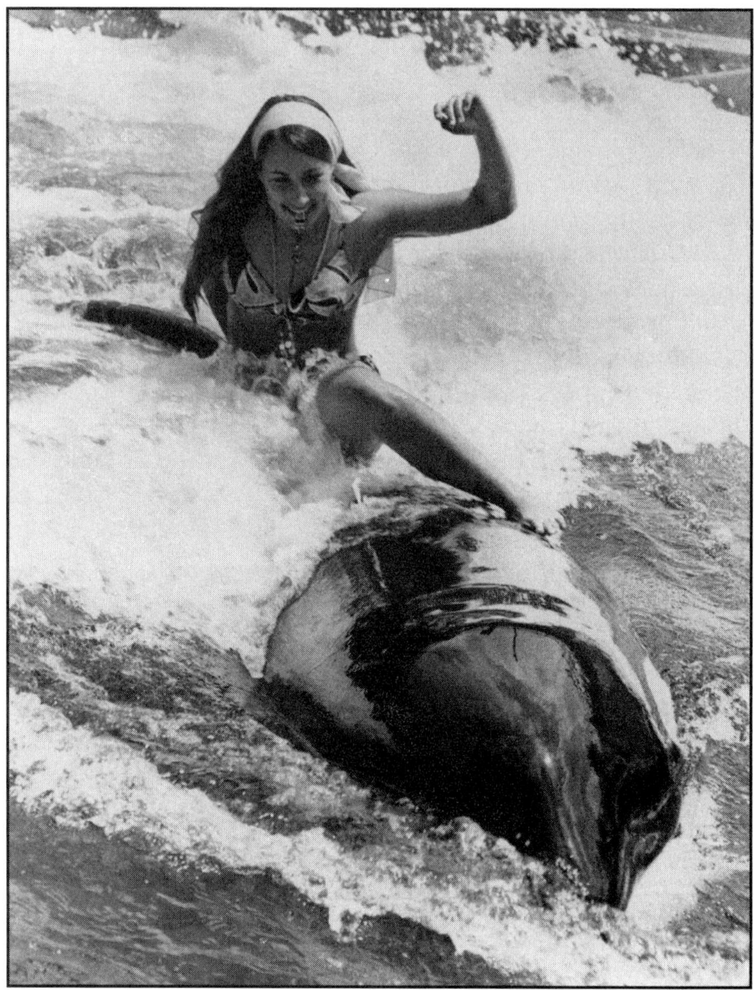

*Anne Eckes during her historical whale ride, 1970.*

George recalls that while the event was very scary and could have been disastrous, "It was a fantastic PR coup for us and made a national star of Shamu." The entire management team was deeply concerned and training policies were modified immediately dictating that only qualified trainers and certain Sea Maids were allowed in the water with Shamu.

**Come on Down, Birdie, Birdie**

In his constant worldwide search for unique shows, George went to Japan and observed a production in which kimono-clad, elderly Japanese women each walked peacocks to the top of a mountain peak and at a designated time, released the peacocks which then flew back down the hill and landed in front of the crowds, all choreographed to a musical track. George came back and told everyone that it was quite spectacular and unique. He told Frank Todd, the top bird guy at the park, and Schultz that he wanted a peacock show just like the one he had seen.

Early one morning before most of the employees had arrived for work, George had Todd take three peacocks to the top of the sky tower while five members of the top management team gathered at the base. George wanted them to see for themselves the beauty he saw in watching flying peacocks. George yelled up to Todd, "Release the peacocks!" All three of them go pfffft, straight down. Schultz recalls that, "They hit the ground right at out feet, a terrible view. All died instantly."

Bob Gault was one of those standing at the bottom and witnessed one of the funniest lines ever delivered by George as he was standing there at the base of the sky tower with the peacocks dropping like rocks. "Gee, it didn't look like this in Japan," George said softly.

Fast-forward 20 years to Schultz and George having dinner one evening and sharing stories from their past. George looks at Schultz and says to him "Damn it, to this day I can't figure out why the peacock act worked in Japan but it didn't work here."

Schultz started laughing and said, "George, Frank Todd clipped their wings because he didn't want to have to do that show at SeaWorld. He sacrificed those three birds so he wouldn't have to have dozens of peacocks performing that show four or five times a day."

Schultz thought George knew, but it turned out he hadn't. "George looked at me in disbelief and he started to get pissed. If Frank would have been there that night, George would have ripped the hell out of him," Schultz said. George recalls that moment of enlightenment. "If I had known that at the time, I would have fired him on the spot."

### *High Divers are a Hit!*

In the early 1970s, Go-Go Gurlack was hired as a comedy diver at SeaWorld Ohio and it was commonly known that Go-Go had the habit of having a few belts before each show. One day, "Go-Go damn near killed himself. He fell off the diving board, missed the water and hit the concrete, ending both Go-Go's career and our diving show," George remembers, noting that he wanted to replace him with a diving pig. "But our vet said he would quit his job and lead an animal rights campaign against the park if we brought in a pig act. I never did like that vet."

Victor Zobel was a comedy diver in San Diego. "He spent an entire summer with us. He was an old man but a very funny comedy diver," said George. "He was brash and he was a good showman. The white-haired and balding Vic showed up sober every day, did his show, never bothered anybody, ate lunch and dinner at the employees' lounge, and he got along great with the young kids. Many people really liked the old guy," George recalls.

### *A Stubborn Pachyderm*

During late spring 1972, George was on the phone with SeaWorld Ohio's new general manager, George Becker. He was bemoaning the fact that Google, an elephant purchased to be the star of the Water Ski Show and that had been a big part of the TV marketing campaign was refusing to water ski.

George's good friend Al Slavik walked in the room just as George yelled at Becker, "If that stupid elephant won't water ski, get rid of her and get an elephant that will!" Slavik howled with laughter and told the story for years about George and his problematic water skiing elephant. "By the way, the little gal came around and became the hit of the 1972 season in Ohio," George notes.

### *A Grand Old Tree, A Yearly Tradition*

Doc Lemmon, the first general manager at Magic Mountain, which SeaWorld built and opened in 1971, was "a hell of a nice guy, a real classic. We were in the middle of construction at Magic Mountain in 1971, and I was up there one day looking at the sky tower which was located at the top of the mountain and had an open observation deck at the top," George recalls.

Lemmon was explaining to George how he wanted to string lights from the very top of the tower down to the observa-

*George Millay, 1976.*

tion deck at Christmas, making the top segment of it look like a huge Christmas tree. "I thought, gees, that's a hell of an idea, and I went back to SeaWorld and started wondering if we could do the same thing with our sky tower. I called in Bill Riley, our head fabricator, a genius metal fabricator and Hank Kotch, our head electrician. I told them what I wanted to do and Riley suggested that we take it one step further and take the lights clear to the ground."

At first George thought he was kidding, but once Kotch and Riley put their heads together and thought about it, they told George they could do it and he gave them the go-ahead. They ran steel cables from the top to the ground and wrapped the strings of lights around them, held in place by small rings. The SeaWorld Christmas Tree premiered in winter of 1972 and has become a San Diego tradition.

- CHAPTER 13 -

# Avoiding Adversities

A book on George Millay's failures, tragedies and disappointments would be a short one. For being such a risk taker, George experienced an amazingly small number of failures or major disappointments in his life.

One of the disappointments, albeit a small one when you consider the scope of the ideas he conceived through the years, concerned a small passenger submarine. George had visited Expo 64 in Geneva, Switzerland and one of the most popular attractions there was the August Piccard, a deep-diving submarine that would take people, 29 at a time, to the bottom of 1,000-foot deep Lake Geneva where they would sit awhile and look out at the surroundings. George immediately thought about bringing it to the U.S. and creating an attraction that would take passengers out to the La Jolla Trench, off San Diego.

He hired Captain Frank Bewar, a retired Navy submarine captain living in San Diego, to study the feasibility of the project. The biggest problem and the one that blew it out of the water was that the submarine had been built outside the United States and Maritime law reads that one cannot transport people in territorial waters of the United States for profit in a vessel not built in the United States. It's one of those old protectionist laws that were passed in the early 1800s to protect American shipbuilding.

The Coast Guard couldn't approve the project and George, who was very excited about the attraction, was broken hearted and didn't buy the submarine.

### *Dirty Politics Killed the Deal*

George was very high at one time on buying Sea Life Park in Hawaii. It was a well-constructed and beautifully designed park in one of the most picturesque settings ever chosen for a theme park of any kind.

The marine park had never been successful and was going broke. George saw an opportunity. He approached the owners and started negotiations to buy the park out of bankruptcy. Sea Life

**Politically Speaking**

*I left UCLA a liberal, not a roaring liberal, but a liberal from the point that I felt the world could be better. I slowly became a radical, screaming conservative. The only time I ever walked the streets of this country for a candidate was for Barry Goldwater. I really went out for Goldwater and for Reagan. During my late 20's, 30's, 40's, and even into my 50's, I was an active conservative. If I ever gave any money to politics it was always to Republicans.*

*My mother and father voted Democratic. The first time I ever voted I cast a ballot for Adele Stevenson but I slowly transformed into a conservative. I was a hawk in the Vietnam War and still am. We should have won that war and I was vehement about it. I really was pissed about losing those kids out there and not winning the damn thing.*

*I started transforming myself during the past few years. I've stayed Republican because I think the Republicans, at least in some respects share my beliefs on social and fiscal issues, but I don't think the Republicans or the Democrats make much difference nowadays when it comes to general administration of the country.*

*I think the Republicans are a little more stringent on defense and on sociological and religious issues. They're more to my thinking so I will continue to vote Republican but I don't think there's a hell of a lot of difference between both parties.*

*If I ever leave the party it will be over so called free trade. For 40 years I have been quite concerned and disgusted about losing industries and jobs overseas. Now look at us. That's why I've really grown indifferent to politics.*

*I scoffed at President Bush's pledge during early 2004 that he planned to put a man on the moon again and then on to Mars. I'm not saying we shouldn't go to the moon but I don't think we should spend a billion dollars going to Mars. I'm not going to crusade about it but I do think they shouldn't spend that money, especially since we don't have it. These politicians keep saying we're the richest country in the world. Bullshit! We're in debt up to our neck and the Japanese and the Chinese own us lock, stock, and barrel. The only thing that keeps us going is that the Japanese and the Chinese keep buying our treasury notes and if they ever start calling them we're going to be in real trouble.* *- George Millay*

Park was started by Tap Pryor, a young man about the islands who had been a military pilot and whose claim to fame was that he was a son of one of the founders of Pan American World Airways.

During late 1970 and early 1971, George attended several Sea Life Park stockholders' meetings. After spending a great deal of money for a high-powered attorney, SeaWorld lost its bid to take over the facility. It was a bitter pill for George to swallow. He felt dirty politics and skullduggery had been played and that he and stockholders of both parks had been deceived defrauded. He loved that park and saw it as a natural extension of SeaWorld - as a holding area and a central point for collecting missions.

**Not Bad Company**

*George is a creative, brilliant guy. You don't have to go too far down the list from Walt Disney to get to George Millay. Yeah, you can throw P. T. Barnum in there and you can throw Henry Ford in, but George will always be in the Top 5.*
*- Jan Schultz, retired SeaWorld executive*

One of George's major personal disappointments in life was the behavior of Kenny Norris, the person who first gave him the idea of building a marine park and a creator of many of the initial SeaWorld concepts.

"I became increasingly despondent over Kenny because he never gave enough time to the SeaWorld project. He was given quite a bit of (promotional) stock as part of his original deal and we paid all of his expenses. Increasingly, Kenny didn't perform for us. He didn't come down to San Diego. He didn't help in collecting and he didn't supervise trainers. He was just totally detached, always traveling and gone."

George said Norris had "completely fallen down" in acquiring top-notch trainers and aquarists in the fish and the mammal areas. "It seemed we got all the dregs from Marineland. A couple of their trainers came down and weren't worth their salt. He did bring down a couple of good fish men, but they lacked any flair. His imagination was fantastic, but his selection of people, the original crews, was horrible."

After SeaWorld opened, George found that during the

previous two years, Norris was not only involved with SeaWorld, but he was also involved with Sea Life Park in Hawaii, and another park in Philadelphia. "Finally, I had it with him because he really let us down and didn't come through when I needed him the most. I insisted he return his promotional stock, which he readily did and within four months of our opening, Kenny Norris was gone and he went back to teaching. I never saw him again."

### *Tragedy Strikes*

The most tragic event during George's career occurred in the early 1970s while SeaWorld was building Magic Mountain. George and Dave DeMotte needed to visit the new park, 150 miles away, quite often, and traveling from San Diego to Valencia, the site of Magic Mountain, was very time-consuming. One day, George got what he calls "a hair-brained idea" that he could buy a helicopter and use it as a revenue source by giving rides at SeaWorld when it wasn't being used for transporting SeaWorld executives.

He figured it would save a great deal of time and energy going back and forth from parking lot to parking lot. "We bought a beautiful new Bell Jet Ranger and we gave helicopter rides to the public and they loved it. We took them over Mission Bay and were charging $15 each and three or four passengers could go together."

The park hired a pilot and a co-pilot, and some of George's top guys, including the park's restaurant operator Larry Crandall, started using it on a regular basis. One day Crandall and Ron Harper flew from the SeaWorld parking lot to Boom Trenchards, a restaurant SeaWorld was building at the airport. When they got back, Harper ran into George and told him "something was wrong with that damn helicopter and I was happy to get out of it." After Crandall and Harper got out, the helicopter took off and headed to Gillespie Field where the pilot was to pick up some new parts that had been ordered for the plane.

On its way, George said the helicopter "just fell out of the sky" from 3,000 feet over La Mesa, about 20 miles east of SeaWorld. It fell into a house and fortunately there was no one at home but both the pilot and the co-pilot were killed instantly. "I went out to identify the men and it was the worst thing I ever saw in my life. That was the tragic end of our helicopter business," George said.

Two years later, Larry Sands, George's former show producer was killed in a similar accident while filming for the Army Corps of Engineers. Since then George has been reluctant to use helicopters.

- CHAPTER 14 -

# On To The Buckeye State

One sunny San Diego afternoon in 1967, George received a call from Earl Gascoigne of Cedar Point amusement park in Sandusky, Ohio. "Mr. Millay, I'm the vice president of marketing at Cedar Point. Our owners would like to chat with you and would like to pay your way out to Ohio to see our park."

George had never been there and was curious what they had in mind, so he agreed to visit. Within days of that phone call, George and Dave DeMotte were on a plane headed to Cleveland.

They rented a car and drove out to Cedar Point where they met Earl Gascoigne and the park's owners, Emile Legros and George Roose, two of the most interesting characters George said he has ever met. He was very impressed with Cedar Point.

They wanted George to build a SeaWorld in Ohio, about 20 miles west of Sandusky, near a state park and a major campground. The Cedar Point officials praised the site up one side and down another. The owners claimed four million people a year visited that park and campsite and the piece of property they had picked out for George was less than a half a mile from the front gate of the campground, adjacent to Lake Erie.

"We went home and in our research of the area, found that those two guys, Roose and Legros owned the property on which they wanted us to build and all the property around it. That rather cooled me and from that point on, I started watching those guys very closely. It appeared they were a couple slippery Ohioans looking to take us beach boys to the cleaners," George recalls.

On a subsequent trip to Cedar Point, George was in Gascoigne's office behind closed doors and was told that a couple Cedar Point officials, including Gascoigne, were going to buy Geauga Lake Amusement Park in Aurora, Ohio, an older traditional park just outside Cleveland. He explained to George that there was plenty of property on the other side of the lake that would make a beautiful site for a SeaWorld. He said, "Forget about Roose and Legros, come on down with us and we'll sell you the land across the lake cheap."

### *Lakeside Venture*

A short time later, George and Ron Harper visited Aurora to look at the property and saw its potential. "I kind of liked the idea that it was on the opposite side of Cleveland from Cedar Point because I thought that park had the potential to bury us. I didn't trust Legros completely and not too much later found I shouldn't have trusted Gascoigne either," George admitted. "Ohio is a great state if you like cows."

SeaWorld decided to buy the property and build a marine park in Aurora, Ohio, across the lake from Geauga Lake amusement park. Harrison "Buzz" Price, the numbers cruncher who conducted the original studies on Disneyland, performed the feasibility work on SeaWorld Ohio, George Walsh designed the park, Dutch Harley was the general contractor, and Ron Harper and his crew from SeaWorld oversaw its construction. The park brought in 1.1 million through the gates that first year, doubling the attendance projections. For a company that started off slowly and struggled on its first project in California, Ohio was a most unbelievably positive situation.

What Price hadn't realized in his original projections was the well-established summer vacation travel habit from Western Pennsylvania and West Virginia up through Ohio to Lake Erie. That was the major difference during that first year.

Bob Gault, a SeaWorld San Diego alumnus who was transferred to Ohio, said Shamu was also a huge boost to the popularity of the park that first year. "Just the uniqueness of having a killer whale in Mid-America, in Cleveland. I mean that was just a mind blower for people. People just had to come out and see it to believe it."

Ron Harper said what happened in Ohio that first year could only be categorized as "a phenomenal" success. "We had to bring in portable toilets and instead of having five Shamu shows a day, we had to present 10 so everyone could see it, I mean, it was unbelievable what happened."

The park also had a huge base from which to draw. Nearly 100 million people lived within 500 miles of SeaWorld in 1970. Both Pittsburgh and Detroit were 90 minutes away. Cleveland was 20 minutes away.

SeaWorld officials were very confident in the Ohio site right from the beginning, as was Buzz Price. If attendance figures had only hit the original projection of 550,000, the park would have made money, George said.

### *The Building of SeaWorld #2*

The overall process of getting the Ohio park going was a bit easier than getting the San Diego park on its feet, but the construction, most of which took place in the dead of winter, was a challenge for everyone. Ron Harper, head of construction, moved his family to Ohio and went about the business of building the second SeaWorld.

Harper notes that the time schedule was tight and if the park would have opened much past Memorial Day, it would have cost the company a fortune, because Ohio was to be a seasonal park and would close by mid-September. "We really had to press. Construction had already started before I got there in January and we did what we had to do and opened that thing on Memorial Day weekend, 1970," Harper recalls.

Going into Ohio, "We had excellent designs in place and knew what we were doing. We had the staff already trained. We had experienced trainers. We had great water quality people. We had the aquarists. We had the operations and we had the marketing. We had everything there except a general manager," said George. "It wasn't like the blind leading the blind; this was a group of professionals."

### *Anxious George Gets into a Pickle*

In his desire to get the park going, construction began before a final contract was signed with Gascoigne, a move that George now calls "a huge" mistake.

"We designed as we negotiated and we were well into hundreds of thousands of dollars in design before we finalized the deal," George recalls. "Earl kept getting tougher and tougher. This was where I really got pissed at him and ended up having no respect for him for the rest of his life. He kept putting a gun to our head. When I got the final contract, I found a couple of things to bitch about that really weren't unreasonable requests."

Gascoigne called George and told him "to either sign the damn thing or forget about it." George wasn't accustomed to being talked to in that manner and he was angry and upset. He and Harper flew back to Ohio, went to the site and sat down on the hill overlooking the property. There was still no deal and the contractor's equipment was already on site. They sat there not

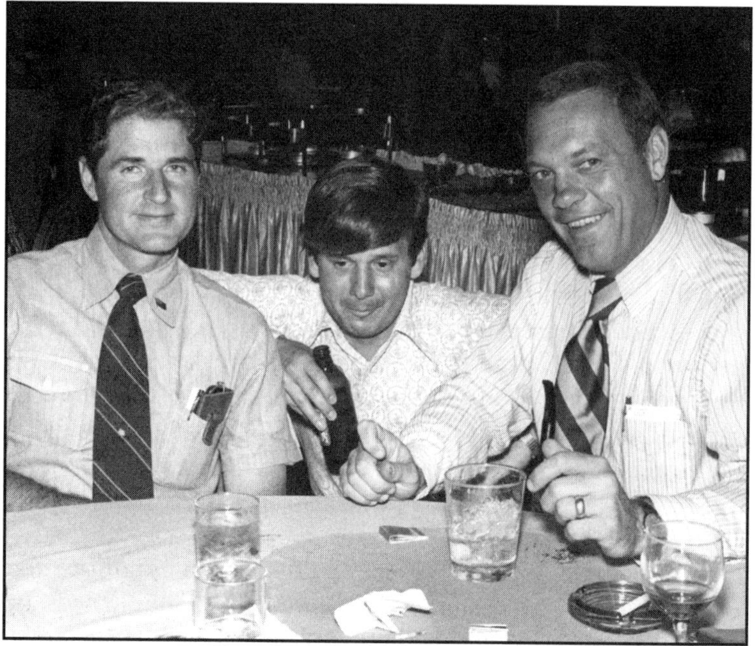

*Dr. Lanny Cornell, joins John Seeker, center, and Jan Schultz, right, for an after-work libation, 1971.*

saying a word for a while and George finally looked at Harper and said, "Let's give the SOB what he wants and get going." He did just that.

"The guys from Geauga Lake proved to be very slick, sly, and conniving," adds Harper. "George has always been so upfront with everyone and he was very enthusiastic about this project. Ever since I've known George, he has taken people at their word, but this time he got taken and we had to jump through hoops to get this land purchased."

Three years later George filed a lawsuit against Gascoigne and Geauga Lake amusement park in the middle of its public stock offering. "There were several inaccuracies in their offering pertaining to their contractual obligations to SeaWorld," George said. "We wanted our relationship and our obligations portrayed correctly." The suit was later dropped, but to this day George recalls, with much glee, the delays in the offering and the hubbub the suit caused.

### Exporting the Best

Gault was one of the experienced professionals who went

to Ohio. "I volunteered to be on the opening team to help with the operations design. Then George chose me to be the director of operations for Ohio," Gault said of his first major promotion. "We opened Ohio in 1970 and I went back to San Diego when it closed for the winter and went back to Ohio again for the 1971 season."

After returning to San Diego after Ohio closed for the 1971 season, Gault found that SeaWorld Florida was on the drawing board and volunteered for that team as well. "I thought my best ticket to growing in the company was to help with these growth projects. I guess you could say I was opportunistic because I really put myself in a position to grow as the business was growing."

Gault said the biggest challenge he had in Ohio, from an operations point, was creating the procedures and finding the right people to come in on a seasonal basis. The season there was approximately a 114-day window and it was difficult to find the right mix of full-time people, part-time people and to figure out how many were needed to be there on a year-round basis to keep the park in condition during the winter months.

Seasonal operation, with each day potentially being able to affect the bottom line, was a new challenge for all SeaWorld veterans because the San Diego park was a year-round operation. "If you had one rainy Sunday in August you could lose 25,000 people and not get them back and that's a big hunk of your business for the whole summer. Learning seasonality and how to manage the costs was quite a challenge," Gault said.

During the winter, when SeaWorld Ohio would shut down, the whales and dolphins would be flown back to San Diego where they were kept in pens built in Mission Bay. Throughout the winter, they were rotated in and out of the shows to keep them sharp. Each spring, it was a big time in Ohio when Shamu and the others came back to the park aboard the Orc Ark, as the American Airlines plane was called.

### *The Park of Many Owners*

What a history SeaWorld Ohio has had since its 1970 opening! It was originally built for $5.5 million. In 1977, it was sold to Harcourt Brace Jovanovich (HBJ), along with the California and Florida SeaWorld parks for $57 million. HBJ built the $200 million SeaWorld Texas in San Antonio and added it to the family in 1988 and subsequently sold all four of the parks to Anheuser-Busch in 1989, along with its Cypress Gardens and Boardwalk and Baseball parks for $1.1 billion. Busch individually sold SeaWorld Ohio to Six Flags in 2000 for $110 million and Busch kept the killer whales and flew them to SeaWorld Florida.

Six Flags shut down SeaWorld and incorporated the marine park into Geauga Lake amusement park, which they had purchased in 1995 and in 2000, had renamed Six Flags Ohio. In 2001, the one big park, including Six Flags Ohio, SeaWorld Ohio, and Hurricane Harbor Waterpark was renamed Six Flags Worlds of Adventure.

In 2002, in hopes of rejuvenating slumping attendance, Six Flags was able to purchase a killer whale. However, even with the whale, the mega-park never caught on with the public in the manner that Six Flags officials had hoped and expected. In spring 2004, the owners of Cedar Point purchased the entire park for $145 million and changed its name back to Geauga Lake. The remaining fish were sold to Ripley Entertainment for their two aquariums and the killer whale and other mammals were shipped to Six Flags Marineland in Vallejo, California.

***The Search for Top Management***

Doc Lemmon was guiding the Magic Mountain development at the same time George was looking for an Ohio manager. Having been general manager of Cedar Point, Lemmon was asked by George for a suggestion on who he thought would be a good GM for the new park.

Lemmon recommended Jim Reed, a young man who worked at Cedar Point, for the SeaWorld Ohio position. "Reed should have been the tip-off of Doc's inability to judge management, but it didn't sink in just then. We hired him," said George. "Reed would show up at the construction site every day in French cuffs and he'd sit in the office, have a cup of coffee, and then just sit there all morning. He didn't have a clue as to what he needed to do," George recalls.

Ron Harper kept telling George that he needed to get to Ohio and talk with Reed. Finally, George had a talk with Reed and sadly had to replace him after he had been on the job for only four months. With only a couple more months to go before the park was to open, George immediately started looking for GM #2. He was given the name of Gil Rigdon, a retired Air Force fighter pilot, by an official of Busch Entertainment, a company that later purchased the SeaWorld parks.

George hired Rigdon. "Gil was a character unlike any I had ever met. His idea of running a park was to throw a party every night for the employees and constantly joke around. He stayed on through the first year and we had a very successful year. I think our first year's huge success was despite Mr. Rigdon not because of him. We had professionals running everything but the day-to-day operation, and that was his job.

"Finally after a year we had to let Gil go. I remember flying back there and taking him to lunch at the Aurora Inn and he had no idea of why I was there. He starts out the lunch by saying, 'You know George, I'm one of maybe two or three people in the United States who is capable of running this park,' and I said, Gil, I don't agree with you and the reason I'm here is to ask you to resign. Well, he was crushed but he took it like a man."

**Loyalty Over Brains**

*What turned out to be a popular mantra for those who worked for George, 'Loyalty over Brains' was first used by George Becker following his first year as general manager of SeaWorld Ohio in 1971. He was describing his predecessor, Gil Rigdon, and it caught on like wildfire. George used it in many a speech through the years. It was a tongue-in-cheek way of laughing at himself and the rest of his staff. The saying jumped to Wet'n Wild after George and many of his loyal followers left SeaWorld and started the world's first waterpark.*

*Bob Gault explains the motto, as he sees it. "George was the smart guy. He was smarter than everybody else or at least thought he was. It was his crass way of saying these guys couldn't be too smart because they're working for me and they're out here busting their ass in this difficult business. I think that was his way of saying you guys are pretty cool."*

- CHAPTER 15 -

# Ohio's Success Had its Price

The immediate success of SeaWorld Ohio caused many unexpected operational problems. A shortage of parking spaces was one troublesome area and another was the lack of enough women's toilets. "I really am sympathetic and ashamed whenever I walk past long lines of females patiently waiting in lines to go to the bathroom. You see them standing in lines at airports, concerts, and sporting events. SeaWorld Ohio in its opening year was no different. We rented Port-a-Potties to add more facilities, but that didn't help much."

That potty parity dilemma was discussed during a phone conversation George had within a month of the park opening in 1970 with Harper, Gault, Becker and Jim Brown, the Ohio maintenance superintendent. Brown finally told the group that he would take care of it and the others, with a sigh of relief, agreed to let Brown tackle the situation.

First, Brown took out the mirrors in the ladies toilets to speed the process up a bit and that helped the lines move a bit faster. Then in a bold move Brown took off the stall doors, presumably to quicken the process even more. For some reason, it worked, and the lines got noticeably shorter. There weren't too many complaints and Brown was a hero to the management team.

Crowded walkways were also a problem during the first several years. George Becker called George one August afternoon during that first year and told him that no one had to clean the walkways "because a wrapper can't get to the ground."

***Becker's the Man!***

The maxim that the third time is a charm proved true here in the search for a general manager. George Becker, who had been at SeaWorld San Diego as an assistant marketing director for about a year and had worked at the Ohio park during the first season in marketing, got the call from George to go back to his native state of Ohio and take over the park. He was happy to go and George was delighted with Becker's performance. He remained in that role in Ohio until late 1974, when he was transferred to SeaWorld Florida.

**Doing it His Way**
*I have had it pretty much my way during my entire adult life because luckily I have worked for myself during that time. As an employee, I was fired from every full-time job I had in my life. Fate determined I should go on my own and that allowed me to achieve some fame and fortune. My only boss now is Anne Millay.*
*- George Millay*

George showed faith in Becker right from the start. Two weeks into his career at SeaWorld San Diego, Becker looked up from his desk to see George standing there. That was in late March 1970.

"You're from Ohio, so I want you to go back there and replace the advertising agency. I want you to fire anyone in the marketing department who in your opinion is not pulling his weight," George told Becker. "I want you to hire a new advertising agency and I want you to get the marketing and sales programs going because we're going to open SeaWorld Ohio on Memorial Day weekend this year."

"It turned out to be a very interesting winter, spring, and summer," Becker remembers. "I packed a bag and went back to Ohio and stayed there all the way through park opening, all summer long, and didn't go back to San Diego until the fall. It was a baptism by fire because when I walked onto the property at SeaWorld Ohio that March it looked like the Third World War. I mean snow and mud and bulldozers sunk in mud. There were huge amounts of work to be done but people worked together and we got it finished."

After the first season when the park closed down for the winter, Becker headed back to San Diego. Within weeks George named him VP of marketing. He spent the winter of 1970/1971 working on both San Diego and Ohio marketing programs. As it grew closer in time to open Ohio for its second season, George filled Becker's doorway once again and asked him if he would go back to Ohio, but this time as the park's general manager, to replace Gil Rigdon. Jan Schultz, who had been originally hired for the marketing job at Magic Mountain, came to San Diego to take over the top marketing position when Becker was moved to Ohio.

"George (Becker) did a hell of a job for us. He kept our attendance up over a million and ran that company with an iron hand," said George. "That's where George Becker really began his management career and started getting his good reputation."

The only trouble the two Georges had between them was when Becker wanted to go to Florida and run that park when it first opened. "I didn't want him to go to Florida because we didn't need him in Florida. We really needed him to stay in Ohio because that was a tougher job. Any boob could make money in Florida during those days in outdoor recreation, and that included me," George professed.

### *Learning Small Town Politics*

During the second year, there was talk that the city of Aurora was considering an admissions tax for SeaWorld Ohio. Ron Harper and George attended the meeting in which the tax was to be discussed. "We were going to sit there in the council chambers and protest when it was brought up." By then George was kicking himself because he hadn't insisted that a no admission tax guarantee be put in the initial purchase agreement. The subject was not brought up and the council meeting adjourned at 9 p.m. and everyone went home, at least that's what George and Harper thought.

The next morning, George found that the council had recessed to the bar at the Aurora Inn, had a couple of drinks, and had gone back into session. Failing to tell anyone they were going to re-adjourn, behind closed doors at midnight, they voted in favor of a 6% front gate tax on SeaWorld.

George was livid. "How could they do that to us?" he ranted. "We had spent millions of dollars there and had brought thousands more dollars into the town. We had employed hundreds of kids and our taxes were already high."

SeaWorld Ohio's attorney, who happened to be the ex-mayor of the city of Aurora, told George that he would work on lowering the tax. The barrister said, "Let me go to work on this and my deal will be that you pay me 25% of everything I save you. If I can get that down from 6% to 3%, you pay me 25% of 3% for five years."

He came back to George in a week and announced he had negotiated it down to 3%. "We later found out that our buddy, the ex-mayor, had given the idea to the council knowing full well that he could go back to them and get it lowered to 3%. He had the whole thing figured out. So much for Ohio politicians," George said.

### *A Whale of a Traveler*

When it was time for Shamu to make her trip to Ohio on the Orc Ark, it was the first time anyone had ever tried to transport a whale across the country and the first time an Orca ever took a ride in a jet. The original Shamu had arrived in San Diego from Seattle in a prop plane. American Airlines accepted the challenge of flying Shamu to Cleveland, knowing they would get a great amount of publicity out of the deal.

Someone had told George that Bill Lear, founder of the Learjet (and years before, the eight-track cartridge tape player) was interested in the Shamu move and wanted to see how it was done. Lear wanted to escort the whale across the country. He wanted to fly alongside Shamu in his own jet, and he invited George to go with him.

"This guy is quite a character. It was always show time with Bill. He liked to scare the hell out of his passengers. He'd

*Two icons play at SeaWorld, 1973.*

constantly argue with his pilot and would grapple with him for the controls and ended up flying his own plane most of the time. He would move in close and be taking pictures of the 707 at 39,000-feet and the captain would warn him to stay further away. Lear didn't listen and finally the captain reported him and he was fined by the FAA."

When the group landed at Cleveland Hopkins airport, the mayor met the plane and rode in his limousine to the park, right behind Shamu, escorted by a dozen motorcycle policemen. A big sign at the airport read: "Cleveland Welcomes Shamu." The Midwest's first killer whale arrived three weeks before the park opened, giving her time to get acclimated and to rest after her stressful trip.

- CHAPTER 16 -

# Water Skiing Comes to SeaWorld

George became enthused about integrating a water ski show into the entertainment mix at SeaWorld Ohio during its first season of operation. He reasoned that a water ski show kept with the water-oriented theme, gave guests a non-animal show option, and he bet it would appeal to a good percentage of attendance.

He had seen the water ski shows that Dick Pope produced at Cypress Gardens in Florida, and recalled that the people loved watching the action and the glitter of a well-produced show. During the summer of 1970, George and George Becker visited Ontario Place in Toronto to see a ski show of which they were both impressed. They went back to Ohio, started the process of getting access to the lake and started designing a large, lakeside stadium.

One of the first steps was to hire the legendary Tommy Bartlett and his number one man, Dick Rowe to produce a show. Rowe produced SeaWorld's first water ski presentation, paid all salaries, and furnished all the costumes. The park provided the ushers and the technicians. Rowe produced it for a total of three years after which SeaWorld took the production in-house.

**Women Love Animals**

*One thing I learned at SeaWorld is that women have a far bigger affinity toward animals than men. I guess it's that mother instinct in them.*

*- George Millay*

"Dick Rowe was one of the true professionals you infrequently meet who always got the job done and always gave you 105%. We corroborated on a number of shows over the years. Dick was one of a kind," George said of the late producer. Total cost for that first show was less than $150,000 for the summer.

Another uncomfortable situation with their amusement park neighbors took place during the construction of the water ski stadium. Halfway through construction, they discovered the surveyors had miscalculated and 10 feet of the corner of the stadium was across the property line, on Geauga Lake Amusement Park property.

"We had to go to Earl and that SOB charged us $250,000 dollars for a piece of land 10 feet by 50 feet, a total of 500 square feet. It was either that or tear up the stadium that was already under construction and start all over again." George seethed.

### *George Wants a Ski Show in California*

With the success of the Ohio water ski show, George wanted to add a similar show and build a stadium at the San Diego park and had picked out an area on the waterfront on the northeast point of the park along the estuary running to the eastern portion of Mission Bay.

In 1972, the California Coastal Commission Act was about to implement the Coastal Zone Conservation Act that would greatly inhibit development along the California coastlines. George and his team were quite aware that the stadium had to be environmentally sensitive in all respects to fit into the new regulations that were soon to be law. They designed a 5,000 seat facility made mostly of wood and were going to surround it with lush landscaping.

Not wanting to be a test case at a Coastal Commission hearing, George asked San Diego Mayor Pete Wilson to place SeaWorld on the City Council calendar ASAP to gain approval for the use of the bay, before it would have to be approved by the Coastal Commission.

Wilson vacillated and said "George, don't worry, the Coastal Commission is no big deal." George phoned him and "I met and pleaded with him but to no avail. I had been quite active in supporting Pete in his run for the mayoral bid and had been warned that Wilson was an unknown and suspected of close ties to environmental and protection groups."

Wilson blocked the attempt to get on the council docket, so up to San Francisco George went and SeaWorld became the first applicant to appear before the commission. George says the commission members "were in a vicious and vindictive mood. It was no contest. We lost and SeaWorld and San Diego lost a great marine stadium, which is still sorely needed. I was and still am quite bitter."

- CHAPTER 17 -

# The Making of a Magical Mountain

Dave DeMotte enjoyed playing the stock market and spent a great deal of time studying it. He was the most informed of all the SeaWorld executives when it came to the market.

He would barge into George's office on occasion, slam his hands on the desk and tell George that they were in the wrong business. He'd show his boss how well Cedar Point and Disneyland were doing. All those positive financial numbers whetted George's appetite and interested him in getting involved in building a park based on rides, not animals. It was a genre of the business that neither George nor any of his people knew much about. That's how SeaWorld initially became involved in the building of Magic Mountain ride park in Valencia, California.

One day in late 1969, George was visiting with his old friend Ben Southland, who had been the senior planning partner of Victor Gruen, the architects that created the original SeaWorld San Diego.

In the course of their conversation, George mentioned that DeMotte was high on ride parks and asked Southland for his opinion about building a park in Southern California. Southland liked the idea and told George that he needed to meet with people from the Newhall Land and Farming Company, a wealthy land, cattle and oil company. Southland had done work for them and knew they were looking for ideas and for partners to develop parts of their huge expanse of land in the north of the San Fernando Valley surrounding Valencia. Southland offered to introduce George to the company's CEO, Tom Lowe.

SeaWorld had a great name and reputation by then and wherever George or his executives went, they were treated with respect. With that reputation, George didn't have to sell himself or the company to Lowe. Within a short time, the two had struck up a deal and selected the property on which to build a ride park.

It was a 50-50 partnership. Each partner was to put up

$2 million and with that $4 million in equity, Newhall Land and Farming was responsible to raise the additional $18 million needed to build the park. In the end, the park ended up costing $25 million. Buzz Price and his team from Economics Research Associates in Los Angeles conducted the feasibility study.

***Got the Deal, Need the People***

SeaWorld had two parks in operation and officials were starting to think about building another in Florida. With all that going on in 1970, the crème de la crème of the SeaWorld organization was busy and couldn't be spared to work on the Magic Mountain project.

The renowned Los Angeles park designer Randall Duell, along with his design team of project architects Albert Lambinon and Ira West, were hired to design Magic Mountain. The Newhall people had approved three potential parcels of available land and Duell flew over all three, visualizing a park on each. He liked the one with the mountain in the middle. "He saw that piece of land and knew it was going to be more of a challenge to build a park on top of and against a mountain, but he knew it would be a magnificent design because of the land itself," said Ira West.

The park was originally designed as a full loop, with a

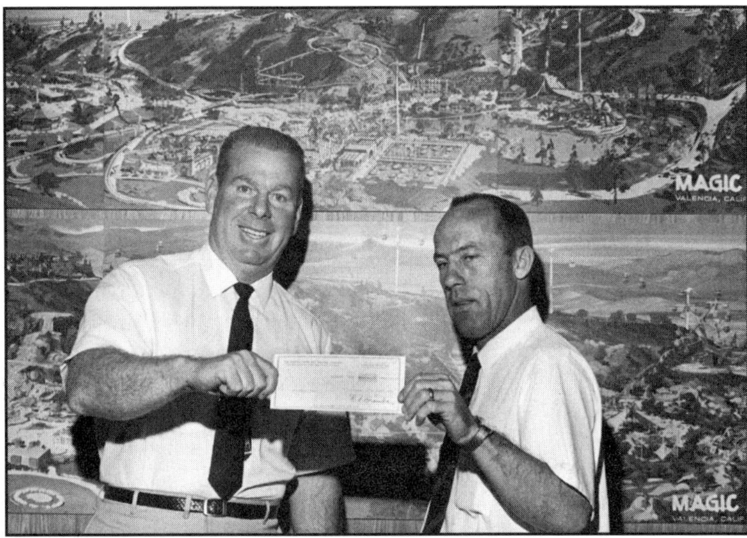


*George Millay and Dave DeMotte proudly display a $500,000 check from Newhall Land and Farming Company, a partial payment for construction work at Magic Mountain, November 1960.*

pedestrian tunnel being bored through the mountain. The budget stopped that expensive idea so the plans were altered. Instead of walking around and through the mountain, guests would first ride up to the top in a Funicular, walk around and enjoy the attractions, and then walk down the front side. The loop was finally completed around the backside of the mountain many years later when more land was acquired.

### *Who's Running the Mountain?*

Once again that proverbial problem of finding the right general manager loomed before George. For a helping hand, he went back to his stable of Disney consultants, including Jack Sayers, Ed Ettinger, and Bob Foster for advice. He also discussed potential GM candidates with Cedar Point and Geauga Lake officials. Doc Lemmon's name kept coming up as a potential GM. George had met him in 1969 while searching for a SeaWorld Ohio general manager. He contacted him again and hired him for the GM position at Magic Mountain. Lemmon had strong credentials and George liked him.

"Doc knew the park business probably as well as anybody in the country at that time. He insisted on hiring Bob Minnick as operations manager right away to work with Ira West and the Duell design team. It was a very smart move because Bob was very instrumental in the design," George notes. Minnick got his initial training at Disneyland and then spent several years with Randall Duell, so the design and operations team all knew each other and respected each other going in, according to West.

Thanks to the helicopter SeaWorld purchased, George and DeMotte were able to visit Magic Mountain every week and keep in close contact with Doc Lemmon during the construction process.

### *Another GM, More Problems*

George said Lemmon started showing some problems early on. He had been given a budget and the power to hire directors for finance, food, marketing and operations who in turn would report directly to him. "Except for Bob Minnick who came in through the back door, Doc hired the biggest bunch of incompetent, dishonest buffoons you'd ever lay eyes on, and it started becoming apparent very quickly," George said. "Tom Lowe and the Newhall people spotted it before I did."

*George Millay being interviewed at SeaWorld San Diego, 1965.*

George Whitney, a San Diego TV executive and a commissioner of the Cal State Fair in Sacramento had suggested to George that he take a look at Jan Schultz, a Chicago advertising executive, for the original marketing director's position at Magic Mountain. Schultz had worked for NBC, Leo Burnett, and Alberto Culver and was very qualified for the position, but George stuck to his promise and let Lemmon hire the first marketing team.

After the original marketing director at Magic Mountain was axed, George followed Whitney's advice and made contact with Schultz.

"I needed to fly back to Milwaukee for another, unrelated meeting and I asked Jan to meet me there at a country club where we could play a round of golf. We immediately hit it off. We played golf, went to a bar, got drunk, almost got in a fight with a couple other drunks, almost got arrested and I hired him to be our marketing director." It was an auspicious beginning to a friendship that continues today.

"I had not heard of SeaWorld, nor had I heard of Magic Mountain. So I certainly hadn't heard of George Millay," Schultz recalls. As they were preparing to hit the links, Schultz witnessed a Millay ritual that he didn't fully understand for many years.

"He took out this tube of stuff that looked like lard and spread it all over his face. I realize now that he was trying to protect his skin from the sun, but it stayed white all afternoon and he looked like a mummy," Schultz laughed.

"I won the golf game but not by much," added Schultz. "More importantly, during that short period of four hours I really started to get a feel for one of the all-time great characters that I'd ever meet in my life. I use character in a very respectful way."

The next week Schultz was on a plane headed to Magic Mountain, which was then just coming out of the ground. "I spent a day there. Then we went down to San Diego and only then, when I saw the quality of SeaWorld did I know that this was the type of company for which I would love to work."

Schultz also liked George and he liked the idea of theme parks, which was a new concept for him. "I thought, wow, this is really something." Schultz began work at Magic Mountain on July 1, 1970 and the park was scheduled to open in May 1971.

***Schultz Makes the Team***

"You know, I got in at the right time. I watched the park being built from scratch and it was a great challenge as well as a great opportunity for me," Schultz said, adding that he joined "an interesting" management team.

"Doc Lemmon had quite a bit of experience and our head of construction was Gene Wade. Max Sloan, our food and beverage guy had been around forever and Ross Stevens was our financial guy. Bob Minnick was our head of operations.

Lemmon would preach to his management staff that in this business "no team has ever built a park and lasted any longer than a year after it was built." That preaching proved prophetic for Lemmon and all the opening team members except for Schultz. The park opened and by season's end, Lemmon was gone, then everyone else either left or was asked to leave. By the end of that first summer, everyone was gone. Terry Van Gorder, who later made a name and career for himself at Knott's Berry Farm,

**George on Recognition**

*Original developers, the real risk takers, are nearly always forgotten and rarely receive the credit they desire and rightly deserve. Admittedly, many entrepreneurial types are poor businessmen. They have made their dreams come true, but lack the managerial and people skills to guide their creation to profitability. Happily this was not the case at SeaWorld or Wet'n Wild. It is no sin to want recognition for a job well done. It's quite human.*

*- George Millay*

then with Newhall Land and Farming Company, was made general manager and Schultz was made assistant GM in addition to his marketing duties.

George said it was evident that Schultz's days at Magic Mountain were numbered and advised him "to hang on as long as possible. We're going to send Becker to Ohio and I want to put you in San Diego, but we're not ready yet." Two weeks later, in October, Van Gorder fired Schultz, who notes, "I didn't last very long but at least I lasted longer than the rest of them." Following that firing, Schultz spent three months working for the SeaWorld advertising agency, with 50% of his efforts on general agency work, the other 50% directly for SeaWorld.

### *The Great Cover-up*

It appeared at the time that Magic Mountain remained on budget throughout its entire construction phase. DeMotte was excited about it, but George kept saying, "Let's wait and see." For some reason, construction manager Wade shoved many construction-related invoices into his desk before anyone else saw them.

"We thought we were on budget until the day we opened and then found we were about $5 million over budget," said George. "The only numbers he presented showed that we were on budget, but the pile of unpaid invoices in his desk drawer showed otherwise and we got rid of him immediately."

Duell's Ira West, who spent a great deal of time at the park during construction, remembers Duell telling Lemmon that something was wrong and that he had better have a talk with Wade about billing and ordering. "Doc never listened, even when he confronted Wade himself," West said.

Despite being over budget, construction went smoothly. Doc had been through it before and was quite knowledgeable. His selection of rides turned out to be excellent and the entire layout and traffic flow patterns of Magic Mountain were very good, working well from day one.

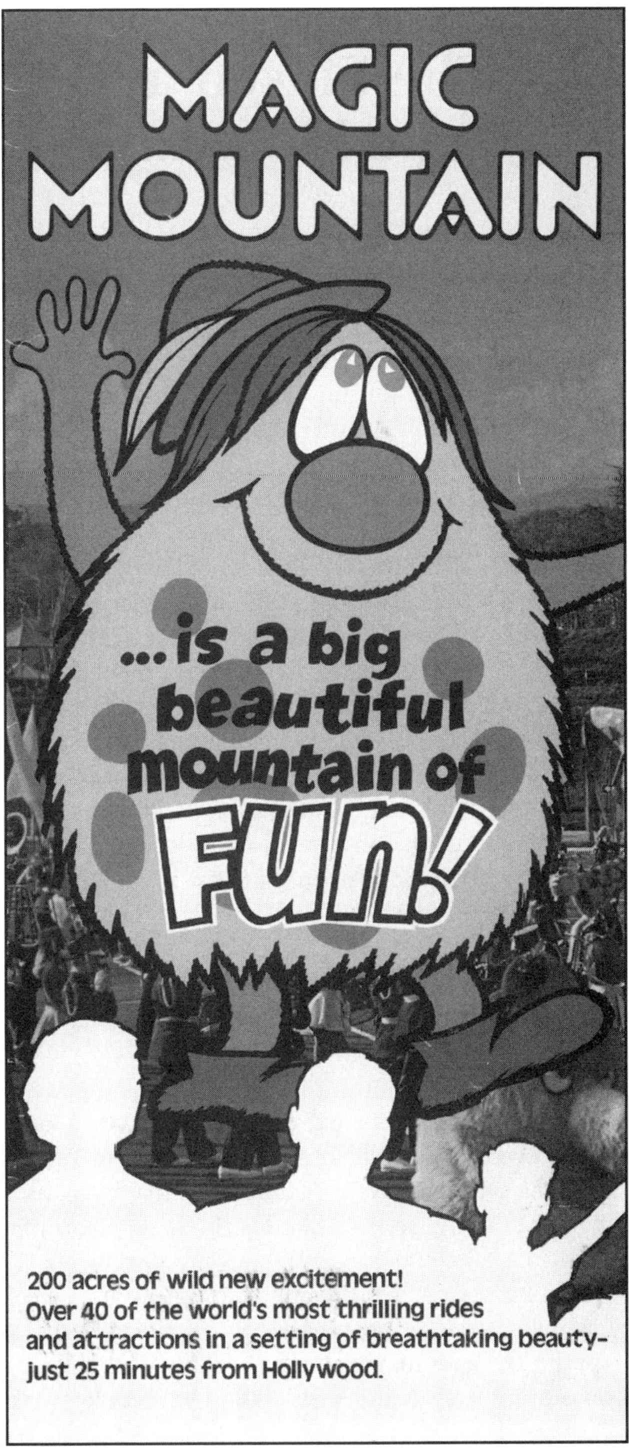
MAGIC MOUNTAIN
...is a big beautiful mountain of FUN!
200 acres of wild new excitement!
Over 40 of the world's most thrilling rides
and attractions in a setting of breathtaking beauty-
just 25 minutes from Hollywood.

- CHAPTER 18 -

# The Fiasco at Magic Mountain

One won't find details of Magic Mountain's opening weekend in a scholarly dissertation entitled "How to Open an Amusement Park," that's for sure. Three of the major rides weren't operating, the landscaping wasn't totally in, there's wasn't enough shade, there was a shortage of working water fountains, the parking lot wasn't large enough, and thousands were turned away from the party to which they were invited.

"Basically, there was not enough of anything in the park, except for people," Schultz recalls with a shudder.

"I asked to go in and see the board a month before the park opened and I explained to them that, hey, I'm no expert on theme park construction, but it looks to me like the park is not going to be ready. I told them that I could still move the two pre-opening events, but a decision had to be made that day."

The board thanked Schultz and asked to see Gene Wade, the head of construction. Wade went in, assured the board that it would not only be ready to open, but that it would come in on budget. At that point, the board took a walk of the park with both Schultz and Wade to see for themselves. After the tour, the board, being once again assured by Wade that everything was fine, told Schultz that the opening would not be delayed.

### *Two Pre-Opening Events*

Magic Mountain opened with two soft events, one a private charity event for a local hospital on Friday night, May 27, and the other on Saturday for Chevron, a major sponsor. The park opened to the general public for the first time on Sunday, May 29, 1971.

Schultz arranged both pre-opening events. The Friday night bash went well and there were approximately 400 people in the park. The Saturday event turned out to be "one of the worst days of my life," Schultz recalls with a shudder.

"I had created a promotion with Chevron to bring in employees on that Saturday. In working with my counterpart on their end I said you are allowed 10,000 individual tickets, no more." Chevron printed the tickets and in allowing them to do so, Schultz lost all control over the ticketing process. After the tickets were printed and distributed, Schultz was given one and at that point, realized 10,000 family tickets had been distributed, not 10,000 individual tickets. Instead of 10,000 people on whom they had planned, there were nearly 40,000 people with passes to get in that day.

Schultz shudders, even now, when he thinks about the "big rookie mistake" that he made. "Our parking lot was full by 11 a.m. and we ended up parking them on our new landscaping and they were knocking down our sprinklers. I'm all over the place. I can't find Bob Minnick, and Doc is home taking a nap. So essentially I'm in charge." Schultz called Doc at home and explained what was going on and that traffic was backed up to Hollywood on I-5. He told Schultz, "Jan, I'm taking a nap and I'll be in after I've rested. The good Lord will take care of you." Schultz couldn't believe what he was hearing. "Well, He better start doing it quickly because I'm in a big deep pile of you know what right now," Schultz recalls telling Lemmon.

The California Highway Patrol was directing traffic and Schultz alerted them that there were no more places to put the cars. They told him the only thing they could do was turn them around at the gate and put them back on the expressway heading back toward Los Angeles. "I said go ahead, meaning that hundreds, maybe thousands of employees of our largest sponsor, weren't allowed into the park. You can only imagine the reaction from my client. The guy from Chevron got fired over this fiasco. I should have been," Schultz noted. Despite it all, Chevron stayed on as a major sponsor.

### *Here Comes the Media*

On Sunday, while the park was open to the public for the first time, Schultz received a call that the entertainment editor for the Los Angeles Times was coming in to do a story on the park and that he was bringing his wife. Schultz greeted them at the gate and escorted them to the Funicular that would take them to the top of the mountain to get an overview of the park.

About half way up, the Funicular malfunctioned and

stopped abruptly. The reporter fell and broke his leg. It took the untrained emergency crew more than an hour to get him down, during which time the reporter is laid out on the floor in pain. "We finally get him in the ambulance and his wife said she would take her car and follow him to the hospital. I offered to drive her but she refused and insisted we take her to her car. That wasn't possible, because during the short time they were there, someone had stolen her car from the parking lot. The only car stolen from the lot was hers!"

**The Millay Formula**
*Take what you already know, combine it with the expertise of incredible consultants and suppliers, and then make it happen, against all odds.*
*- Pat Millay, son*

Everyone held their breath while they waited for the article. A week later it appears and starts off by explaining that there's a new amusement park in Southern California. It's located in Valencia and it's a ride park. Then the ax falls. "The owners call it Magic Mountain. It should really be called Tragic Mountain," and the article tells the story.

***Sorry I Missed it***

The opening at Magic Mountain took place on the same weekend as did the debut of the water ski show and the 4,000-seat stadium at SeaWorld Ohio. George was there, and as such, missed the excitement in California. He was anxious to see the water ski show to see how the new departure from the traditional marine park show lineup would go over with the Ohio, Pennsylvania and Michigan crowds. It was of course a huge hit, so he really had nothing to worry about.

George heard about the fiasco in a phone call from John Campbell, who had been sent to Magic Mountain to lend a helping hand. That was the weekend, according to George, that Doc Lemmon's future at the park was sealed.

Imagine spending nearly a half-million dollars to promote the opening of a $25 million park and have the entire world laughingly call it Tragic Mountain within a week of opening? The name stuck, mostly within the company, but George still looks back, shakes his head, and calls it Tragic Mountain.

Schultz said he couldn't laugh about the turn of events

that weekend until he moved into his position at SeaWorld San Diego a year later.

### *No Carry-Over Problems*

Luckily, the bad rap Magic Mountain was getting had no effect on SeaWorld attendance or SeaWorld stock, mostly because George had gone to great pains right from the beginning, to separate the two. In retrospect, if the SeaWorld team had actually gotten involved, there might not have been the Tragic Mountain scenario.

In all the parks George opened after the initial San Diego SeaWorld, both at SeaWorld and Wet'n Wild, he would bring in an experienced opening management team that had done it before and knew how to control costs and manage the construction. However, in his desire to keep this park separate and because his existing staff was so busy with the other parks, he let the new team make the decisions.

Magic Mountain didn't do well at the gate that first season, either. "I think we had a loss of about $800,000 that first year but we were writing off a tremendous amount of expenses and had other opening costs. Schultz did everything in his power to make the thing go, but we found you can't beat a dead horse," George added.

### *No More Ride Parks*

By the end of the 1971 season, George and the SeaWorld board knew they needed to get out of the Tragic Mountain deal. George wanted to sell and Tom Lowe of Newhall Land and Farming Company wanted to buy, but neither was aware of the others intent, so the ritual began.

George went to Lowe with a bluff and started telling him that the SeaWorld board had realized that the ride park business wasn't for them and that their skills were in the marine park business. They were still friends, so George felt comfortable saying, "You know Tom, we've got to run this our way if we want it to be a success, or maybe the best thing for us to do at this point is to sell to Cedar Point or another park operator. We don't have much cash, but we'll get you your money back. We'll transfer your debt to a new owner."

Lowe countered by telling George that he also wanted to take control and wanted to buy out SeaWorld. George acted surprised and said he would have to think about it and left having accomplished exactly what he had hoped for - to sell their share of the park. In the end, SeaWorld got its $2 million initial investment back and another $1 million over a five-year period. "Needless to say, we were delighted to get out of Magic Mountain with our shirts," George notes.

Meanwhile, unbeknownst to George, who was elbow-deep in getting SeaWorld Florida, open, the Magic Mountain fiasco was the beginning of the end of his career at SeaWorld, a drama that would play out in the boardroom less than six months later. Board chairman Milt Shedd started sowing seeds of doubt about George to the board and they in turn began to see that George Millay was not omnipotent. Ron Harper says the Magic Mountain project "was the first shot across the bow at George."

- CHAPTER 19 -

# George Thrilled to Meet Ray Kroc

One morning in 1971, during construction of Magic Mountain, the switchboard operator at SeaWorld called George's secretary DeEtta Sharp and said there was a Mr. Kroc to see Mr. Millay.

"Mr. Kroc wants to see you," she relayed to George. "I don't know any Kroc, is it Ray Kroc?" George asked. Still on the phone she asked the operator, "Is it Mr. Ray Kroc?" The operator asks him, "Are you Mr. Ray Kroc?" He says yes and the operator relays that affirmative to the secretary who relayed it to George. "I said good God, get him in here." Ray Kroc, the head of McDonald's restaurants, was quickly waltzed into George's office.

Kroc had arrived at the park in a big black limousine that had parked in George's personal parking space. George had jogged to work that morning allowing for his prime space to be vacant. Two of Kroc's young VP's, both sharply dressed in suits, accompanied Kroc who was casually dressed. George recalls that meeting.

"He came in and pulled up a chair to my desk, and the two young vice presidents sat military style one or two chair-lengths behind him and off to each side." Kroc got right to the point, he says, "Mr. Millay, I have heard that you are quite successful here in San Diego and in Ohio and I know about your Magic Mountain project. Now, I want to interest you in my project."

George had no idea of what was coming next because he had not heard that Kroc or McDonald's was interested in getting into the parks or attractions business.

It turned out that Kroc owned quite a bit of property in North Los Angeles County and he wanted to build a large, permanent world's fair-type attraction. Kroc admitted that he had already talked with Walt Disney who had declined the offer. "I've come to you guys, because you've got a good reputation," he said to George.

He described the project as a place where different countries would offer changing exhibits and other forms of entertainment. Ronald McDonald and his friends would promote the park heavily. George recalls that all the while Kroc was explaining, his two assistants were slyly shaking their heads back and forth and secretively making negative gestures to George, all the while trying not to be seen by Kroc. "They were trying to let me know that they didn't like the idea and that I shouldn't go along with it." To this day, George thinks no one at McDonald's was interested in the project but Kroc.

George recalls saying, "Mr. Kroc, it looks to me like it would be a conflict of interest with our Magic Mountain park because it's only 30 miles down the road. I asked him to let me think about it and that I would call him. We stood up, shook hands, and he and his guards left. I called him a few days later to say almost the same thing. Our people felt there was a conflict of interest and we were turning the opportunity down. I never heard from him again, and never heard of the project again."

- CHAPTER 20 -

# Move Over Mickey, Shamu is on Her Way

One could hear a huge collective sigh of relief coming out of the SeaWorld camp when the company got its money back from the Magic Mountain experience. Luckily, they got out with all their original investment back and made a few additional dollars along the way. The also learned a valuable lesson: They were great at marine park development and operation, but they weren't ride park people.

Planning for the Orlando park was well under way when SeaWorld exited Magic Mountain. At the time, Disney was just getting established in the Florida market and SeaWorld executives felt their future was also in the Sunshine State. A five-man team under Ron Harper's leadership was already hard at work, and George Walsh was once again leading the team of architects. Walsh would later design the first two Wet'n Wild parks.

George originally became interested in Florida as a potential SeaWorld site in late 1970. Bob Foster, Disney's attorney and a part-time consultant to SeaWorld, had been telling George of Disney's plans to construct a park in Orlando and he urged George to acquire land in Central Florida and help add to the area's attraction base. Buzz Price was commissioned to do a feasibility study.

Foster pulled out a map and told George to "buy here." He pointed at a site and explained the land was owned by Florida Land, a subsidiary of the Florida Gas Transmissions Co. George set up an appointment with Jack Bowen the chairman of Florida Gas, and Harper, DeMotte and George flew to Central Florida to inspect the site and to get a price commitment. The property was at the intersection of I-4 and the proposed Bee Line Expressway, a short drive from the Disney entrance and at the intersection of two of Florida's busiest freeways.

Before committing to that specific site, George began looking at some Disney-owned property much closer to Walt

Disney World that was then being set aside as a future recreational area for Disney employees. It was across I-4 from where Disney had planned to build four or five hotels and it had a large lake in the center of the property. George's proposal to buy that land went all the way to the top of the Disney organization, but when it was denied, plans to build SeaWorld went back to the original site.

### *The Big Land Deal*

"We went back and made a deal with Florida Land. We made a hell of a deal," George said. "We bought 100 acres for $2,000 an acre and got an option on the 10 acres of land where the big Wyndham Hotel is now, for 10 years at $10,000 an acre." There were more options to adjacent land that officials purchased after George left the company in 1974.

The Bee Line Expressway was under construction and due to the high traffic anticipated at the park, it was imperative the expressway be open before the park could open its gates. The most efficient entrance had to come off that expressway.

George and Harper went to Tallahassee to see Florida Governor Rubin Askew during the summer of 1973 to discuss

*Construction work was well underway at SeaWorld Florida in 1972. From left, are Ron Harper, George Millay, Mike Demetrios, and an unidentified construction supervisor.*

*Ron Harper, right, and George Millay, flank Florida Governor Rubin Askew during a visit to Tallahassee in early 1973. Gar Millay, left, and Jeff Harper, in front, went along to meet the governor.*

the construction timetable for the Bee Line. "Mr. Millay," the governor said. "When do you want to open?" George said, "Governor, we think we'll be ready to open later this year." The governor smiled and told George to "give me 60 days notice of your exact date and the Bee Line Expressway will open on the same day."

At 10 a.m. on December 21, 1973, Ron Harper went over to the road superintendent and said, "We're open," and the superintendent said, "We're open, too." They dedicated the expressway, and the traffic started to flow into SeaWorld.

### *Building SeaWorld Florida*

"By the time we approached SeaWorld Florida, we were the class of the industry, and we could hire anybody we wanted for any job we wanted, and we assembled a hell of a team to go down there," George noted.

Years before, the expansion at SeaWorld San Diego had been handled by Nielsen Construction Co. and George had become an admirer of that company and its founder and namesake Falck Nielsen. Company officials became quite interested in the Florida project and asked George if they could negotiate a contract that would allow them to bring in a major southeast contractor as a partner. SeaWorld officials were amicable to that arrangement because above all, they trusted Falck Nielsen.

Moffatt & Nichol and Bill Dunn were the engineers and the architectural design process went smoothly. George's team of professionals was able to strut their stuff on this project. Ron Harper knew how to handle and encourage input from the staff and at the same time control their every whim. Farris Wankier, Dave Powell, Kym Murphy, Bob Gault, John Rognlie and two senior trainers rounded out the design team for SeaWorld Florida. Kent Burgess had left the company before the Florida project.

Falck Nielsen ended up bringing McDevitt and Street, a big construction firm from South Carolina, into the project as partners and they-co-ventured the deal. Construction started in mid-1972 and the crews had to contend with a rainy summer during initial grading. Every time an area would get graded, it seemed that a thunderstorm would come along and wipe out all the work.

"The great part of this project was that we were starting with a big, flat palmetto field and we were able to master plan it properly right from the beginning so that we could create it exactly the way we wanted," said Bob Gault, who by then was an integral part of the development team. "The biggest problems we had were water table issues. You know if you go down a couple of feet in Florida, you hit water. So we'd have huge dewatering issues whenever we dug holes and that presented us with some interesting challenges."

### Falling Behind Schedule

The crews started falling behind in construction, and there was starting to be a great deal of acrimony on the labor side with the sub-contractors.

McDevitt and Street had promised Neilsen that their top man would be put on this job but "they brought in some guy from Miami to be the superintendent and he quickly proved unable to deal with subcontractors, contracts, or labor situations," said George. "He was also all talk and no progress. If you sat and talked with him, you'd think he knew something, but his talk was much better than his actions. Thank God Neilsen had some of his top boys down there, and they struggled along with Harper and his crews to create a good product, and nearly on time."

George is quick to point out that McDevitt and Streets' top guy may have been perfectly competent, but that he could have easily been overwhelmed by the scope of the project. A $25 million job was huge for those days and not too many construction companies had tackled a project this large, either in cost or in scope. Due to various problems and delays, the opening had to be postponed from October to December 1973.

**George on Fish**
*I love to eat fish, but fishing bores me. I caught a fish once, that's enough.*
*- George Millay*

Gault recalls that one of the principal labor problems was the difference between the work ethic in the Florida workers and the workers the SeaWorld team had worked with in California and Ohio. "We perceived a tremendous difference in the speed with which stuff gets done. It's hot and humid in Florida and there was a different culture in terms of the speed with which people transact business," Gault added.

That difference created a "huge frustration level" during construction. "George just couldn't understand why things couldn't go faster," Gault added. "The productivity was much less than we had anticipated and that created a great deal of frustration and schedule issues."

Into that atmosphere sailed the brand new, beautiful SeaWorld Florida. The park opened without incident just prior to Christmas, and because of a colder-than-usual winter, attendance for the first several months was terrible. Total gate count for the first year was 800,000 people against a projection of one million.

### *Murphy & His Ozone*

The water quality systems at SeaWorld Florida were based entirely on ozone, not chlorination. It was the first time ozone had been used exclusively on such a large scale and its subsequent success ended up revolutionizing water quality techniques and standards throughout the total industry. Prior to SeaWorld Florida, virtually all aquariums and mammal displays in the world used chlorination. Today, most use ozone.

Kym Murphy began tinkering with the idea of being able to use ozone instead of other, much harsher chemicals, in 1967. The zoology graduate, hired at SeaWorld San Diego in late 1964 as an aquarist, said re-circulated water, based on chlorine, was similar to a YMCA swimming pool environment and very stressful on the animals. "Even though our systems were very sophisticated, the chlorine was hard on them," said Murphy, now senior vice president of Environmental Policy for The Walt Disney Company

George provided research and development money for Murphy's idea that an ozone system would be much better for the animals and at the same time, provide a much clearer water quality throughout the park. A tank was dedicated to the research and Murphy's hunches quickly proved to be right.

However, three months before SeaWorld Florida opened, George had his doubts, about Murphy and his ozone concept. Shamu was on her way to her new home in Orlando, the tank was full, and the long list of media invitees were ready to arrive. Unfortunately, a check valve was installed incorrectly in the tank's water system, and when the button was pushed to start re-circu-

*Shamu is treated to a drink, courtesy of George Millay, center, and Chimp, 1967.*

lating the beautiful, blue and crystal clear water, everything turned a milky gray color, due to backflow into the tank.

"You couldn't see six inches into the tank," recalls Murphy. "George wasn't too happy. When everyone was there and the celebration was about to begin, I kind of disappeared off to the side to avoid his stare."

The evasiveness didn't work, George saw him, and as he greeted the VIPs and the media and started talking about Shamu over the microphone, George stopped the procedure, pointed out Murphy to the crowd and said, "Ladies and gentlemen, you can thank Mr. Murphy over there for the wonderful clarity of our water today."

One fact about Murphy that George is proud to point out is his post-SeaWorld success at Walt Disney World, in Orlando. Murphy's first project at Disney was the creation of the Living Seas Pavilion in Epcot. The 6.2 million gallon aquarium attraction is still considered the largest aquarium in the world.

What makes it special for George is that it was the first major Disney attraction created by a SeaWorld-trained individual. Through the years, Disney executives were helpful, as consultants and friends, in the creation of SeaWorld and Wet'n Wild, but the creation of this attraction by a SeaWorld alumni signified to George, that SeaWorld had officially come of age.

### *The First of the Wet'n Wild Dreams*

It was during the course of construction at SeaWorld Florida, during those hot Florida days, that George first started thinking of a water-oriented family leisure park concept. "Anyone who goes to Central Florida in the middle of summer, walks around on hot asphalt for a couple of hours and sits on concrete benches, soon realizes there must be a better way to be entertained. It had me thinking."

Due to the extreme heat and the need to keep guests comfortable and happy, George decided it would be smart to air condition the outdoor stadiums at SeaWorld, which added another $4 million to the construction price causing the total cost of the project to come in close to $27 million.

Milt Shedd didn't like the additional expenditures and continued planting doubts in the board's mind about George's ability to lead the company. Shedd kept telling DeMotte that he should be the one running the company, not George. "We don't

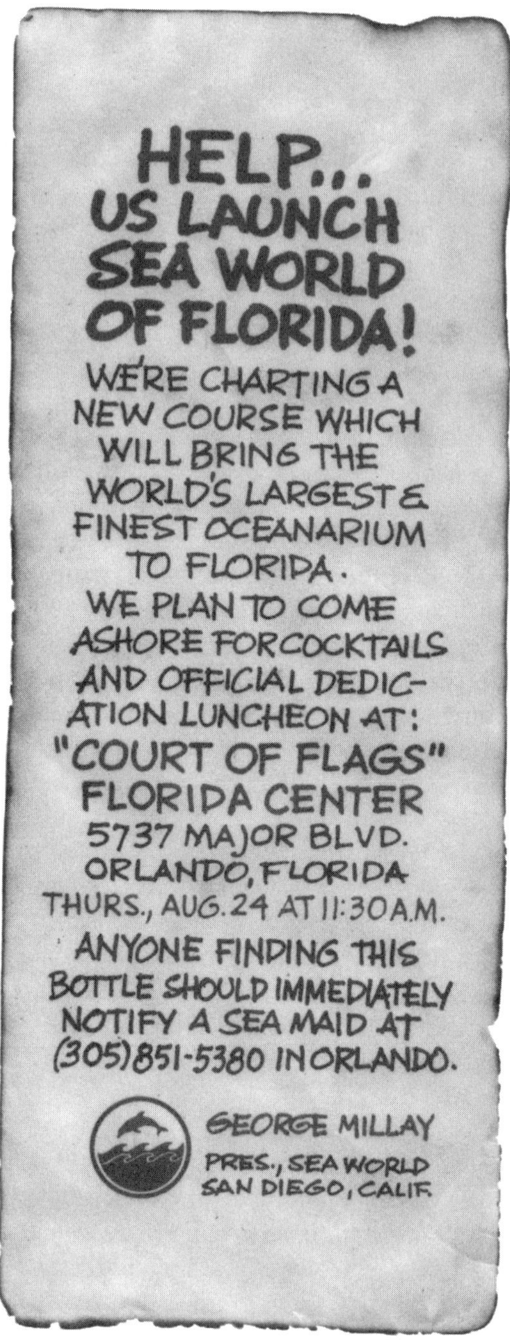


*A parchment promotional message was delivered to the Orlando press and VIPS, wrapped up in a bottle, 1972.*

need a creative guy," he was heard to say. "We need an accountant running this company." Shedd had also gone behind George's back and started talking to the local lenders about George's ability to run the company. It got to the point that the bank's representatives started criticizing George for the "glitzy, expensive shows" at the park.

### *Bad Time to Open a Great Park*

The conditions of the time were not kind to George's reputation within the boardroom as a big spender. The park opened on December 21, 1973, in the middle of nation-wide gas rationing. Oil prices were going up and even Disney, then in its second year, was having trouble. Family auto trips as well as commercial airline flights were cut back due to the gasoline and jet fuel shortage and Florida tourism went in the tank as a result.

During the same period, interest rates grew beyond belief. "When we first borrowed the money to build Florida, we borrowed it at 8% interest, and by the time we opened, it was at 14%. Shedd, DeMotte and the other financial guys, along with the bankers, began to panic," George recalls.

The company had borrowed $18 million from several banks, including Security Pacific, Cleveland Trust and Sun Bank of Florida. SeaWorld had put $8 million of its own money into the Florida venture. At 14%, the higher interest rates meant additional interest payments of approximately $750,000 per year. "I don't think we had projected more than a million dollars a year in profits for the first couple of years, so it was a dangerous thing that was going on, a real dangerous thing," George said.

In addition to the interest rates climbing, SeaWorld stock dropped drastically from $63 to $30. Everything combined only fueled Shedd's claim that the company needed an accountant at the helm.

### *Board Becomes Concerned about Money*

George said his "perceived" reputation for spending too much money was "total bullshit. I watched my money very, very closely, but I never wanted to do anything unless we did it right. We needed to present something to the public that was well designed, well maintained and original, a park that would last for decades. Sometimes to do that, it costs money that you just can't accurately project."

**On His Honor**

*George had many opportunities where he could justifiably take advantage of other people, but he didn't do it because it wasn't in his makeup. On the other hand if you screwed him, look out. He'd bury you. If he had a fiduciary obligation to you, you could always be assured that he would carry that out to the absolute degree.*

*- Gary Zuercher, ride manufacturer*

The inexperienced board was deeply concerned about money, continued to talk about cutting back and was becoming worried that the company was growing too quickly. They also began expressing their concerns vocally that George was spending too much money on unnecessary things.

The first example of what Shedd considered "unnecessary and expensive," was the air conditioning of the stadiums. Another example focused on Foremost Dairy, a large corporate partner. They wanted to sponsor a major snack bar in the park and it was going to cost SeaWorld nearly $800,000 to develop the complex with Foremost's name on it. They would pay $50,000 a year for the naming rights.

Jeff Asher, a board member, asked George why that particular expenditure had to be made. Asher asked George, "Why don't we just put a Foremost Ice Cream cart out there and make do with that?" George hated talk like that. "Our guests want shade. They want to sit down and rest. We want to give them a menu with many choices because they will buy more," George replied.

Several employees had warned George that Shedd and DeMotte had been talking big time behind his back. "I started seeing that something was afoot as early as November, more than a month before we opened. I didn't think I needed to do anything about it. I didn't canvas the board and I didn't go talk to Buzz Price, who was by then a member of the board, like I should have."

- CHAPTER 21 -

# George is Doomed

The board's first official move against George occurred in November when they established development and show committees and required George to report to those groups to discuss any new show concepts and all costs. George acquiesced to it, had one meeting with each of the committees and then went back to the board and told them that it wasn't going to work. "I wasn't going to take all day trying to justify why we needed to do something to a lawyer or an accountant or someone else not in the business who didn't know what the hell I was talking about."

Shedd and some of the members of the board started putting serious pressure on George in December, just before the park opened. George said he had gotten word that Shedd was starting to quietly gather a consensus among the directors. In an early February meeting, the board "promoted" George to chairman, effectively taking him out of the day-to-day decision-making process.

"I just said the hell with it and walked out of the meeting. I admit I was pretty arrogant at the time. I don't want to make it look like I was a little lamb and did nothing wrong." When George was promoted, Dave DeMotte became president. George didn't stick around for the actual vote. "I saw the way the thing was going and decided I wasn't going to sit there and listen to that shit, so I just got up and left."

Shortly after the meeting, Shedd called George at home and told him about the vote. "I was stunned, shaken, confused, and really pissed off, because I owned more stock than anybody on the board and here they voted me out of there."

**Remember George?**

*How will George be remembered? As an original. As a great entrepreneur. As someone with lots of guts who was willing to take great risks. As a creative innovator.*

*- Marty Sklar,*

*Head of Creative for The Walt Disney Co.*

Individually, George owned 8% of the stock at SeaWorld, Milt Shedd owned 7%, and Dave DeMotte owned approximately 2%.

George had lost his power and the control of the company and only went back to the park once after that February meeting. A week before the scheduled May board meeting, he sent Shedd a letter officially resigning from a chairmanship he had never accepted in the first place. That action officially closed the doors and at that point, George Millay, the founder and most of the brains behind SeaWorld was no longer a part of the company he had built.

Giving up his $60,000 a year salary, his car, and his insurance was hard to do and was quite a gamble for the high-rolling executive. Those were tough times in the world and George sensed they were soon to be tough times for him as well. He didn't know where he was going or what he was going to do. All he knew for sure was that he wanted no part of the organization that shunned him.

***You've Got to be Kidding***

From what George had told them, Jan Schultz said he and Ron Harper had a strong feeling that George was going to be reprimanded. "I can remember George being in a terribly foul mood the morning of the board meeting. He stopped by my office and said if anything was going to happen, it was probably going to happen at that meeting."

Neither Schultz nor Harper ever thought the board would really do it. They might try shaking him up and scaring him, they thought, but they surely wouldn't get rid of him. Shedd had developed his scheme with consummate timing.

The board meeting took place in San Diego, and word spread quickly throughout all three parks. George left the building before the meeting was over, so no one saw his immediate reaction.

By literally kicking him out of the organization he founded, the board reached George "the manager" and George "the boss," but they "never really got to George the person," Harper notes. "To this day, I have never truly heard him publicly badmouth the people who, in my opinion took advantage of him at SeaWorld and stabbed him in the back."

He brought much of it on himself, Harper admits. "He wouldn't take counsel from the board because he was so sure he was right, and that's a trait that has always been a shortcoming in George, but it's also the trait of a genius. If he had been more contrite and more willing to work with the board, he never would have been kicked out. People who get things done however, don't listen to the naysayers claiming it can't be done."

Jan Schultz, who stayed on with SeaWorld for more than a decade after George left, says George was prone to argue with everyone. It was a sign that George had so much passion about the project at hand. "It wasn't that he hated you or thought less of you. Arguing was his way of challenging you when he thought he was right. He wanted to see if there were real reasons why you disagreed with him. It was an interesting and mostly misunderstood management style of his."

***What Now for George's Followers?***

George Becker, who was still VP and general manager of Ohio at the time of George's dismissal, said that for the members of "George's team" who were left behind, "it was very confusing. There was never a real explanation given to any of the management or the staff on the reasons why George was no longer around."

Becker said surprisingly, no one feared for his or her jobs. "I think if Dave (DeMotte) did anything in terms of communicating the difficulty to us it was to assure us that we were doing a good job and for us to continue focusing on the things we needed to focus on."

Bob Gault said people left behind by George were more concerned about what changes would take place rather than a fear of losing their jobs. "The fact that Milt, George, and Dave were so close during all those years and that they could break up like this, sent a significant ripple through the organization. It created much uncertainty and anxiety," Gault remembers.

There were also many questions of loyalty that arose during the transition, according to Gault. "It was like being a kid in a divorce where you love both your mom and your dad. You don't want them to break up but when they do, your own loyalty is often questioned. With whom do I side? Don't put me in a position of having to side with one or the other," Gault said, noting that most people in the company were frustrated and confused. If you continued to work there, you had to have loyalty to the company and the people who were signing your paycheck. By the same token we all had great loyalty to George who created the company and gave us tremendous opportunities."

It soon became obvious that the corporate culture was changing, Gault notes. "Dave DeMotte was a very conservative financial guy so we went from a very aggressive growth posture to a let's haul it back and control costs mode. Clearly there wasn't the impetus to grow the business as rapidly."

***Testing the Loyalty***

Within 20 minutes of that fateful board meeting, Schultz was summoned into the boardroom where Milt Shedd and the directors were waiting for him. "Jan, we know how close you and George are and we would like you to know that we want you to stay. With George leaving there's a big void on the creative side of the business and we need you to step in and to help fill that void," said Shedd.

Schultz saw right through that rhetoric. "One thing they were afraid of from the beginning was that George would somehow find a way to get back in and get somebody to buy SeaWorld or that he'd buy it himself." Schultz said he got the feeling they were trying to tell him they didn't want him to have anymore contact with George.

**Get them Talking!**

*George had great pride of authorship in the business and was always very concerned about guest perception. At SeaWorld in those early years, we had a minimal advertising budget and the entire business had to be driven by our guests' word of mouth referral.*

*- Bob Gault, president Universal Orlando*

"I said to them, look, he's one of my best friends. He's been my mentor. My loyalty, however, is with SeaWorld. I love this company and I'm going to stay here and do the best job I can, but George Millay will always remain my friend and if you guys want to tell me that I can't see him or I can't have dinner with him then I'm going to have to think about whether or not I want to stay here," Schultz told Shedd.

True to his word, Schultz continued meeting George for lunches and dinners and the two were able to keep their friendship alive. Nearly a year after George left SeaWorld, he invited

Schultz over to his house to show him "a new concept" that he had been thinking about. "I left the office about six and drove over to his home which is a mile away and he introduced me to the Wet'n Wild concept. I thought it was wonderful."

The next morning, a Saturday, Schultz went to work and was greeted by Shedd and DeMotte who immediately said they knew that Schultz had met with George the night before and they wanted to know why. He said George had shown him a new concept, one that would not compete with SeaWorld. Schultz was fired on the spot and he packed up some things and went home.

Three hours later he received a call from Shedd who rehired him. "What had happened and I didn't know it at the time, was that they were trailing some of us and somebody followed me as I drove over to George's house. They were still very nervous, very paranoid," Schultz added.

### *George Always was Lousy on Defense*

In retrospect, George realizes he should not have resigned, but should have stayed and fought the board. He now thinks he could have won. "I could have stepped into the market and bought a big chunk of stock in 1975. It had bottomed out at $6 a share and I could have purchased enough to give them a good scare. I could have kicked the bastards out, but for some reason, I didn't. Milt Shedd said to me one time, 'George, you're great on offense, you're the shits on defense.' He was right."

One of the most asked questions of George through the years has been: "Would you do the same thing again? Would you walk out and leave SeaWorld without putting up a fight?" Even today, 30 years later, he is asked that question several times each year.

"I look back and although it still hurts, I now realize I had supporters on the old SeaWorld board. Buzz Price, Joe Powell, John Moffatt and Bill Burrud, all proved to be on my side. There was support, but I wasn't interested in returning to a situation that I felt was stacked

**George as a Pioneer**

*Yes, I do see myself as a pioneer, but the feeling is mixed. I see a lot of pioneers as losers. Poor creative wretches who had great ideas but fate and good common sense weren't with them. I have been lucky.*

*- George Millay*

against me. My freedom was gone and could never be resurrected," George said.

Marty Sklar, principal creative executive with Walt Disney Imagineering, has known George since college, when they would have water balloon fights between the fraternities at UCLA. Sklar, while not having any direct dealings with George, followed his progress through the years. He thinks George's attributes as a risk taker and a creative innovator made it hard for him to work in a corporate environment.

"He wasn't cut out to work for someone, especially a board of a corporation," Sklar said. "George is an entrepreneur and in many ways a throwback to a time in our business that we have moved away from, the days of P.T. Barnum."

At the time he walked out, the call of a new concept was inching itself into George's psyche. "I don't think I realized it then, but it was time for me to strike out again on my own. The only difference now was that I had capital and a good reputation. My pocketbook was readily open to pay for the pursuit and design of unique water activities. The designers were on board and the suppliers were calling. Do it again, show them, cried my very soul!"

Distancing himself from the past, he was able to begin another creative journey.

"Was I a fool? Maybe, but I don't think so. Only time would tell."

- CHAPTER 22 -

# The Post-Millay SeaWorld

George looks back with wonderment on how he was voted out. He had so many successes and so few failures under his belt.

"First of all, I know I didn't pay enough attention to the board. I didn't think I had to because what I had created had been so successful. Many board members had benefited financially from what had been accomplished. We started SeaWorld and made it work. We started Magic Mountain and that didn't go very well, but we got out of it. We started Ohio which was a winner right from the start and in 1972, our stock was selling at 40 times earnings, while Disney stock was selling at only 20 times earnings."

George thinks Shedd started to become his enemy because he had told him in so many words, "to keep your nose out of where it doesn't belong."

The day George resigned, Shedd said to him, "I want to turn this company back two years," and ironically within two years, they were all gone. Less than a year after George left, Universal made an unsuccessful bid at an unfriendly takeover of SeaWorld. That bid however, left the company vulnerable and in search of a friendly buyer.

The Universal takeover bid remains a mystery to George. Why were they interested in the first place and how it came about. He has heard many contradictory stories over the years. In the mid-1970s when the Universal bid took place, the company had not yet announced plans to build the second Universal Studios park in Orlando and there wasn't room to build another park adjacent to SeaWorld, so George can't see to this day why they were interested in SeaWorld at that time.

Jan Schultz told George that Universal's Lou Wasserman called Dave DeMotte and asked for a meeting and Schultz joined DeMotte at that meeting. Wasserman told them he was interested in buying SeaWorld and DeMotte said, "We are not for sale," and the meeting ended. Two weeks later Universal made its

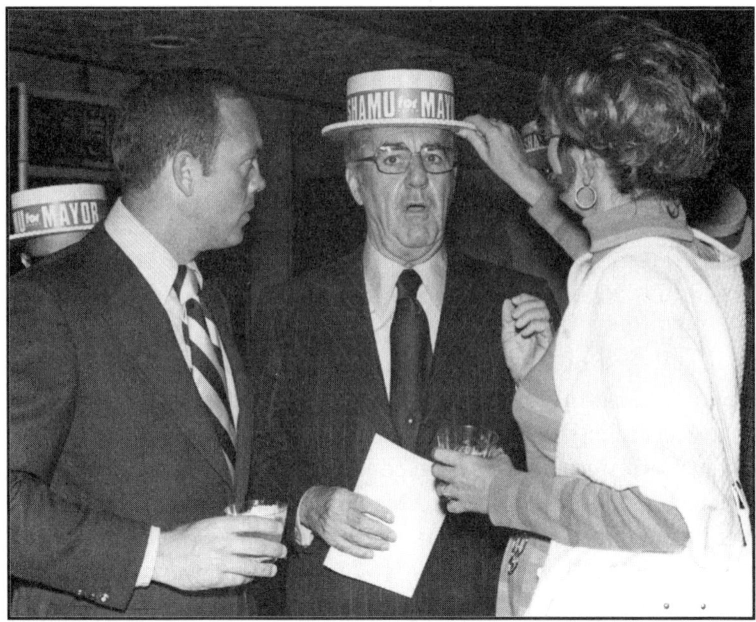


*Actor Jim Backus served as honorary chairman of the Shamus for Mayor campaign during the early 1970s. Jan Schultz watches as an unidentified Shamu fan helps Backus with his hat.*

unsolicited offer and Shedd and DeMotte scurried for a white knight, which turned out to be Harcourt Brace Jovanovich that eventually bought the parks. "SeaWorld stockholders suffered enormous loss during that sell-out and got nothing compared to what they should have, and I think I suffered the most," according to George.

***George's Dream Sold for a Pittance***

The three parks were sold to HBJ for approximately $57 million in 1976. "To this day I shudder at the enormity of the financial debacle. Bill Jovanovich came in and stole the company. The one good aspect is that he let Bob Hillebrecht, a real pro, run it for four years," George notes. "I was so impressed with Bob (Hillebrecht) that I later asked him to serve on the Wet'n Wild board."

When SeaWorld was sold to HBJ, DeMotte and Shedd each received five-year work contracts. "Bill Jovanovich soon tired of Shedd's hypocritical preaching and bought his contract out after two years," said George.

A short time later Shedd ran into George's wife, Anne, at

a small grocery store in San Diego and apologetically, with tears in his eyes stated, "Please tell George I made a terrible mistake." A surprised Anne replied as she backed away, "It's too late Milt."

Dave Demotte was dismissed the day his contract was up in 1980. "They tell me he was flabbergasted and bitter at that turn of events. Dave passed on a few years later as a result of a brain tumor," George said. "We lunched several times during the period just before his passing and we made our peace."

Bob Gault, general manager of SeaWorld Ohio when the sale took place, said initially HBJ was good for the company, due in part to them being an educational publishing company and understanding the company's educational and conservation mission. Plus they were supportive in terms of providing capital to grow the business. They understood the need for capital spending to keep the product fresh and new. From that standpoint they were very positive, according to Gault.

George disagrees with Gault's perspective. After the buyout they never put a dime of HBJ money into the existing three parks. All expansion capital came from within SeaWorld, through its revenues and profits, not from HBJ pockets, George notes.

In addition to expanding the three existing SeaWorld parks, HBJ opened SeaWorld Texas, the world's largest marine park in May 1998. The 250-acre, $200 million park in San Antonio opened as a year-round park but went seasonal within a couple years.

### *More than SeaWorld to Offer*

Other HBJ additions to the SeaWorld family of parks included Florida's Cypress Gardens, which it purchased in August 1985 for $23 million, and Circus World in Haines City, Florida, which HBJ purchased in May 1986 for $18 million. The company turned Circus World into Boardwalk and Baseball, a sports-themed amusement park.

In January 1987, HBJ purchased Marineland in Rancho Palos Verdes, California, the park that sparked George's original idea to build a marine park. They closed the park within a few months, and moved the two killer whales to SeaWorld San Diego. By 1987, HBJ had grown into the second largest theme park operator in the country, behind the Walt Disney parks. However, by mid-1987 financial problems started to surface and in August of that year, HBJ was forced to lay off 729 park division employees.

The company limped along, but by the end of the first quarter of 1989, HBJ carried nearly $2.7 billion in debt and was no longer able to reinvest in the parks.

"We ended up with a leader who was very autocratic and aggressive and who tried to grow the business too quickly. They were forced to re-capitalize the company because money from the employee profit-sharing plan had been used to expand and in doing so, they destroyed the business. HBJ ended up with nothing and they ended up out of the attractions business," Gault said.

**Generous George**

*George was always really protective of money being spent. He didn't pay himself a big salary and through the years, he never took a bunch of money out of the company. He ran a company the way it should be run, for the benefit of the shareholders. He was very generous and he gave a lot of people a great deal of stock when he took SeaWorld public.*

*- Ron Harper, president, Harper Construction Company*

Rumors that HBJ was ready to sell off its park division began to gain feet in early 1989 when several suitors publicly made their desires known. One of the first groups to go public with their intention was headed up by George. He, Jan Schultz, and former SeaWorld CEO Bob Hillebrecht formed a partnership and said they wanted to buy the parks. They assured the media they would have no problem funding the purchase.

"I received several phone calls from investment bankers asking if I would be interested in leading a group to buy back the parks," George said. Hillebrecht was a good one to have on the team. He had engineered HBJ's purchase of the parks in 1976.

In June 1989, HBJ officially announced its park division was up for sale, and it wasn't long before analysts started predicting who the suitors were and who would end up with the prize. The Walt Disney Company, Anheuser-Busch, MCA, The Rank Organization and Paramount Parks were all listed as candidates. The team of Millay, Schultz, and Hillebrecht got lost in the media dust.

In late September 1989, it was officially announced that Busch Entertainment, the parks division of the Anheuser-Busch

Company, had won the prize and had agreed to buy HBJ's park division for $975 million. Including the extra land sold along with the parks, the total price came to $1.1 billion. While HBJ officials said they were deluged with many offers to buy the parks, the price ended up being at the low end of what most analysts had predicted it would sell for.

- CHAPTER 23 -

# George Falls for a Zsa Zsa Line

In the early 1970s, while still heading up SeaWorld, George "foolishly" invested in Zsa Zsa Gabor Cosmetics, a startup company based in New York City. "I was dragged into the deal by Bob Foman, the West Coast manager of E. F. Hutton and Company," he said. Foman lured George into the deal by noting that "only a select few" were going to be able to get into this deal. "He should have said only a select few pigeons."

George put up $100,000 and was a stockholder. "We had a guy from Estee Lauder as president, and we had guys coming from all over to head up the company. It was the greatest crew of experts in cosmetics you could have found at the time, plus we had Zsa Zsa Gabor to front the thing. E. F. Hutton co-sponsored the deal with Shearson Hammel raising $6 million for the deal, and they wanted to put me on the board."

The other West Coast board member was Al Slavik, whose family owned a major share of the Granger Corporation fortune. According to George, Slavik put up $250,000 in the company, "which was peanuts for him since he was worth nearly $500 million."

Slavik and George became buddies, traveled together and were enjoying their board seats on this new cosmetics venture, until the company went bankrupt within a year.

In true entrepreneurial fashion, the two decided they would take over and save the company. George and Slavik came up with $500,000 worth of personal guarantees and used the $3 million worth of inventory sitting in a Brooklyn warehouse as collateral. Zsa Zsa had agreed that if the two could turn it around and make it work, she'd come back and help.

Re-organization was underway when a New York judge granted a New York businessman the right to come in and take the then defunct company over. The new owner told George that he planned to take over the inventory as well, and he personally

**On Being Irish**
*Celtic blood runs deep in my veins. It is definitely a part of me. The Irish have been under a brutal heel for nearly a thousand years. Yet we survive and prosper. I think our sad history has been a major reason for our drive and many accomplishments here in the U.S. If I had been closer I probably would have been a member of the IRA.*
*- George Millay*

guaranteed George and Slavik's $500,000 worth of guarantees from Citibank. It wasn't long, however, before he went broke and reneged on those guarantees. "He eventually went bankrupt and we fought this guy for two years, going right up to the Appellate Court of New York and we won," George said.

One day during that process, George received a call from Citibank saying, "Mr. Millay, get back here, your guarantee is in jeopardy because nobody has paid on these loans." The VP of delinquent accounts who George remembers as "having the personality of a penniless undertaker," told George and Slavik that he was sorry, but their certificates of deposit and other guarantees had been liquidated.

George was still president of SeaWorld at the time and he and Slavik hired a New York City law firm to go after their money. It took three years, but the two got most of their investment back.

Ever the promoter, George talked about his Wet'n Wild ideas with both Slavik and with Tom Curnin, the head of the New York law firm representing the two. Curnin later became an early shareholder in Wet'n Wild. Slavik also jumped into the Wet'n Wild deal when it appeared that his friend George Millay, who had proven himself to Slavik on many occasions, wasn't going to get enough capital investors to build his dream park. Both men did well by believing in George.

- CHAPTER 24 -

# Once a Restauranteur, Always a Restauranteur

With his entrepreneurial roots in the restaurant business, and with the success of the Atlantis restaurant he built at SeaWorld in 1967, George got the urge to build more themed restaurants in early 1970.

He got the bug to do so while visiting the Proud Bird restaurant that his old friend and mentor, David Tallichet had built on the glide path at the Los Angeles International Airport. "What a fantastic concept he had there," George recalls. "The diners could watch the planes coming in and taking off and they could put headphones on and listen to the pilots talking to the control tower. The people loved it and the restaurant was immensely popular from day one."

George left the Proud Bird that day knowing he was going home to San Diego to begin working on another themed restaurant in that city. In his mind, he had it designed by the time he got home. In a short time, he had secured a piece of property near the runway at Lindbergh Field and SeaWorld began to build a themed restaurant called Boom Trenchard's Flarepath, after the English pilot who turned the Royal Air Force into a potent fighting machine during WWI. "Boom's" opened in late 1971.

***Let's Eat in a Flying Saucer***

Originally, George's idea was to build a space themed restaurant at Lindbergh. It would consist of two discs, ala flying saucers, seemingly suspended in the air with green lights flashing from beneath the discs.

He hired Larry Crandall who was the director of development for Lowery's Specialty Foods in Los Angeles, to help create, then after it was built, to run the restaurant. He lived nearby in La Jolla and George liked him the minute he met him. "He was a conceited kind of a guy and full of bullshit, but he had a great creative mind and he was able to get me to drop the space ship theme and build a World War I themed restaurant instead," George said.

They used the headphones concept that Tallichet had come up with at the Proud Bird, and the restaurant was heavily themed to the war and to aviation. "Crandall did an unbelievable job," George said. "Tallichet came down to look at it and he was so jealous he couldn't see straight. He went home and created the 94th Aero Squadron restaurant chain that eventually was built at dozens of airports across the country." Crandall, as planned, stayed with SeaWorld after Boom's was built and took over the responsibility of the Atlantis as well.

**Tell-a-George**

*For the most part, George would let us do what we did best, but we always kept him informed. An informed Millay was a good Millay.*

*-John Seeker, VP, MARC USA*

Crandall also gave George an idea for another restaurant, 10 Downing. The SeaWorld board didn't want to invest in any more restaurants, so Dave DeMotte, George and his brother Bud, took the concept, formed a partnership, and built two on their own. The downtown San Diego location opened in late 1973, and the Solana Beach location, without DeMotte, opened in 1978.

"Larry turned out to be a creative genius but he couldn't run a restaurant worth a damn and I had to let him go. That's too bad, because I really liked him," George said. "I think he was so creative that everything else just didn't matter."

### *George Gets Lucky Again*

After Crandall left, George said he got lucky. His brother, Bud, had become friendly with Joe Gauci, one of Tallichet's top managers and he had discovered that Gauci wanted to move out of Los Angeles to San Diego. It was good timing because George was in dire need of a good, experienced, tough manager. Gauci went in for an interview and as George describes him, Gauci was "a rough, tough, cynical, hard-working bundle of energy." He was hired and took over the Atlantis, Boom's, and the downtown 10 Downing.

The SeaWorld people liked Gauci and he easily fit into the verbal kidding and mental jousting that was so prevalent in the organization. He produced immediate results in all the restaurants and continued to do so for years. When George left SeaWorld in early 1974, his relationship with DeMotte understandably became strained and about a year later, George bought him out. George and Bud remained as the two owners of 10 Downing.

Gauci left SeaWorld shortly after George did but continued to run 10 Downing for George and Bud. Gauci wanted to expand the concept and talked George into opening the second 10 Downing in nearby Solana Beach. By then, George had nearly $300,000 invested in the two restaurants.

The 10 Downing location in downtown San Diego was the true star of the two. The English pub setting was extremely popular as a watering hole for the downtown people after work. It had an English-style menu, had an excellent chef and Gauci was running it. "We made pretty good money, averaging a profit of between $50,000 and $70,000 a year after all the expenses and salaries. In our good years, we grossed about $1 million with an average dinner tab of $8," George said.

The downtown restaurant relied heavily on traffic from a couple of large hotels and the Fox Theater, located a short distance down the street. The eatery would get 50 or 60 diners a night from the El Cortez Hotel alone. When the hotel closed and the Fox Theater was closed and demolished, the restaurant saw a sharp decrease in business. George wondered if he was going to be able to pay off the $100,000 in loans still out on the restaurant.

### *Enter HBJ, Again*

The downtown restaurant was in the basement of a high-rise building, ironically owned by Harcourt Brace Jovanovich, the same company that owned SeaWorld at the time. The building agent, employed by HBJ, came to George and said Bill Jovanovich needed the space and wanted the restaurant out of the building and asked George how much he wanted for the business. George threw out $500,000, a figure way more than the business was worth. The agent countered with $400,000 and the deal was done and Jovanovich got his additional space. That was in mid-1982.

"We paid off the note and had $300,000 to distribute between the two of us, Gauci, the chef, and our bookkeeper.

Everyone was happy," he said.

The Solana Beach location was in a shopping center and did well, but was never as lucrative as the downtown location. A new owner took over the shopping center and wanted to expand the liquor store that was next to 10 Downing and offered to buy George out at a ridiculously high price. The deal was made, the restaurant was closed in 1984 and the liquor store was able to expand. Today, it's a Long's Drug Store.

After those two restaurants were sold, Gauci went to Wet'n Wild Las Vegas when it opened in 1985, where he became the park's first food and beverage manager. He retired from that position in 1998 when George sold the company.

Within a few years of George's departure from SeaWorld, Boom Trenchard's was sold to San Diego hotelier Doug Manchester who operated it until it was torn down during an expansion of Lindbergh Field.

- CHAPTER 25 -

# The Sociable Boss

Wherever George held office, there was always a large amount of horseplay that went on among the vice presidents and others who reported to him. He loved and encouraged the interchange. However, during all the frivolities, there was never a question of who was in charge or who had the final say.

He trusted in his management staff and while relying on them to help grow his company, he enjoyed their company. "No matter how much we played nor how much we goofed off, we were serious professionals and continually pushed ourselves to achieve our goals," said Schultz. The goal at SeaWorld San Diego during those early years was to be a strong number two, behind Disney, in the outdoor recreation industry in Southern California. Another goal was to put Marineland out of business, which we did.

Through the years, George was often criticized for getting too close to his management team. "I stayed very close to my top guys because they were the people who were making the thing go. I would get involved in certain areas more than others because I had some proficiency in them, and in some areas, like insurance and accounting, I stayed out of the way for many years until I felt comfortable with them," George said. "We drank and played real hard and interacted socially during the early days of SeaWorld right through to the final days of Wet'n Wild."

**Semi-Social George**

*I don't believe I'm a social person because most people bore me, especially since I quit drinking. I truly enjoy my wife and family and a dozen or so good friends, but I have become cynical of mankind in general. I try to be courteous to everyone but I can't say I'm friendly.*

*- George Millay*

Today, George doesn't drink, but does admit he drank way too much during most of his career. "I never drank during the daytime. In fact, I usually didn't drink until 6 and 7 at night and then I'd consume anywhere from five to eight ounces of alcohol on a regular night and on some of the big nights, I'd go out until 4 or 5 a.m. and would consume a fifth of vodka, plus some wine. My prime drinking age ran from 29 to 60."

***Too Poor to Drink***

Not surprisingly, George's early success in the restaurant business led him to drinking. "I got into that business and all of a sudden I went from a guy who couldn't rub two nickels together in my jeans or pay for the hard stuff to having free martinis," he remembers. "I started drinking moderately when I was 29. Up until that time I really didn't drink very much because in reality, I didn't like beer and I couldn't afford anything else. All of a sudden I have this big successful restaurant, and later two or three more restaurants, and I could drink as much as I damned-well pleased, free."

Then, when he opened SeaWorld, he could drink free in the park's restaurants. Also, by that time, he had more than enough money to buy anything he wanted. "Starting with SeaWorld, we all drank pretty heavily." Atlantis, owned by SeaWorld, was his favorite hangout.

"God bless my wonderful wife, Anne. She never ever jumped me about my drinking. Once in a while she'd ask me to cut back, but she never made a deal out of it," he said, noting that he seldom let his drinking interfere with his family life. "Don't get me wrong, I drank only at night and most of the time I was in bed at 10 but I went to bed goofy for 30 years. My children were aware of this stupid habit and put up with it. Thank God their mother's good influence (and prayers, Anne adds) prevailed, as none of the kids have a drinking problem and never dealt in drugs."

***A Gregarious Drunk***

Was he a mean drunk? "No, I just got a little more gregarious when I drank and sometimes my quick temper would get a little quicker. I'm spoiled. I'm impatient and I have a quick temper. Those three things might have added up to a dangerous situation from time to time, especially when you add alcohol to the mix."

There is no question that drinking brought a more carefree and venturesome attitude to George. "When I drank, I took more chances, especially when driving my boat. I used to love to jump in my Bertram 38 with a fifth of Smirnoff by my side. I would race out to sea four or five miles, play Wagner's Valkeries extremely loud and charge around the Pacific in the dead of night."

On many a night, George was a party waiting to happen. He would go around the office and round up as many of his compatriots as he could to go out for dinner and drinks, or maybe a boat cruise around Mission Bay. He'd go around and say, "Hey, let's take a quick boat ride around the bay and have a quick dinner." Harper recalls that "quick" meant 10 p.m. if he was lucky. "It's not something you want to do several times a week, even with George Millay," Harper states.

**George the Pugilist**

*I was on the UCLA boxing team in 1952 and fought in seven fights. I was a fairly good boxer, the biggest guy on the team. I fought middleweight, light heavyweight, and sometimes heavyweight. The heavyweights were easier except they hit you really hard.*

*- George Millay*

Jan Schultz remembers that everyone drank too much on those mini-cruises, including the boat driver creating the potential of crashing into a ship, a pier or a breakwater. Those "cruises" were primarily drinking junkets, joke telling opportunities, and "the man against the sea thing," Schultz adds.

Jim Ring, a crew-cut student at the University of California at San Diego, worked part time in maintenance and would also drive George's boat on many nighttime forays. He was one of George's "good guy students." He kept his hair short, he was in Navy ROTC and his motto following a nighttime boat ride was, "I know nothing."

### *Afraid to Stop*

Luck helped George succeed in business as luck helped George stop drinking. For 10 years before he quit, until he reached his early 60's, George often told himself that he had to stop, but he admits today that he was too afraid. "It was actually a phobia and I kind of overly visualized people going through the withdrawals. You hear about shaking hands and lying awake in bed at night. I thought, my God, can I go through it? I knew I had to, but I didn't have the courage to start."

He felt that way for a number of years but was not ready to seriously do anything about it. His fears were based on the potential ramifications of sobering up. Ironically he hadn't decided to quit when he actually did.

Anne and George had sent their daughter Chrislyn, to a language school in Cuernavaca, Mexico. She lived in the home of a Mexican family and was there for three months. "I flew down to visit and I caught a severe case of tourista. I had rented a car and driven it from the Mexico City Airport out to Cuernavaca. I spent about four or five days with Chrislyn."

**George is Thrown into the Slammer**

*George loved to go out on the water at night and feel the fresh air in his face. It was a stress buster for him. On one of those trips, he got a citation for speeding on Mission Bay at 2 a.m. in his Bertram 31, a fast sports fishing boat. In true George fashion, he either neglected or forgot about the ticket, even after he received a notice. One day several months later, he was sitting in his office at SeaWorld and there came a knock upon his door. It was the sheriff. "Mr. Millay, I'm sorry I have to do this," as he put the cuffs on George.*

*With his hands cuffed behind his back, the president and founder of SeaWorld was led out of his office through the park to the parking lot, in front of many of his employees.*

*George said it was only a little bit embarrassing. He always said that he didn't have much use for any man who hadn't spent a night in jail. He himself had previously spent several nights in various Navy brigs so it didn't bother him to get locked up. They put him in jail with two other guys. "They asked me what I was in for, and I said for not paying a speeding ticket. One guy was in for vagrancy, the other for murder. At lunchtime, they served us dry, cheese sandwiches on white bread, and I wouldn't eat it. I divvied the sandwiches up between the other guys and you wouldn't believe how thankful they were. When they found out I had cigarettes, man, I was the local hero." He was behind bars for less than three hours before someone posted bail.*

George became quite sick and was running a temperature of about 104-degrees the day he was to fly home. "I drove back to Mexico City, about 100 miles or so, and I had to stop along the road five or six times to relieve myself on the side of road. The Mexicans would drive by and laugh. I got to the airport and I climbed on the plane. Fortunately, the American Airlines flight attendants were fantastic and they iced me down right away and got my fever way down and I had a fairly good flight back to Dallas, nonstop."

He returned home, went to bed and the next morning went to the doctor. It turned out that he had a serious bug. "I had picked up one of the two worst bugs you can in Mexico." The doctor gave medicine to George but warned him sternly that he would get even sicker if he drank any alcohol while taking the medicine.

### *Not a Drop Since*

"I went home and went to bed and took the medicine, no booze. I woke up feeling better than I had felt in the morning in 30 years. I had forgotten how good it was to wake up without a hangover. I said that's it and I haven't had anything to drink since."

After hearing so many drinking stories from the past, Gar, George's second oldest son, talked with his dad once about the amount of drinking that George did in his earlier days. "I asked him what he regretted most about his drinking years," said Gar. "I thought he would say hangovers or feeling bad. I was totally surprised by his answer. Here's a man who has done more than most mortals and he looks at me and tells me he could have done so much more if he hadn't drunk so much. If that's the case, I wonder what he really could have accomplished."

Quitting smoking was more difficult for George to do than quitting drinking. He didn't start smoking until he joined the Navy. Prior to that he played ball and didn't have enough money to buy cigarettes. He smoked through college and into his early SeaWorld days. "I quit a couple of years after SeaWorld opened, in the late 1960s, when I was 37. I stayed off them for about seven years, and then I stupidly started chewing and puffing on cigars. I went from one a day to 14 or 15 a day. I kept smoking until the first of three cancer bouts hit in the late 1970s."

### *No Moderation for George*

Whatever George Millay does, he has a tendency to overdo and there has been little, if any, moderation in his life. "I don't believe in moderation and I see that as a good thing. Anne is the epitome of moderation. She runs her whole life that way. I have never seen her smoke or take more than two or three drinks during an evening. I've become moderate in my older life, but in the early days I wasn't. If I ate a doughnut, I would eat a half dozen. If I wanted a martini, I'd have four."

- CHAPTER 26 -

# Wet and Wild Thoughts

It is now late spring 1974. George is out of SeaWorld and in a fresh creative state of mind. He's germinating ideas for what is to become the world's first waterpark.

It was a brand new concept, one never done before and there were many questions. What should a gated water recreation facility consist of? What would it entail? How much of a critical mass would need to be created to attract the hundreds of thousands of paying customers needed? Would people pay money to go swimming? Those were just a few of the questions that pioneering George had to tackle, and he loved every minute of it.

While creating the waterpark concept, George was also looking at several other opportunities in which to become involved. Those included Waweep Lodge in Page, Arizona on Lake Powell, Campland on Mission Bay in San Diego, and a new concept he was calling Gardens of the World that he would have built on 75 acres close to Disneyland.

If he could have secured the land, he says he probably would have gone forward on the gardens attraction. He was keen on the idea, but looks back now and doubts it would have been a success. The attraction would have consisted of several distinctly different botanical gardens. Guests would pay, board a boat and go from one garden to another, spending as much time as they wanted at each. It was a similar idea to one of the original concepts that he, Bob Nichol and Farris Wankier had toyed with during the planning of the original SeaWorld more than a decade earlier.

### *Looking for Ideas*

The idea of a gated water recreation facility kept coming back to George and soon consumed him. He had completed some preliminary sketches and had developed a few ideas, but he was still several attractions short of having a critical mass, one for which he could sell a one-price ticket. Orlando was his choice to build such a facility, the closer to Disney the better.

George hired architect George Walsh, the designer of two SeaWorld parks and who was now working for Ron Harper, and Bill Dunn, a mechanical engineer, both based in San Diego close to his home. Together, they created rough drawings of what George thought a waterpark should be.

Don Stewart was still working with Economics Research Associates at the time and was asked to conduct the feasibility study for the new park idea. He said it was a fun challenge. "Being a totally new concept we didn't have much to base the study on. We used our experience with evaluating theme parks and other attractions and applied this knowledge successfully to the waterpark concept," Stewart said, adding that the International Drive area in which George chose to build was nearly empty at the time. Wet'n Wild was the fifth development along the drive. "Even his early sense of selecting a site in a new untested market was uncanny," Stewart said.

### *Wet'n Wild's First Employee*

George was chatting one day with Dick Evans, a friend who had previously been with Disney, and told him that he was looking for a good administrator with park experience. Evans knew just the guy, a former Disney financial planner named John Shawen, who was looking for a job. He had left Disney to go with Irving Feld to build Circus World in Haines City, Florida where he was chief financial officer. When that park failed, Shawen was out of a job, with a family to support. George called up another one of his Disney buddies, Bob Allen, and he too confirmed that Shawen could be the man for whom he was looking.

After learning about Shawen's background, George called him in April 1974 and offered to fly him to San Diego. Shawen recalls that first meeting, held in George's office at the time, a boat. "It was a very interesting day. I had never had a meeting on a boat tied up to somebody's dock in the front yard before. George laid out his plans and wanted me to work up a feasibility study."

After George left SeaWorld, he set up office in the boat at the dock in front of his penthouse condo on Mission Bay. He said it relaxed him being on the water and there was plenty of room on it for everything he needed. His secretary reported to work on the boat every morning, and he would walk out to the dock and go to work, often in his pajamas.

When the government decided to do away with all the docks on the bay, George had to tear his down. By that time, he had created an office in the building in which he and Anne and their children lived. Anne jokes today, saying the time George was out in his boat office, was the happiest time in her married life.

George hired Shawen as the first full time employee of Wet'n Wild, paying him $1,500 a month and promising him that if the park was built, he would get at least 2% of the deal to start with. To put that in perspective, when Wet'n Wild sold to Universal in 1998, Shawen became a millionaire.

After being hired by George and discussing what needed to be done, Shawen asked if things could slow down until his wife gave birth to their child in June. George agreed, and within a couple weeks of that birth, Shawen left his newborn child and wife in Florida and moved to San Diego for six months during the summer of 1974. He lived in George's brother Bud's extra apartment.

During those initial planning months, Shawen crunched the numbers and went water skiing behind one of George's boats. "One day," George recalls, "John fell while water skiing, got into the boat, said he had enough for the day and when we got back to the dock, he quickly left. That night, he came to dinner and had a cast on his arm. He had broken his arm when he fell and didn't say anything. Instead he went to the hospital and had it set and put in a cast."

*The simple but effective, Wet'n Wild mascots, Splish and Splash.*

Shawen was an important asset to George, especially during those early formative years. "He was my right hand, keeping me orderly. He has a very disciplined mind, and he was good for me to talk with because he's the exact opposite of me. He was the right fit for Wet'n Wild." George recalls.

### *Cashing In*

Between 1974 and 1976, George sold about a third of his SeaWorld stock, which amounted to approximately 30,000 shares. He knew he was selling them at lousy prices, but knew he had to in order to finance the early stages of his waterpark dream.

He had learned a great deal from his experiences at SeaWorld and had pledged to protect himself right from the beginning on his next venture. Before he had taken in a penny from the other Wet'n Wild investors, George had already invested $400,000 of his own money into the project.

Even with his dreams of creating something new now dominating his time and energy, his departure from SeaWorld was still looming in his psyche. George said he was still "bitter, bitter, bitter, very, very bitter. I was disillusioned, disgusted, mad, and frustrated. I don't have the vocabulary to fully describe my feelings. I went through two years of mental hell."

He was embarrassed that he had let the situation at SeaWorld develop as it did and says he had a hard time handling it. "But you know, maybe I did handle it right. I've always believed in that old axiom, that when one door closes in life, another door usually opens, and that's exactly what happened, and I was far more happier creating the waterpark concept and building and controlling Wet'n Wild parks around the world than I would have ever been under the constraints I would have had if I had stayed at SeaWorld."

In a way, his later success at Wet'n Wild saved his life. "I didn't shed any tears but I lost many a good night's sleep for a couple years. Had I not been blessed with the ability to get Wet'n Wild going and have it be successful, I think I would have been a very sorry, bitter man for the rest of my life."

The success of Wet'n Wild was a salve. "All the SeaWorld guys know that George went out and did it again. Instead of fighting them, I decided to go out and show those bastards, so I built a successful park within a mile of them in Orlando."

- CHAPTER 27 -

# Sailing the Seven Seas

In 1975, George ended up having one more go-round with a marine park before he could move on to building the world's first waterpark. He was asked to take over the city-owned Seven Seas marine park in Arlington, Texas and it was an offer he couldn't refuse. The background to his taking on that park goes back to the early 1970s.

After the successful opening of SeaWorld Ohio in 1970, George received a phone call from Cleveland Smith, the executive VP of Six Flags in Arlington. He asked George to come out and meet with Angus Wynne, the president and founder of Six Flags Over Texas.

George had once met Smith at SeaWorld San Diego. "It wasn't easy finding a time when these two titans could get together," Smith recalled. He was able to get them together for one afternoon and the talk centered around the possibility of George bringing a SeaWorld to Dallas and building it near the Six Flags park in Arlington, about half way between Dallas and Fort Worth.

Wynne, Dave DeMotte and George went to the Great Southwest Club that afternoon for a drink. "In those days, Angus was the classic rich, free-spending Texan. He was big, he was good-looking, he was powerful, he was influential, and he was at the top of his game in life," recalls George.

The two spent a couple hours with Wynne, who told George that a marine park would work well in Arlington and then pointed out to where a SeaWorld could go on the adjacent land. He quizzed George on all facets of the business and they talked about how successful the park could be, tucked into Arlington next to Six Flags.

### *How about 40 Freebies?*

Two months went by and nothing else transpired, and George got busy doing other things. One day, George got a call from Luther Clark, Wynne's construction manager. "Hey George,

I'm out here at your front gate," the Six Flags' executive tells him and George replied, "That's great, you want a ticket to get in, how many you need?" Clark answers, "There are 40 of us out here. Angus has decided to build a SeaWorld-type park himself, and I brought all these engineers and architects out here to see your park." George was miffed, told Clark to "Go screw yourself," and hung up on him. But George did sell 40 extra tickets that day.

The group went in and photographed the park up one side and down the other. They stayed for two days, and George never spoke to them once. They went back to Arlington and Wynne started building the Seven Seas marine park for the city, next to Six Flags.

Tommy Vandergriff, who was Arlington's mayor from 1951 to 1977, said he liked the idea of a SeaWorld type park and thought it would work well in Arlington. Vandergriff had attended college in Southern California and had visited SeaWorld San Diego. "All you had to do was go to that park one time and you were completely convinced that you needed one just like it in your own backyard," Vandergriff said.

***Couldn't Get Mickey***

The mayor had tried to get Walt Disney to build a Disneyland in Arlington and when that attempt failed, he convinced Angus Wynne to build a Disneyland-type park in the industrial park that Wynne was building. That park, Six Flags opened in 1961 as the first major regional amusement park in the country.

Vandergriff was also the main force in getting the Texas Rangers Major League Baseball team moved to Arlington from Washington D.C. in the early 1970s. Part of the deal with the team was that the city would make an effort to build up the tourist attraction base in the area.

The mayor went to Wynne and said if he could come up with a workable idea, design, build and manage it, the city would put up all the money. One of Vandergriff's suggestions to Wynne was that of a SeaWorld-type park. That's what led to that first meeting between Wynne and George.

The original idea, Vandergriff said, was to get George to come in and build an "official" SeaWorld on his own, but when George didn't get back to Wynne immediately following their discussion, he went to Vandergriff and suggested they do it themselves. George doesn't think there was ever an intention of bringing SeaWorld to Arlington. "Wynne wanted the city's money to himself, he never seriously intended for us to be a part of the picture," George suggests. "But Tommy Vandergriff didn't know that at the time."

"Angus was always a man in a great hurry and he thought the way to get it done was to do it himself," Vandergriff recalls. "That's why he became so intent on it becoming a reality."

### *Doing it Themselves*

According to Stan Wilkes, who served Arlington as its city attorney from 1965 to late 1974, obtaining municipal funding for the project was no problem and construction began on the $15 million park in 1971, with Six Flags serving as the major contractor.

During that period, Wynne bought out the rest of his family from the Six Flags organization and had gone to Penn Central Railroad to help refinance that process. By the time construction on Seven Seas began, Penn Central started having financial problems of its own and went bankrupt.

"Construction had begun before all the financial problems of Six Flags and Penn Central surfaced and it was too far along to back out when it did surface," said Wilkes. "The city decided to take over and finish the construction ourselves and to either find someone to run it for us, or to do it ourselves."

*George Millay, right, with ABC's Elton Rule and John Campbell, at Seven Seas, 1975.*

Vandergriff, along with Wilkes, the city manager, and other city officials then paid a visit to George at SeaWorld San Diego in late 1972 to see if he would have any interest in running the still unfinished park for the city.

They sat down in the conference room, and Vandergriff says, frankly, "George, I don't know what I'm going to do with the thing." They started talking about the possibilities and George said he could see right away the talk from Vandergriff was all a show for his group and that he wanted to run the park himself. "He wanted to be able to say that we couldn't come to an arrangement, so he would have to do it himself. He always dreamed of being a showman," George adds. "This was his chance."

### *Seven Seas Opens in Arlington*

Seven Seas opened, and it operated for two years, 1973 and 1974, two seasons that George terms "disastrous." The people managing the park, a Six Flags splinter group, knew nothing about fish and mammals and the management was weak and inexperienced, according to George.

The marine park had a good design and it looked good, having copied much of its elements from SeaWorld. However, George feels it was too crowded with attractions. They had crammed what should have been a 20-acre park on to 10 acres.

During the fall 1974, several months after George left SeaWorld, Vandergriff called him at home and asked him to take over the park and run it for the city. George went to Texas, took a look, and decided to take on the challenge, and soon realized that he was going to need some additional financial help. In the meantime, his Wet'n Wild dreams would have to wait.

It was going to take approximately $750,000 to get the park in shape and to get it opened. He was to assume responsibility of the park in February 1975. "I think I tried to push them as far through the winter as I could so I wouldn't have to be the one to absorb those winter losses. Trainers were there all winter with the animals, and the grounds crews kept the park in immaculate shape all winter."

### *George Calls for Assistance*

Seeking a partner in the deal, George called John Campbell, the ex-SeaWorld marketing and productions VP who was now running the Weeki Wachee and Silver Springs parks in

Florida for their owner, the American Broadcasting Corporation. George asked Campbell if ABC would like to joint venture the park with him. "Let me talk to Elton Rule, (ABC President)," Campbell replied and a day later he called George and said, "Let's do it."

"We created a joint venture with ABC putting in more money than I did. I put up $150,000 and they put in $350,000. We did all the work however," George recalls. Campbell helped a great deal by sending support staff from Weeki Wachee and Silver Springs.

A one-year lease with an option for further leasing or purchase was worked out with the city and the partnership received a management contract to run the park. George and ABC had to supply the money to keep it afloat from February when they took it over, until May when it opened for the season.

John Shawen, who was still involved in the creation of Wet'n Wild, moved to Arlington to help George run the park and they had three and a half months to get ready for opening. Fred Brooks, another Circus World executive was invaluable in readying the park.

***Fortune Smiles***

The city didn't contribute a dime after February but "we performed a miracle. We went in there and had it opened by May 1975. I don't know how we did it. Thank God ABC was there, they had their Weeki Wachee girls and producers there for our underwater show. ABC brought their foods guys to the park to help out and that's where I found Gary Daning who later turned out to be one of our best Wet'n Wild managers. I brought John Seeker from SeaWorld, Bill Riley from SeaWorld, and two top SeaWorld trainers, Mike Verdeckberg and Gary Priest, to lead up our training program. Between SeaWorld personnel and ABC personnel we did it!"

Fred Brooks, a former Disney operations manager, joined the group as the Seven Seas operations director. "He was a godsend and brought law and order and hubris to all employees," George said. Brooks later helped open Wet'n Wild Orlando.

All that said and done, "We weren't able to make a go of it. They had let the park's reputation run down and we had trouble convincing the public that a new, more professional team was in there. We put on some damn good shows. Our diving show was the best I've ever seen in my career and Newtka, the little killer whale was fantastic, but we weren't quite making it."

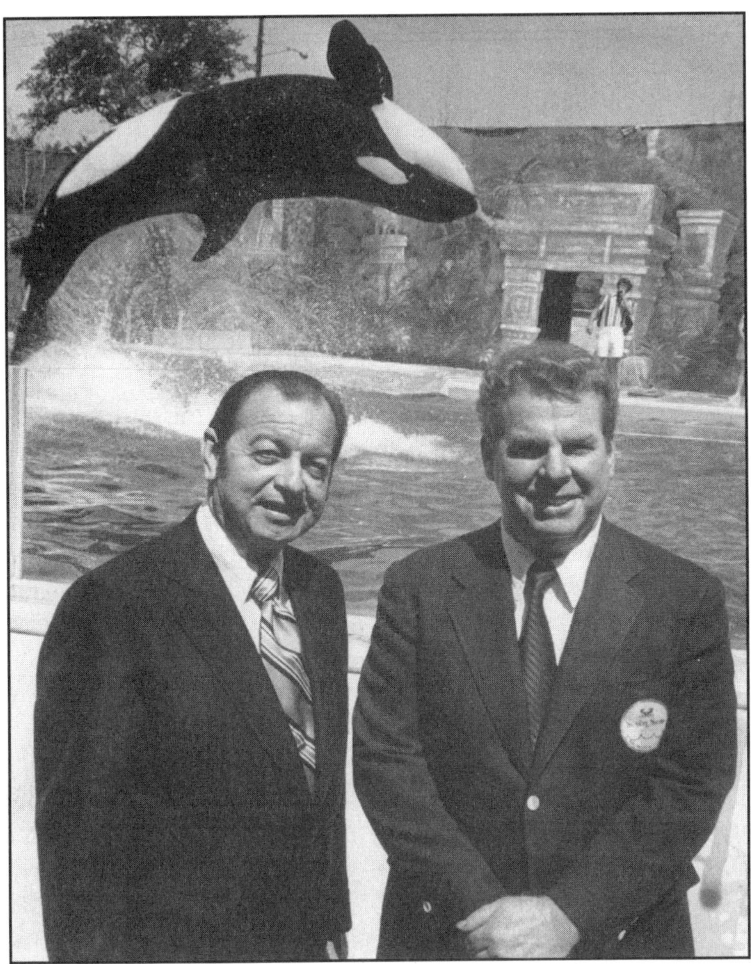

*George Millay ran Arlington's Seven Seas for Mayor Tom Vandergriff, left, 1975. That's Newtka showing off in the background.*

Leonard Goldenson, the chairman of ABC visited the park in late July with Elton Rule and John Campbell and wanted to know what the plan was. They were seriously concerned following two consecutive months of mediocre financial results. It didn't look promising; the attendance numbers had never been hit and the projection of a $300,000 first-season profit seemed like a pipe dream.

### *God Bless Hollywood*

In early August 1975, the movie "Jaws" was released and sharkmania swept the country. Local reporters visited the small shark tanks at Seven Seas and within days, the park became the most talked-about attraction in the market. "We had been sucking wind all summer and were ready to close the doors and all of a sudden, we're celebrities," said John Seeker, marketing manager for the park. The media descended upon us, asking for interviews and wanting to see the sharks. Numerous stories were published, with most urging the locals to go out to the park and take a look for themselves. It had already been common knowledge that the park was probably going to close in September, possibly for good. People decided to see the sharks and visit Newtka one last time.

During the last three weeks of August, the park was deluged, doing 9,000 or 10,000 people a day during the week and 12,000 on the weekends. The small park couldn't handle those kinds of numbers. They ran out of parking each day, the food stands had constant queues and kept running out of food. The walkways were crowded. "We made up our losses and made nearly a half a million dollar profit in that three-week period," said George.

By demand, Seeker became an "instant" shark expert. He spoke with Dave Powell, the former curator of SeaWorld and then curator of the Steinhart Aquarium in San Francisco and in four or five hours learned enough about sharks to talk with the media. The park didn't have anything compared to Jaws, just a couple of nurse sharks and a brown shark or two. However small in stature, those sharks were big money makers, being primarily responsible for turning a losing season into a winner in just three weeks. "However, we give ourselves full credit for the turn of events," adds George, with a smirk.

### *Selling the Seven Seas*

After the park was closed and all bills paid, both George and ABC each took home about $200,000. Part of the lease deal with the city was that George had the responsibility to find homes for all the animals if the park closed permanently. He sold Newtka to John Holder at Marineland in Niagara Falls, Ontario for $125,000 and the other animals to various zoos and wildlife parks. All proceeds from the animal sales went to the city.

Vandergriff and George became good friends during that summer. Vandergriff said there were few people he trusted as he did George. "I don't know of any man on earth other than George, who could have talked me into putting my head into a whale's mouth," laughed the ex-mayor. "I'm convinced he could talk anybody into doing anything." Several years later, George would call on that friendship to help find land to build a Texas Wet'n Wild and as could be expected, Vandergriff came through with a prime find.

The city turned around and leased Seven Seas out again the following year to Don Jacobs, a dolphin collector from Southern Mississippi. The park struggled one more season as Hawaii Kai, and was then closed for good in fall 1976.

Seven Seas was located in the area where the current Rangers baseball stadium is and adjacent to the Wyndham Hotel. "The park's Japanese Gardens and some other remnants can still be seen in back of the hotel," claims Cleveland Smith, the ex-Six Flag executive who helped create the park. The pumps now used for the pool at the hotel were once used at Seven Seas and many of the walkways and a few smaller buildings still remain.

### *Goodbye for Now, My Sweet Arlington*

George's wife Anne and their four children lived in Arlington during the Seven Seas season. As George and his crew were closing down the park after the season, Seeker got a call from the boss. "Hey Seeker, how would you like for me to pay your way back to San Diego for a visit," George asked. Seeker jumped at the chance and assured George that would be a great idea. George said, "Great, you can drive Anne and the kids back for me."

Seeker was in a jam. "What was I supposed to do at that point? Change my mind? I realized he had me." Seeker recalls the interesting journey.

"They had this 1975 Cadillac and we loaded up Anne and the four kids. Gavin was in diapers. First of all, George didn't check the tires and we're driving along and we hear this thumping and I have to pull over in the middle of some damn desert. He didn't have a spare so we had to find a tire that would fit this Cadillac. We did, and once we were on the road again, all I wanted was to get across to California as fast as I could. I was a single man and didn't want a wife at that time and I had no children, except on this trip.

"We're going along and all of a sudden they decide we've got to stop and spend the night. We've got like five more hours of daylight. Well, it turns out that was the night that Evil Knievel was jumping the Snake River Canyon and they all wanted to watch it on TV. I went out, brought dinner back to the hotel and we all watched it.

"I don't know what people thought. That woman has an awfully young husband because I would have been in my mid 20's and Anne had four children. They must have just thought I was a remarkable specimen or something. Looking back, I guess it was a compliment that he trusted me with his family. I didn't look at it that way at the time though."

One of the main reasons George was willing to take on the Seven Seas project was to get his foot into the Dallas market, thinking all the time that he might create his first Wet'n Wild there. "I wanted to convert Seven Seas into a Wet'n Wild. I thought it would be ideal. The big filter systems were already in, and several of the pools and most of the infrastructure could have been used for a waterpark," said George. "It was my plan, especially with ABC as a partner, to convert it."

However, Goldenson pulled the plug and said he wasn't interested in doing anymore outdoor recreation projects. "Smart man, that Goldenson," George now chides.

-CHAPTER 28 -

# Visualizing a Waterpark

Following ABC's decision not to partner with George to build the world's first waterpark in Arlington, George and John Shawen thought things over and decided to stay with their first choice, Orlando. The two went to Orlando and struck a land deal with a local developer, Major Realty. They were given an option on 17-acres of land on International Drive, which was just starting to be developed. They got a split piece of property, a parking lot on one side of what is now Universal Drive and the park was on the other side, next to the lake.

That was during the winter of 1975, a few months after they closed down Seven Seas. The tough economic times that began several years earlier, continued into late 1975 and it was hard to get financing for any major project. George and Shawen were losing confidence in their ability to raise money and investors were not as confident as they had been in the 1950s and 1960s.

The original Wet'n Wild was projected to cost approximately $3.5 million and by the time the first few investors bought in, George had nearly $500,000 of his own money into the project. He was getting concerned because it was taking him so long to reach the investment level he needed.

A number of his SeaWorld investors had said they would participate in Wet'n Wild if George could get the major piece of financing in place. Shawen claims that was not an easy task, even with George's vast array of connections. "We talked with Sun Bank and numerous other financial institutions, as well as a number of insurance companies, looking for long term financing. It was a hard sell for a new concept. We were in the middle of an energy crisis and we were going to charge money for people to go swimming. Investors just couldn't see the sense in that kind of thing and had their doubts we could do it successfully," Shawen said.

George had not lost contact with his cosmetics partner, Al Slavik, who had also been a small, but satisfied investor in

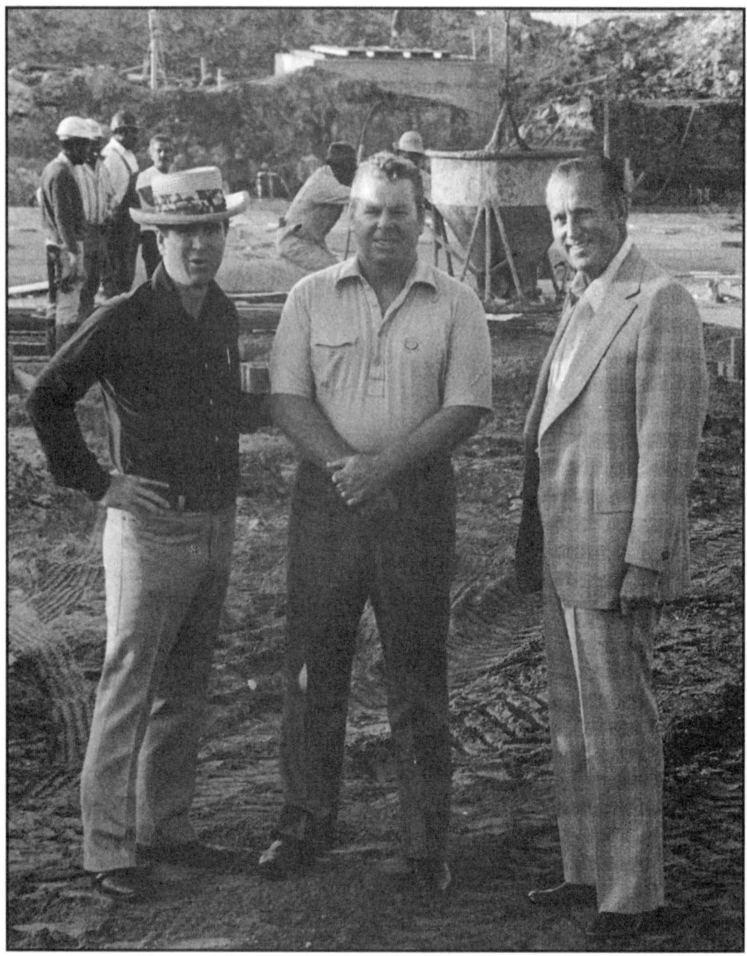

*George Millay, center, with Ron Harper, left, and Al Slavik at the Wet'n Wild Orlando construction site, 1976.*

Seven Seas. Slavik had great faith in George and at one time during their relationship, told George that he would gladly be a part of any of George's future projects.

### *Big Al to the Rescue*

Remembering Slavik's comment, George called and invited him and his wife Joy down to Orlando to see the property and the plans for the waterpark. Slavik saw that site on International Drive and was ready to invest. He says, "Okay, George, I'll buy the land and own it, and lease it back to you for 40 years, and I'll also build two or three of the rides. You select them and I'll build them. I'll own the rides and I'll lease them back to you over a seven-year period and after that you will own them."

Slavik's agreement to become a landlord instead of an equity investor finally solved the puzzle of "how in the world do we raise enough money for a prototype project that allowed George to maintain total control," Shawen noted. "Once Slavik came forward, most of the other potential investors, all of which George had dealings with in the past, came aboard."

SeaWorld contractor, Falck Neilsen and his wife Charlotte, became equity partners in the world's first waterpark. Builder John Buchanan and his wife Jeannie, became equity investors as did Paul Hughes, who had been an original investor in SeaWorld with his Hawaiian Punch company. Tom Curnin, the company's New York attorney came into the deal as did Kelly Smith, their Orlando attorney.

Slavik's total contribution amounted to nearly $1.5 million, and George and the other investors came up with the rest - about $2 million. With financing in place, the legal corporation for the Orlando facility was formed in March 1976.

### *Keeping the Faith*

Shawen said George never lost faith that he would get the required financing. "He never had a doubt that he was going to be successful, and when he did get everything in line, it was no big deal for him," Shawen said, noting that it was like George knew it was going to happen and his attitude was more like "would somebody hurry up and step up to the plate so we can get this damn thing going."

Two businessmen who passed on investing in Wet'n Wild in 1976, paid George the supreme compliment when visiting the Orlando Park a month or so after its opening. Burt Arnds, President of Sparklett's Water Company and Bob Jackson, a top producer for the old E. F. Hutton Company, had both spurned requests to invest in George's new venture. "They were both golfing and drinking buddies of mine and visited me shortly after the park opened. They had a ball, saw the happy crowds and loudly lamented that they had not taken me up on the offer. In 20 years they would have made 1,000% on their equity. Fortunately they didn't need it," George laughed.

**The Wet'n Wild Layout**

*The design of the original Wet'n Wild in Orlando was created to provide plenty of relaxing and comfortable areas for the guests. Amenities included a large AstroTurf deck around the wave pool, plenty of room for sunbathing and lounging and many shaded picnic areas. As the perspiring tourists walked into the park, they were greeted with the sound of crashing waves and the sight of a big green beach overflowing with comfortable beach chairs. These features helped attract a larger demographic than would normally be expected at a water facility and it proved that it could keep them here longer, allowing them to spend more money. As a result, when they left, they spread a positive message about the park because it had surpassed their initial expectations.*

*While the kids played in the water, mama could sunbathe and dad could relax with a beer in the shade or kick back and take an afternoon snooze. Even if mom and dad didn't go on a slide or take a swim, they still had a fun, relaxing time and they usually left the park happy and satisfied. The Orlando market had always been a rat race for parents and we gave them an opportunity to kick back and relax. This was a key factor in our success.*

*So many of the people who tried to copy the success of Wet'n Wild in the 80's and 90's neglected to provide the huge wave pool deck. Their close-minded architects couldn't spot its effectiveness on moms and dads; they missed the point in the design. And that's just one reason so many failed. Huge decks around large wave pools, all surrounded by Lazy Rivers, became the Wet'n Wild trademark. The design worked in Brazil and Mexico as well.*

*- George Millay*

***More Money Please***

During that first season the park lost money, and George had to go back to the stockholders for more cash. Shawen said that was one of the lowest points in which he ever saw George.

"We had to go back for more money and he didn't like doing that. He took it personally. He knew the thing would survive, that it would be okay, but he hated to have to go back to people and say that's it's just not working yet. It just needs more time and more money."

Slavik put in $200,000 more, George put in another $100,000 of his own money, and the other stockholders chipped in with another $100,000. That $400,000 was enough to keep the doors open, and from the second year on, the park was a profitable venture.

A Wet'n Wild board meeting was convened in Orlando a couple months after the end of the first season. The Buchanan's, the Nielsen's, and the Hughes' all flew into Orlando to listen to a barrage of bad news. George and Shawen did their best to smooth things over, stressing that "we'll be ready to give 'em hell next year."

As Charlotte and Falck Nielsen were leaving to return home, George walked out of the building with them, stressing to them that times would soon get better. Charlotte Nielsen smiled, kissed him on the check and without mincing words said to George. "Never mind the BS George, just get the place in the black!"

In essence, Slavik financed nearly 50% of Wet'n Wild on that first visit to Orlando. To this day, George doubts whether he would have been able to build the park if it had not been for Slavik. It was a good deal for George because he got to create his park and maintain control, and it was an extremely good deal for Slavik. The land that was purchased in 1976 for $600,000 is worth approximately $25 million today and during the 23 years that George owned the company, Wet'n Wild paid nearly $20 million to Slavik and his family in lease payments.

When Slavik died, his three sons took over ownership of the land on which the park sits today. "That's one of the reasons we sold to Universal in 1998. Our lease terms were extremely favorable for the first 20 years, but it had started to escalate a little each year and by 2007 it would have been overwhelming. Starting in 2012, it would have gone through the roof. We were looking to the future," George said.

Recognizing that the park had such a very favorable lease, Slavik's sons were after George for more money. "We were only paying $700,000 a year in rent, but since the land had escalated so much in value, the sons thought they should be getting more money. I wouldn't negotiate. We never went to court, but they were chaffing because we were so successful."

Universal Orlando, which now owns the park, will move Wet'n Wild from its current location to Universal property before the 2012 escalation in the lease, George predicts.

**Don't Touch Big Bertha!**

*Our first year at Wet'n Wild was devastating. It was a rough year for all of us, especially George. His wife Anne has an 18-carat diamond that George always referred to as 'Big Bertha' and times were so tough that first year that George was going to his pocket quite often to make payroll. He thought about selling Big Bertha until he realized that little Annie would beat the stuffing out of him if he touched Big Bertha.*

*- John Seeker, VP, MARC USA*

***Protecting George***

During the early stages of his search for investors for Wet'n Wild, George could have been funded several times, with him as a minority partner, but he kept turning down those deals. "It was tough because we were looking for companies that would joint venture this concept with us. George would provide the creative juices and the recreational experience, along with the team necessary to build the project. All we had to do was find a company that wanted to put in most of the required millions and be happy being a passive partner," Shawen said.

In creating the ownership structure of Wet'n Wild, George was careful to protect himself so the same thing that happened at SeaWorld couldn't happen again. He formed a company called Leisure Marine Corporation, of which he and Anne, his brother Bud, and Anne and George's four children, collectively owned 60%.

Leisure Marine, in turn, owned 55% of Wet'n Wild stock. George controlled Leisure Marine, and Leisure Marine controlled Wet'n Wild. With that structure, it was unlikely that he could ever get voted out.

"I made a commitment to George early in the summer of 1974, that I would never allow him to lose control of that company and that he would have 50% control forever unless he deliberately changed it," said Shawen, who ended up with 8% interest in Leisure Marine. George eventually gave a few shares to Fred Brooks, John Seeker and Gary Daning. Mike Hulme, a former SeaWorld compatriot, had a few shares and Ron Harper had purchased 2% equity in the company as well.

"Early on, we even gave some stock to Kelly Smith and Milt Beavis, our attorneys in Orlando, because we couldn't afford their retainers," Shawen said, adding that much of the early stock was given to people in lieu of compensation because George was funding this initial start up out of his pocket, "and after a period of time, that pocket started getting a little empty."

***Go Public? No Thanks!***

George never took Wet'n Wild public. "No, I'd gone public twice in my life, at Specialty Restaurants and at SeaWorld, and I didn't particularly like it. When you go public, the Wall Street analysts, the lawyers and the accountants own you. Don't get me wrong, I'd been very lucky with two public IPO's, and three secondary offerings, but this time around, I wanted to stay private, and never really entertained any thoughts otherwise."

Ironically, it was that strong urge on George's part to maintain control and never go public that dictated a great deal of how Wet'n Wild was developed.

"I can remember sitting in his office during our planning stages, and he had just sold a big chunk of his SeaWorld stock," Shawen said. "Here I am a little accountant sitting there going, good God, how does somebody get that much money? He sold it and took a tremendous loss because the stock had tanked in value. However, he needed the money to keep investing in the waterpark until he could get additional investors. He insisted on keeping control and that meant we needed to use his own money."

Shawen said George had a SeaWorld ego on a Wet'n Wild budget, and it was "my job to balance those elements and make things happen for the amount of funding we had, not make things happen as he saw they should be happening. From the get-go, he and I would debate about his plans. I'm trying to keep a lid on the thing, and he's trying to build this grandiose thing for which we had no money to build, and that kind of thing continued until the day we sold it in 1998."

- CHAPTER 29 -

# What's a Waterpark?

The concept of Wet'n Wild, the world's first waterpark, was one of innovation more than one of invention. George was the first person to bring various water-based elements together into one environment, put a fence around them and charge admission. George's vision was of a water playground and his biggest early challenge was finding enough viable activities to put into this playground to make it an attractive adventure for paying customers.

During his SeaWorld years, George discovered many of the elements that would later be a part of his waterpark concept. His first "discovery" was in 1970 on the grounds of the Canadian National Exposition in Toronto. He and George Becker, then GM of SeaWorld Ohio, went up to look at a water ski show. While there, George became totally impressed by the water playground creation of Eric MacMillan, a Canadian architect. MacMillan would later be inducted into the IAAPA Hall of Fame for the creation of the interactive wet and dry playground industry.

"I was really overwhelmed by it. Here are these Canadians playing in six inches of water on all sorts of interactive contraptions. Mothers would bring their kids dressed in a pair of shorts and they could play for a while and then go onto something else. It was a perfect attraction for the exposition. Guests had not come necessarily to play in the water, but during the hot afternoon, the play area gave people, who didn't need a bathing suit to enjoy it, an unexpected opportunity to cool off. I put it in the back of my mind that the play area could even fit inside SeaWorld," George recalls.

### *The Slide that Started it All*

The next big discovery took place during the summer of 1974, after George left SeaWorld. He, Anne and the kids were heading up to Lake Tahoe from San Diego to spend a week with Larry Sands, who had been one of the show producers at the original SeaWorld. They were driving through the little town of

Placerville when George's son Gar got excited about something he spotted in front of a trailer park they were passing. George saw what he was talking about, turned the car around and drove back to the RV park. There he saw something that impressed, as well as surprised him. A group of kids were sliding down a hill into a natural, dirty watering hole.

"Here is the dirtiest, crummiest little hill full of brown weeds with a pathway up to the top and here's this little gunite flume, crude and hard. The total drop was no more than 25 foot, so it was over before you knew it. It dumped riders into a water hole where the cows would come to drink. It was about three feet deep. I didn't go on the slide but Pat and Gar and Chrislyn all did

**Where has all the Creativity Gone?**

*The golden days of waterparks are over. Where are the parks going in the future? I really don't know. There are few positive and some alarming negatives going on right now.*

*The stand-alone waterpark is sadly disappearing and if a creative and entrepreneurial injection is not forthcoming, they will soon be reduced to an adjunctive role in outdoor recreation. That's sad because when that happens waterpark management will be entrusted to secondary operations managers and concept and direction will be in the hands of ride park operations. Not a pretty picture; an industry with so much more potential run by operational grunts.*

*I cannot say the indoor waterpark concept is a Messiah, just because it may work in the Wisconsin Dells doesn't qualify it as a winner everywhere.*

*Where waterparks go from here depends on creativity. If the entrepreneurial challenge is gone from the industry, it will disappear into the bowels of the ride parks. The concept of aquatic recreation is immense and challenging but the imagineers and risk-takers that are needed to make it grow are now few. Quien sabe?*

- George Millay

and they loved it. I did get into the pool surrounded by eight or 10 kids having an absolute ball. I thought to myself, my God, this is really something."

During the rest of the drive that afternoon, George thought back to when he was a kid and how much he enjoyed riding down slides into pools of water. He often went to a big indoor pool in San Jose called Allum Rock. There was a huge tile slide where he and his buddies would ride for hours. Another place San Franciscan kids enjoyed in those days was the Sutro Baths. It was out by the Cliff House on the coast in San Francisco and consisted of a series of pools at different levels, all with different activities.

As George looked back on that rustic slide in Placerville, he remembered those early experiences, all of which added up to great fun for a kid his age. The family went back to San Diego after their vacation and George knew he had at least two elements for the waterpark: slides and an interactive playground. He knew he had a good start, but realized he needed much more.

In August 1974, George told Dick Evans, his friend who had earlier recommended John Shawen, that he was progressing on the waterpark concept but was still in need of more suitable elements. Evans told George of an attraction that he had recently seen. "They just built something they are calling a wave pool down in Decatur, Alabama. Disney officials were down there looking at it," Evans said.

George was amused by the concept. "You mean it actually makes waves in a swimming pool, no kidding." Big Surf in Phoenix had been in existence for 10 years and it had a large tsunami wave pool that offered swimmers one big rolling wave. It was too big, didn't have enough capacity, and was too specialized (for surfing) for what George was looking for.

### *George Plays in a Wave Pool*

The next morning George was on a plane to Decatur. It was in the middle of August 1974 and he got there around 7 p.m. It was a hot night, the lights were on and the wave pool was packed. "I put on my bathing suit and got into the pool, and I had a ball." By the time George finished playing that night, he knew he had found that one large, missing element for his waterpark. He now had slides, a children's playground and a wave pool. That was the core of the first Wet'n Wild, along with all its auxiliary gift shops, restaurants, first aid, and maintenance. No one had ever combined those elements into one large offering.

Once he saw the wave pool, he liked it even more than he thought he would because of the capacity potential. "You can only put so many people down one slide an hour, but look at all the people who can get in and out of that pool in an hour," he said. As soon as George saw the pool, he knew it would be the focus, the central attraction in his park, one that all others would be built around.

Shortly after that trip to Decatur in August 1974 to see the wave pool, George met for the first time, a man who would become a longtime business associate, friend and traveling buddy, Gary Zuercher. George told Zuercher, who was selling the wave pools, he wanted one for a new type of park he was building in Orlando. "It sounded like an interesting idea and he got my attention," Zuercher recalled. "George's project was the first that incorporated all the features that are now common to waterparks."

Zuercher had brought that first wave pool to Decatur after discovering one operating in 1967 at the Central Baths in Dusseldorf, Germany. "It was installed by a German group and we got real excited about it because it was just a dynamic concept of putting waves in swimming pools," Zuercher said. "Waves in swimming pools go back hundreds of years when people used paddles and all kinds of things to try and create them. This concept used air with no machinery in contact with the water and it created a natural wave."

Zuercher and his partner George Raike started Wave Tech in 1972 solely to market and install wave pools in the United States. After Decatur, the next wave pool was at the Louisville Marriott in Kentucky and the next was installed in Pontiac, Michigan in a county park.

The fourth wave pool installation, and the first that was a part of a group of other attractions was at George's Wet'n Wild Orlando waterpark.

### *George Buys a Wave Pool*

George drove a hard bargain when he sat down with Zuercher to buy the wave pool. "George wanted an exclusive for the world. I said, George, that's really good for you but it isn't worth a damn for me and I'm not going to do it. After reconsidering, he asked for only a few exclusives: Orlando, Boston, Washington, D.C., Chicago, San Francisco, and Los Angeles."

Zuercher couldn't believe George's gall in asking for so many exclusives. "Are you out of your damn mind?" Zuercher proclaimed. "He ended up with an exclusive for Orange and Osceola Counties in Florida for two years." Nice try!

**Brutal, But Loyal**

*George was brutal in his management style but he was relentless and totally blind in his loyalty and his friendship.*

*- Gary Zuercher, ride manufacturer*

George is given the credit for creating the first waterpark and is fondly known as the "Father of the Waterpark Industry." He had the forethought to be the first. Zuercher notes that the products were all appearing, one at a time without George, but he was the one who had the vision to put them together to create the concept. George saw them and was smart enough to know they could all be combined together to form a unique complex with a unique experience, a waterpark.

"Would waterparks have happened without him? Yes, it was a natural evolution that would have occurred sooner or later, but by building the first, George served as a catalyst. Once someone does something it's damn easy to copy it if it's successful," Zuercher said. "And as we know, that's what happened, much to George's dismay." George takes credit "for making" Zuercher. "He didn't have two nickels to rub together in his pocket when I first met him."

Walt Disney World's River Country had been open a year when Wet'n Wild Orlando opened. Many today consider that park the first real waterpark, but John Seeker said that while Disney's park contained several water attractions, it didn't have a wave pool and had only one major slide. However, it was the closest thing to a "water park" that existed at that time.

During the construction of Wet'n Wild, George wanted to inspect River Country. Seeker, through his friend Bernie Bullard managed a tour. George wasn't impressed. It was well landscaped but he thought its two flumes were only ho-hum. The one ride that stood out, however, was what Wet'n Wild later called the "Raging Rapids." George had an architect and a designer with him and he instructed both to photograph and measure all elements of the ride. Dick Nunis, who was running Disney's theme parks at that time, would have had Bullard's scalp for letting a potential competitor into River Country to commit such piracy.

The ride was copied and rushed into the Wet'n Wild arsenal of rides. It became one of the park's star attractions during the second year of operation. Later, Nunis found out how Wet'n Wild was able to get a similar ride so quickly and harangued George for years.

That situation was reminiscent of the day when the shoe was on the other foot, the day a group from Six Flags arrived at SeaWorld San Diego and did exactly what George and his group did on this visit to River Country.

### *The World's First Opens - Ta Da!*

When Wet'n Wild Orlando opened, business was slow. The concept was new and fun, but George found that its scope wasn't large enough. "He realized very quickly that the number of elements and the entertainment value were not enough to give it the breadth and value to make it a standalone park. He immediately started looking for other attractions to build, how to expand the park, and how to broaden its appeal," Shawen said.

As per any new, successful concept, it wasn't long before copycat waterparks started showing up all over the country. George had been warned of that possibility by a venture capitalist years before. He spotted something before construction even started on the first park, when George was out trying to raise money. He said, "You know, George, you have a great idea here, and wouldn't it be great to build five of these at one time in strategic sunny locations across the country so nobody could compete with you?"

That's the first thing that came out of his mouth. Sage advice, but it all came down to money, and nobody was doing anything in venture capital in those days.

According to Shawen, that conversation with the venture capitalist stayed fresh in George's mind and during the feasibility phase of the Orlando park in late 1975, George started thinking again that he should develop multiple parks. He envisioned them in Atlanta, St. Louis, Orlando, Phoenix, Dallas, and a couple other markets.

George's original idea for a waterpark is not what ended

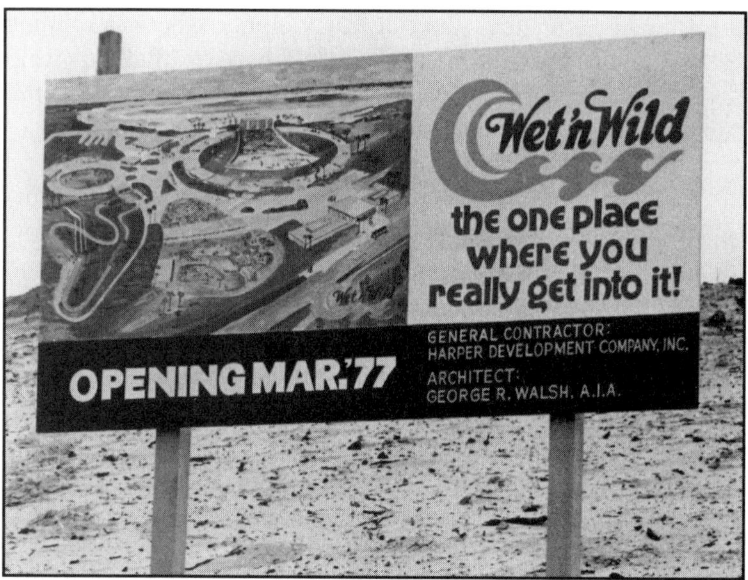


*The world's first waterpark is coming!*

up in Orlando. The initial concept, created by George and architect George Walsh, had many of the same elements, but also had an outdoor movie theater, tennis courts and an old Navy plane floating in the middle of the lake. "Yeah, we refined it quite a bit, didn't we," laughs George today when he looks over those original sketches.

George also had quite a bountiful idea at that time for the park's lake, later known as Lake Millay. The ship, The HMS Bounty, docked on St. Petersburg Beach had always intrigued George as an attraction. He felt it was not promoted well and was not visited as much as it should have been, mostly due to its location. If it were in Orlando, he thought, it would be a sure winner. He wanted to park the Bounty on the lake, adjacent to Wet'n Wild as a separate paid attraction and build a small "Bounty Village" on shore.

"I struck a deal with the MGM people and offered $3 million for it and we would move it," he said. "We were going to float the ship upriver and through some locks into Kissimmee Lake, cut her in three pieces and truck it to the Wet'n Wild site." After studying it further, George found the cost of the move was going to be too expensive.

Coupled with the fact that he was having problems securing adequate financing for the Wet'n Wild project itself,

George had to abandon the Bounty efforts.

***What's in a Name?***

When George first envisioned this water-based concept, he didn't call it a waterpark. He was calling it by several names, including a water playground and an outdoor water recreational playground. Nobody knows for sure who first called an attraction of this genre a waterpark. Gary Zuercher, who first brought the wave pool to the market in the U.S., thinks it was a natural progression and that no one can rightfully lay claim to the name.

"I agree," said George. "I know some of our original material called it a water park, but we didn't emphasize that as much as our Wet'n Wild name." John Seeker, who was director of marketing at that time, said they didn't officially start calling it a "waterpark" until the third season. "Right at the beginning, we used the tag line that Wet'n Wild was oceans of fun in Orlando, and we stuck with that until we started calling it a waterpark."

Shawen concurs that they started calling Wet'n Wild a waterpark during the third season, after it had expanded and had enough breadth and scope to be called a "park." He thinks the idea of calling it a waterpark may have come about as a result of smaller competition springing up in Orlando. "Three or four doctors built a half dozen concrete flumes down the road on I-4 and we initially thought that might be the death of us, that they could potentially take half our attendance," Shawen said.

"We started marketing our facility as a waterpark, calling attention to all the things we had to offer to differentiate between our large scope of activities compared to the individual attraction's limited scope."

Shawen said there was no doubt among any of the original Wet'n Wild team that George had the creative juices and the drive that would make all this possible. "It was his concept from the start and we all contributed a bit here and there. We helped him make it work. George had and still has the uncanny ability to look at something and not see what it is, but rather see what it can become. He sees in his mind's eye a finished product before it ever hits paper, and it takes a while to make that conversion for us mere mortals of what it's going to be."

- CHAPTER 30 -

# Wet and Wild Becomes Wet'n Wild

By early 1976, George had a concept, had proposals, pro-formas, and feasibility studies, but no name. Rollie Crump was in on those early design meetings, and Shawen calls Crump a "wild-card" type of guy. "He was a designer extraordinaire and a free spirit, and I can remember to this day Rollie lying on the floor in George's condo. We were all trying to figure out what to name this water-based concept," said Shawen.

Crump was lying there in his bib overalls, and he started talking. "Let's see. This thing is wet, yeah, and it's kind of wild." Everyone looked up. "It was Rollie who initially came up with those two words, but we didn't put them together to name the park at that time," Shawen noted.

Jan Schultz, who had joined George during the construction of Magic Mountain, and was at SeaWorld when George was building the first Wet'n Wild, suggested that George visit Chuck Pratt, a Hollywood producer and acquaintance of his. Schultz thought he might be interested in investing. George called him up and arranged a meeting at the Bel Air Club in West Los Angeles.

They sat down for lunch, and George went through his dog and pony show and during the conversation, George explained the concept, using Crump's words, "You know, it's very wet and wild."

Pratt stopped George, looked at him and said, "That's the name of the place right there, wet and wild!" George liked it and when he got back to San Diego, he sat down with a graphic designer who created the Wet'n Wild logo and the two mascot characters, Splish and Splash. The project finally had a name. Pratt did not become an investor, but perhaps he made the largest contribution of them all.

***The Pros Know***

When George and his team walked into Wet'n Wild, they were a bunch of seasoned professionals who had all proven their worth. Former Disney operations director Fred Brooks was on the opening team, as was financial planner John Shawen, marketing guru John Seeker, and ABC Park's veteran Gary Daning.

Ron Harper left SeaWorld shortly after George did in 1974 and went back to San Diego to start the Harper Construction Company. In late 1975, he got a call from his old friend George Millay, and in 1976, he led the original Wet'n Wild construction team. "We laughed about it because it seemed we were building something for George in the snow, like I did in Ohio. It actually snowed in Orlando that first winter we were down there. We were trying to build water slides in the snow. People were saying, you idiots, what are you doing?" Harper remembers.

Harper said he enjoyed the new challenge. During his years with SeaWorld, he built everything from sky towers to bathrooms to water ski stadiums. Now, he was constructing Wet'n Wild, the first waterpark ever built.

"It was fun building something that had never been done before," Harper said. George had an understanding of the development business but he pretty much let Harper do his own thing. "He required that everything I built was up to code and up to the highest safety standards. He would tell me to put everything in the ground that was required, but not to spend one dollar more underground than was necessary. He said he would rather use that money to put up flags and things in the park that people were going to see," Harper notes.

***No Stock Footage***

In creating the first television spots for Wet'n Wild, John Seeker realized more than ever, that he was dealing with an entirely new industry. "We had no stock film to use, as everyone does now," Seeker said. "We had to gather up film to promote a type of park that didn't exist a year earlier. We ended up working with photos and film that weren't of our park."

The first trip Seeker and his crew made was to Decatur, Alabama to shoot footage of the original wave pool. "We shot footage, but never did get any model releases from the people, but we used it anyway," he said. Next they needed water slide footage. George said there was one in a campground in California and that he would arrange for Seeker and a crew to film it. A couple weeks later Seeker shows up at George's door in San Diego only to find that George had not made any arrangements; he had forgotten.

He told Seeker to just show up at the slide and start shooting. He hired a local cameraman and they got enough footage before the owner came out. He was quite angry, even after Seeker explained what they were doing, and kicked them out of the park. Again, no model releases. "Thank God we had enough we could use for a TV spot. He had no idea we used the film in Florida," Seeker notes.

The shooting of MacMillan's kid's water playground went much better. "We had plenty of total footage and we spliced everything together to show what our park had to offer, with none of the material actually showing our park," Seeker said, noting that first TV spot "wasn't good enough to be bad."

***The First Led the Way***

George conceptualized and built the waterpark and he had the pride of authorship but he didn't have the benefit of ownership of the concept. "It was a concept that could easily be duplicated by others and he didn't like that, for which I don't blame him. I wouldn't have liked it either," Zuercher pointed out.

George, Zuercher and John Campbell were all friends, but shortly after Wet'n Wild opened in Orlando, the three got into a real tiff. Zuercher had sold George a wave pool and the two had traveled together. Campbell was a partner, through ABC, in the Seven Seas marine park in Texas and had worked with George at SeaWorld. The major bout came when Campbell and ABC decided to build a waterpark at Silver Springs, an attraction near Ocala, Florida. Zuercher recalls the day Campbell called him.

"He said he wanted to build a Wet'n Wild type of park and wanted me to come to New York City to ABC's offices to discuss it with him. Shortly after that meeting, he gave me a contract for the wave machine and we started to work together on that waterpark. I said something to George about it and he went absolutely through the roof because he thought John was stealing his idea. He raised hell with me and he raised hell with Campbell," Zuercher recalls. "He didn't like competition."

- CHAPTER 31 -

# George The Ride Builder

George and his team at Wet'n Wild Orlando created a new genre of park. They were pioneers who constantly defined and refined an entire industry within a three to five year period. They also created a new genre of rides and some of those rides created in the late 1970s were as relevant in 2004 as they were then. Many of the rides in waterparks throughout the world today can be traced back to George Millay's drawing board.

In 1974, shortly after George left SeaWorld, he needed some down time and decided to take his 75-year old mother on an extended trip through the Pacific Rim. As they were riding through an industrial area in South Tokyo on the way to the airport, George looked over and saw a large tower sticking out above the other buildings along an estuary. He could see slides coming off the top.

He asked the cab driver to stop, got out, and walked over to take a closer look. It was a big tower with two fiberglass slides coming straight down at a steep angle dropping riders into a shallow pool. "It was dirty and it was rusty. A nearby worker said the thing hadn't worked in a couple of years, but I was impressed with the concept."

### *No Fiberglass for George*

There were no fiberglass slides in the park when Wet'n Wild Orlando was built. The original two major flumes were made of gunite, because at the time, and his mind would change within a year, George felt fiberglass was too limiting. "When you use fiberglass, you're limited to the shape of the molds that the manufacturer already has, unless you go to the expense of having new molds built. With gunite you could create as you pleased and mold your own ride."

George sent his favorite contractor, Ron Harper to Japan to photograph and to measure the ride that he and his mother had seen. "I told him that when he came back, we were going to redesign and modernize it and build it for our park," George

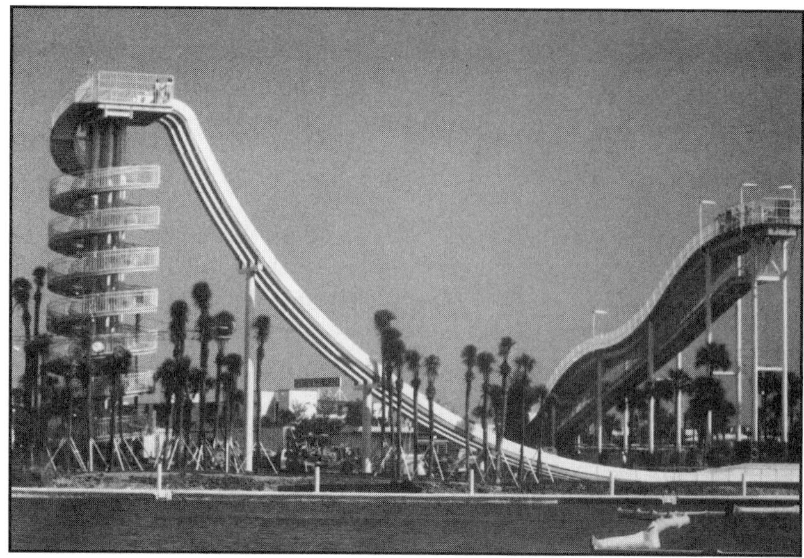

*The Kamikaze, 1979.*

recalls. Harper took his wife Kay with him to Japan to see the ride, which had reopened to the public. Harper wouldn't ride it, but Kay did, and in so doing, was the first American to ride the soon-to-be world famous Kamikaze.

It was built in the center of the park and debuted in 1979. George says the introduction of the Kamikaze is what started the Wet'n Wild explosion. It was a thrill ride; the first major water speed slide in the United States and it's what distanced Wet'n Wild from all the copycats. This was also the slide that convinced George that fiberglass was okay. Mac Clark, a talented jack-of-all-trades manufactured those early slides for the park.

### *Developing Additional Rides*

"Only about a third of the rides we developed came completely from my imagination," said George. "Most of the attractions we created were innovations where we would take something already out there, or an idea that already existed and modify it to our own needs. By doing that, we gave our audiences something new, special and unique." That kind of thinking is what kept Wet'n Wild at the top of the industry for many years.

George received a call one day in the late 1970s from a Canadian named Ken Bailey who exclaimed "I visited your park a couple of weeks ago and I've invented a little ride that I think you guys could use." He lived about 50 miles north of Toronto out on a little lake. His invention, the Boggan (as in toboggan), which Wet'n Wild eventually named the Bonzai Boggan, was a ride on which passengers went down a slide sitting on small sleds and at the bottom of the chute would go scooting across the water. On the lake in front of his house, Bailey had rigged up a tower and a chute and had manufactured a little fiberglass boggan.

George recalls that the water in the lake was freezing cold the day they visited. "I got on the damn thing and rode it. Rick Faber, our development director, went with me and he panicked about halfway down and jumped off into the water. He only fell about 10 or 15 feet and wasn't hurt," George said.

George rode it three or four times and thought it was "one hell of a ride." Gary Zuercher, who had sold George the wave pool, had gone with Faber and George that day to see this new ride.

Shortly after returning to Florida, George called Zuercher and suggested they go back and make a deal to buy the concept outright from Bailey and market it themselves. They started negotiating with the ride builder and got a contract where Bailey would get $50,000 upfront and 5% of all rides that were sold.

### *New Company Formed*

George and Zuercher teamed up to create a new company, Wave Tech International, to develop and market the ride. Zuercher would run the company, along with his own established company; Wave Tech. Wet'n Wild owned half of the new company as equal partners. Bailey told George and Zuercher he had a U.S. patent on the ride, which turned out not to be true. After the purchase agreement had been negotiated, George said Bailey got greedy and wanted more money.

By this time, they had found there was no patent and because Bailey was being difficult, George and Zuercher agreed they didn't need Bailey and decided to build a similar ride on their own.

Zuercher said they didn't go into the deal to create their own ride, but Bailey would not cooperate. "We wanted to be fair with him, so we sweetened the deal to give him what he wanted, and then he came back and moved the goal post a couple more times and we just said the hell with it and left," Zuercher said.

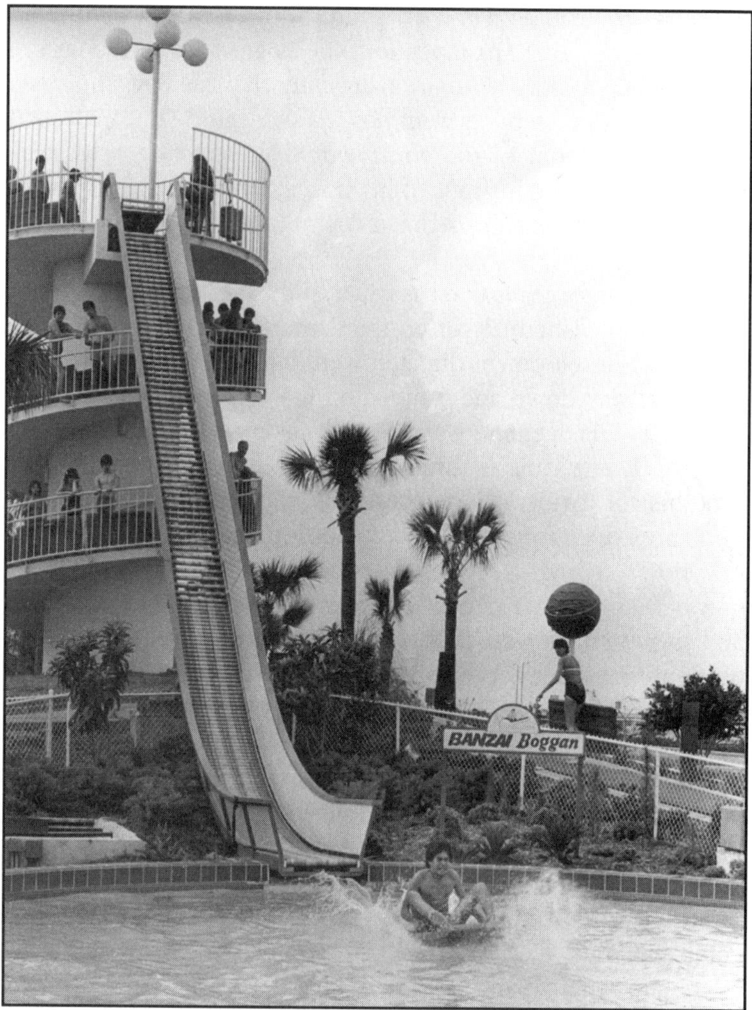


*The Bonzai Boggan, 1981.*

"We went back and started producing that ride and eventually Zuercher sold 70 or 80 of them over a five year period and we made a great deal of money," George recalls. "We had capitalized the joint venture for $50,000 each and at the end of the second year, we both took out a dividend of about $250,000."

The first Bonzai Boggan opened at Wet'n Wild Orlando in 1981 and had a distinctive tower with a spiral walkway up to the top and a 45-degree angled chute going down into a shallow pool. It had a contemporary and symmetrical architectural edifice and the first of many spiral stairways that Wet'n Wild would use on future attractions.

The first ride went into George's park because there was a certain cache about an attraction being in Wet'n Wild. Once a new product was in the park, everybody in the waterpark industry would visit and take a look at it and say, "Gosh, we've got to have one just like that." George realized that fact early on and thought as long as it was going to happen, he might as well capitalize on it. That was one of the motivating factors for his wanting the joint venture with Zuercher. "If I'm going to put it in and everybody wants to buy one, I might as well make some money from it," George notes.

Bailey's version of the boggan sled had rollers on the bottom. George's version had no rollers, using Teflon instead, which George said worked out better than the rollers. Even if Bailey had a patent, Wave Tech International would have not been infringing on his patent because of the major changes it made.

### *Showing off on the Tube*

John Seeker created the first TV commercial for the Bonzai Boggan and it's still one of George's favorite. Seeker hired a Japanese sumo wrestler and on film, he was in the park with a little boy who kept telling the big guy that they needed to ride the Bonzai Boggan. At the end, the wrestler was standing on the loading platform at the top of the ride in his sumo garb. He looked down and then backed away, screaming, "No, no, no, I give up." The little kid hops on and rides it with a big smile on his face. It positioned the ride well. The attraction didn't have great rider capacity but it had great TV exposure.

George's next innovation was the Corkscrew. By the early 1980s there were many waterparks in existence in all regions of the country, and George would visit as many as possible in hopes of picking up a new idea. "I wasn't impressed with most of the junk being built by dentists and real estate promoters and guys who thought they could run a water park," he said.

One waterpark he did like, however, was Water Country USA in Williamsburg, Virginia, owned and managed by Pat Cartwright. "I was very impressed with Cartwright's park. He didn't have much money to invest, but he had this one small slide that was a circular translucent fiberglass tube. It was the first enclosed slide I had ever seen," George recalls.

"After he walked through the park, he came to the office

and introduced himself to me," Cartwright recalls. "Of course, I knew who he was and was quite happy he liked my park. He said he had gotten a couple ideas and I was flattered. I laughed and told him to go ahead and use any ideas he picked up here because enough people had certainly stolen ideas from him!"

The innovator side of George's brilliance kicked in as he left Cartwright's park. He recalled seeing an open slide earlier that year in Tampa that had a small corkscrew shape to it. He and Rick Faber were quite impressed with that slide. Now, armed with two concepts they liked, they combined them and created an enclosed corkscrew attraction. It was the first totally enclosed major ride in the industry and it became very popular.

### *Innovating His Own Innovations*

As the years went by enclosed slides proliferated the industry, getting larger each time a new one was built. George kept innovating his own innovations and came up with the original Black Hole attraction. He not only made the Black Hole bigger than the rest, but he made the flumes black and opaque. To make room for the huge new ride, they tore down the original corkscrew. The flumes on the new ride were 84-inch diameter tubes in which riders would go down sitting in inflatable rafts in total darkness. Special effects lighting and sound were added to the black flumes.

The story line to the ride was that guests climbed the stairs into a waiting black spaceship. Once they got there, they were propelled off into the black hole. It worked and became the first major themed waterpark ride in the world. "I give a great amount of credit for that ride to Rick Faber," adds George.

They hired a lighting firm out of Los Angeles to do something that had never been done before, create lighting effects for a totally dark water chute. They came up with red strobes and neon but the strobes had to be taken out because park officials were told the lights might cause epileptic seizures. Toward the end of the ride, which is still a popular attraction, passengers speed through a dense fog before they shoot out the end of the tunnel into a splash pool.

### *Always on the Cutting Edge*

Through the years Wet'n Wild remained in the forefront of ride building and was one of the first to build large multi-passenger rides, which opened up water thrill rides to the entire family. "Many who wouldn't go on the rides by themselves were now able to ride with their family and at the same time, enjoy a thrill," George pointed out. "Multi-passenger rides really expanded the usage of rides by a new segment of the demographic."

The first time more than two people could ride together in the same raft on a water ride at Wet'n Wild was on the Bubba Tub. Again, George took an existing concept and expanded it. Jack Herschend had a smaller version in his White Water park in Oklahoma City and that's where Bob Gallagher, the Wet'n Wild operations manager spotted it. It was a three-person tube and an eight-foot wide chute. As soon as George saw it, he visualized all kinds of opportunities for it on a larger scale.

**Creative Guy!**
*George Millay will go down in history next to Walt Disney, as the most creative person ever in our industry.*
*- Larry Cochran, CEO, Palace Entertainment*

"You learned early on at Wet'n Wild that nobody but George picked the colors and the names for rides. That was his area totally, but I think I might be the only one who got away with it," said Cleveland Smith, who had joined Wet'n Wild from the Six Flags organization. He recalls that instance.

***The Bubbas Get a Ride***

"George was traveling and before he left, he said he couldn't come up with a name for the new five-passenger ride," Smith said. While he was gone, several managers spent some time putting different funny names and strange things on the blackboard in the conference room and Smith added Bubba Tub to the list of 15 other names. When George came back and walked into the conference room, he stopped, looked at the list and pointed to the Bubba Tub entry and notified the crowd "That's the name of our new ride!"

According to George, the ride "went like gangbusters" after it was first introduced at Wet'n Wild Arlington in the early 1990s. "Then in 1992, we took out two of the Kamikaze slides in Florida and put in a Bubba Tub," George recalls.

Seeker again was assigned the task of creating the TV commercial for the new ride. George would usually let his people do their own thing, but sometimes he had his own ideas and that was the way it was going to be done, no matter what, Seeker notes. The Bubba Tub commercial was one of those instances where George's vision was going to prevail.

The commercial featured what George called "a typical" Texas family - an overweight father and mother and three chubby little kids. The father looked at the camera and said, "I'm a Bubba." Then the wife said, "I'm a Bubba." Then the kids said, "We're all Bubba's and we've got a new ride named after us called the Bubba Tub." The spot ended with the father noting that this "ain't no sissy ride." The public reacted to the commercial and

**George Looks Down a Gun Barrel**

*The construction of Wet'n Wild Orlando was a non-union job and the local unions tried on several occasions to shut the project down. Ron Harper, the park's construction boss had several verbal confrontations with union stewards and some of those confrontations turned into shoving matches.*

*As a result, Harper advised the Orlando police department of the potential danger and on one morning, a dozen men in blue responded quickly to a call they received from the park.*

*George was set to go quail hunting in Southern Georgia with Butch Von Weller, one of the main sub-contractors on the job. To expedite things, Von Weller suggested George wait at the gate of the park and he would swing by and pick him up. That morning, dressed in his finest camouflage hunting jacket, a large bag and a shotgun over his shoulder, George was casually walking to the front gate when the superintendent for the framing contractor spotted him and called police. He didn't know George and thought he was an armed troublemaker.*

*Before he knew it, George was looking down the gun barrel of an Orlando policeman and was being told to drop his gun. He was shoved up against a wall, forced to his knees and hand cuffed. About that time, Harper arrived and saw what was going on. He went over and said, Wait a minute guys, this guy owns the place. George told his story, everyone laughed, the police left, and George went hunting.*

George said, "Once that spot started running, they knocked our doors down."

"Some of his ideas were kind of weird and bizarre and the rest of us would wonder where they came from, including the Bubba Tub commercial. We'd try to kill some of them if we really felt strongly but for the most part, George's instincts were right on," Seeker said.

When the ride was built in Orlando, the same commercial was used and again, it proved to be a winner.

### *Floating Down the River*

George was responsible for bringing to life another ride that revolutionized the waterpark industry, the Lazy River. In the early 1980s, George and Gary Zuercher were on a round-the-world trip and were in Jakarta visiting the large Jaya Ancol recreation park, which had a small waterpark.

He went into the waterpark and as he walked along, he crossed a bridge that spanned a deep circular moat, approximately 1,700 feet in circumference with shallow water in it. The only people in the moat were a few fully clothed Muslim women up to their waste in the muddy, filthy, un-circulated water. What he remembers most is the fun they were having, all laughing and having a wonderful time. They weren't swimming, but were just walking around.

"The circulation system had broken, which was understandable because when we started building the rivers, we had many a session trying to figure out how to get the thing to consistently work the way we needed it to," George recalls.

He liked the concept of a river that people could play in. When he got back to San Diego, he got together with Bill Dunn, Wet'n Wild's design engineer in San Diego, who had also been a SeaWorld engineer. He went to work on it immediately. The Texas park was being planned and George wanted the ride for that park.

During the planning meetings for the Lazy River, George and the designers created what would become the famous Wet'n Wild layout with the wave pool sitting on a little island with a great deal of room for pool decks, all inside the circumference of the meandering Lazy River. "We kept that element in practically every park we designed after that," George said.

The Lazy River was 12 to 15 feet wide and three to four

feet deep. It had jets of water spaced every 100 feet or so, that helped move the water along. There were multiple entry and exit locations. People could either float on a tube, or walk and float along. No swimming "per se" was allowed.

Once they decided to call it the Lazy River they immediately copyrighted the name so nobody else could legally use it. George made sure all his rides were patented and the names copyrighted, but he never had much luck in legally protecting either.

"No, we weren't too successful. First of all, the Europeans and Japanese were copying the rides. The Australians were the worst in the world at stealing names and concepts. They built a marine park and named it SeaWorld and then they built a waterpark and named it Wet'n Wild. Every park that built a Lazy River type ride, called it the Lazy River. Legally, we couldn't keep up with them all. It was a losing proposition," he admits.

### *More of George's Rides*

Two rides that are near and dear to George's heart are the Willy-Willy and the Bomb Bay, both of which were his ideas. The Willy is a tight 100-foot diameter circle with an island in the middle. A high-speed variable pump throws 50,000 gallons a minutes into the circular pool, catapulting rafters at 6 mph in a tight circle. Swimmers and non-swimmers alike love it because of its intense action. The ride proved to be as popular as the Lazy River at Wet'n Wild Las Vegas, the only place where a Willy was ever built. The Japanese liked the Willy-Willy best of all the Wet'n Wild rides.

The Bomb Bay was an off shoot of the famous "Der Stuka" where riders dropped 60-70 feet down a flume in a near vertical drop, relying on the gravity to hold the person in the channel. Only a small percentage of park guests, approximately 20%, were brave enough to ride the Der Stuka. Those who rode it loved it and those who didn't ride it would crowd around the bottom to enjoy watching those who did.

George began wondering what he could do to increase the thrill for the daredevils who rode the Der Stuka and came up with the idea of lifting them up to a parallel plane with the flume and then dropping them into the chute, thus giving them momentum even before they hit the slide. George was the first human to ride it.

Seeker and the park's agency came up with some drawings that made the apparatus look like a bomb. Riders would walk into the "bomb" and not be able to see around or down. Then the trap door at the bottom of the bomb would open, dropping the person straight down into the flume. The ride was introduced in Texas and was immediately rushed into Las Vegas and Florida to the same fanfare and success. It was the most talked about ride in the water-park industry for years.

*The Bomb Bay, 1993.*

Prototypes of the Willy and the Bomb Bay were fabricated at Scripps Institute of Oceanography in La Jolla, California, just north of San Diego, by "a genius named John Powell. He was a rare breed of scientist, engineer and backyard rigger and manufacturer. I think he had more fun building the prototypes than we had watching him. I don't think he even saw his work in its final form at the parks, but millions have enjoyed his efforts," George points out.

### *Lake Millay Needed Something*

Lake Millay at Wet'n Wild Orlando was the perfect place for more traditional water-based attractions. The park had rented paddleboats and little speedboats, but had stopped the latter because of safety issues and maintenance costs. "We had this huge lake and we weren't taking advantage of it and we didn't have much land to play with, so we needed to use the lake to provide more offerings."

In his endless search for unique attractions George got the word one day in the late 1970s of a water ski contraption in

Houston that he could potentially use on the lake. He headed to Houston, and near Galveston he saw what he had come for in a large runoff lake beside the highway. "I came upon the most dilapidated, rundown, bunch of tin shacks with this ski machine out on the lake. There were weeds growing all over the place and there was swamp grass growing in the water.

"A German doctor owned the place and he had hired a bunch of hippies to run it. There weren't many paying customers using it the day I was there, but the concept was unbelievable. A cable system, not a boat, towed the skiers." It was a Rixon ski machine, made in Germany by Bruno Rixon, and this one was the first in this country.

*The popular Willy-Willy, with the Blue Niagara in the background, at Wet'n Wild Las Vegas, 1990.*

### George Goes to Germany

George tracked down Rixon in Munich, Germany. He called Gary Zuercher because of his contacts in Germany and the two climbed aboard a plane to go and have a talk with Rixon. Ursula Rose, Zuercher's German representative, lined up the meeting and served as the interpreter. They negotiated a deal, and George bought Wet'n Wild a Rixon ski machine. He started redesigning it for his own use the moment the deal was sealed.

First, he turned the course into a hexagon from a square to cut back on the angle of the curves, thus making it less of a jerk as the skier went around the corner. In addition, George turned it into a knee-ski attraction. Instead of standing up, skiers would kneel on the skis as they were towed, by cable, around the course. The park did not charge extra for the attraction at the beginning, but did later on. Less than 25% of the park guests, however, would pay for it, so they turned it back into a free attraction.

The last ride produced at Wet'n Wild by George was an improved version of a ride he had seen at Jack Lazarus' park in Myrtle Beach. George called it the Hydra-fighter. People sat in swings and held onto a water cannon. The force of the water, as the passengers would swing around and shoot at each other, propelled the ride around in circles. "Unfortunately we complicated it too much, a weld failed and an accident occurred. No one was hurt but safety engineers were called in and shut it down and there went a great concept. It's still a real water ride sleeper for the industry," he notes.

George said a waterpark operator should never dismiss the importance of the kiddie play area. "We first introduced it to our Florida audience and then refined and expanded the concept at all our succeeding parks. Catering to the non-swimming demographic was the smartest move we ever made. The water got a little yellow in the kids pool but turnstiles clicked faster and faster."

### *The Urge to Thrill*

"In the beginning, I wanted as many thrill rides as I could get, but I began to realize early on that while thrill rides are fine and are a necessity, we also needed attractions that would entertain that 35-year-old woman who didn't want to be thrilled," said George. He notes that once he started thinking about it, he started paying closer attention and found that less than 40% of admissions to the park rode the big thrill rides.

Wet'n Wild never built a thrill ride with more than two chutes because George knew that most of the people weren't going to ride them. Why go to the expense to create an over abundance of rides that the majority of your gate doesn't want?

George said it took him four or five years to learn that

lesson. "It was an evolution of thinking and at the same time, it came as a result of paying attention to our paying customers," he said. "It was amazing how many people would pay $25 in those days and come into the park to just sit in the shallow part of the wave pool or sit in one of the activity pools. They would sit there, get wet, get up, get out, but never go on any rides. They got wet and they cooled down, and that's all they wanted.

They did the wet, not the wild.

- CHAPTER 32 -

# Surviving Cancer, Three Times

George has survived cancer three times. However, the operations that saved his life have left his face disfigured and have cost him his right ear, his right eye and the ability to smile. George has shown the world how tough he really is during his journey through cancer and today says the bouts have certainly mellowed him a bit.

He says he was always "too cavalier" about being out in the elements and knows that he's now paying the price for those long hours in the sunshine.

The first indication of problems came in late 1976, about a year after he and his two oldest boys, Gar and Pat, took a rafting trip on the Colorado River. George always tried to protect his skin and would use sunscreen, but he didn't use it on his ears during that trip and his right ear got badly sunburned. A couple months later, he noticed a white scab growing in the inner skin of his right ear. He didn't think much about it. "I'd just pick it and flick it for two or three months. Finally it got much bigger and started to hurt a little."

He went to a dermatologist in La Jolla and found that he had skin cancer, which the doctor cut out. Three months later, it had grown back and it was larger and it hurt more than it had earlier. "I went over to Scripps Hospital and they started me on radiation. I was traveling back and forth between Florida and San Diego and the doctors didn't require me to maintain the necessary schedule for the radiation to work. I would ask if I could skip a week to travel, and then come back and they always told me not to worry about it," George recalls. He now knows that he should have had that ear radiated for a solid month every day, but the way he had it done, the treatment was stretched out over four months.

### *The 1979 Surgery*

The following year, some growth had come back and he

went to a cosmetic surgeon in Florida. The doctor looked at him, shook his head and said, "George, I can't do anything for you. You've got a real problem there and I don't think there's a doctor or a hospital in Orlando that can help you." He told George that he had better get a "serious look at that thing by somebody who knows what they're doing."

That doctor's candid honesty "scared the hell out of me. I went roaring back to San Diego and visited a doctor who was supposedly the best eye, ear, nose and throat surgeon in town." The doctor examined George and told him, "If I were you, there's only two men in the world I'd let touch me at this point, and that's some doctor in St. Louis and Dr. John Connelly in New York."

He told George those were the two best head and neck surgeons in the world. George liked the sound of the Irish one and the doctor said he knew him. He called Dr. Connelly and arranged for George to meet with him in New York. "I was on a plane the next day, at Dr. Connelly's office the day after, and on the operating table at St. Vincent's Hospital three days later."

### *George Goes Under the Knife*

Surgery took off half his right ear and the doctors thought they had cut out all the cancer. It was during his recovery in the hospital when George decided to never smoke again. "I laid in a room with a guy dying of throat cancer and he was a real character. He would beg me for a cigarette. He had a big hole in his throat and the nurses would come in every hour and drain him out. He was going to be dead in two or three weeks.

"He'd say, 'Red, Red, give me a cigarette' and I'd say are you nuts? There are oxygen tanks all around here. You'll blow us to smithereens. He said, 'dammit, I'll be dead in two weeks; give me a cigarette.' So I'd give him a cigarette and I'd get him all set up and I would go outside while he smoked. I was all bandaged up but I could walk. Lying in that cancer ward in St. Vincent's Hospital I quit smoking. You want to quit smoking? Go to a cancer ward."

George's impending operation was not widely known within the company or among friends. "I didn't think it was going to be such a big deal," he says now.

"Don't come along, because it's nothing important," George told Anne as he prepared for that first surgery. Anne,

**Don't Sweat the Small Stuff**

*He didn't miss a beat after his cancer operations. He came home and I never heard him complain or feel sorry for himself. His relationship with us kids and his wife continued as if nothing happened. His attitude was that there is so much more out there in life, don't sweat the little things. That's a cliché, for sure, but this guy walks it and talks it.*

*- Pat Millay, son*

knowing it wouldn't do any good to argue, stayed home.

A week later, he checked out of the hospital and went home to San Diego. Anne greeted him at the curb at the airport as she always did. "I see him approaching the car. He's wearing his gorgeous three-quarter length blue-gray suede coat, which always made him look fabulous," Anne recalls. "But this time, there on top of his head was perched a woman's blue and pink flowered shower cap over one side of his head. I was speechless, popped the trunk for his luggage and fought back tears as I drove him home."

Jan Schultz remembers the first time the two met following George's 1979 surgery. They met for lunch at the La Jolla Country Club. "I get there first and sat down at the table to wait. He comes walking in wearing a blue and pink flowered plastic shower cap," said Schultz.

"We're sitting there and I try to ignore this cap as everyone else in the room is trying to do. I finally said, George, I know what you're trying to do here, until your hair grows out, but you know they make hats that can hide those things. I mean why the shower cap? He was almost offended, not because of my discussion of his deformity, but the fact that I didn't like the shower cap. I said, George, it serves its purpose but you know I think a hat would be more becoming."

***Back to Work***

He went back to work in Florida at Wet'n Wild after a short recuperation period in San Diego, but within a few months, "it started itching like hell. I'd lie on the floor at night screaming with the itch. Then it got to where if anyone touched me near there I'd scream in pain. I thought it must be the healing process because everyone itches after surgery. Well, the itch kept up and then the pain started. I couldn't even touch that side of my head."

George went back to see Dr. Connelly in New York and was told, "We've got a real problem here, George. I didn't get it all. I thought I over-cut enough, but we didn't get it. In order to get it all the next time, I'm going to have to really disfigure you, George. You're going to be disfigured the rest of your life. I want to tell you that right now and even then, I can't guarantee I'm going to get it all."

George had squamous cell carcinoma, the kind of cancer that grows out little tentacles but doesn't get into the blood stream. It had grown into the lymph node but it hadn't metastasized. George looked at Dr. Connelly and didn't hesitate, "OK, doc, let's go." It was just about a year after his first surgery. This time it was at Columbia Presbyterian Hospital in New York City.

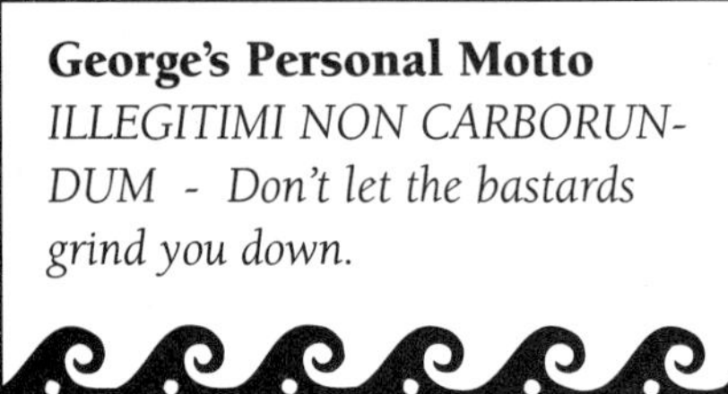

**George's Personal Motto**
*ILLEGITIMI NON CARBORUNDUM - Don't let the bastards grind you down.*


Planning had already started for Wet'n Wild Arlington at that time, but George knew, as he was heading off to the hospital that he was leaving the company in the good hands of John Shawen, John Seeker and Gary Daning.

Once again, Anne wanted to go, but George told her to stay home with the kids because this go-round was just going to be a "clean-up." His brother Bud went with him to represent the family and to keep in touch with Anne. After the 12-hour surgery, Bud called and said George was doing fine. "The Irish nurses are buzzing around and he loves every minute of it. He'll be home in a couple days." In actuality, it took him 10 days to get home.

### *George Scares a Pilot*

As he was boarding the American Airlines flight to go back to San Diego, the captain looked up and abruptly said to George, "What the hell happened to you?" He apologized, noting that George had scared him, all bandaged up the way he was.

In San Diego, George underwent intensive radiation with Dr. Chuck Roland, a well-known San Diego radiologist. "It knocked me on my ass for about six months. I spent most of the summer of 1979 in bed." George didn't make contact with anyone at work for some time, but then started briefly communicating with Shawen. "I wasn't capable of working. I was just so weak and devastated by the surgery. They went into my brain and they cut all the way down my neck. It was what they call a radical section. They took out a big chunk of my head and that's probably as much as they could do without killing me."

Shawen recalls that George "was almost totally out of it" for a couple of months, and then he stayed in San Diego for another six months. "We communicated on the phone, and he was running the show from back there, long distance." Even though George knew the company was in the hands of people he had the most faith in, Shawen said it was obvious that George was missing the front line action. "It was driving him nuts at the time, being back there, and the company was in its infancy, and we were struggling, and the last place he wanted to be was in San Diego, out of the fray."

Anne says she considers herself quite observant and never did see "a change in personality or attitude either publicly or privately" in George during the two major surgeries. She says she never saw a tear and never heard an "Oh, why me, God." His faith "became even stronger," she claims.

"Externally, of course he changed, but his whole life continued like maybe he'd just come home from an adventure vacation." Anne said that after his daily radiation, they would go out to lunch and the only repercussion from the radiation he showed was a weakness and a need to rest. "Of course, he was very anxious to get back to work," she recalls.

### *Not Again Lord, Not Again!*

Within a month of going back to work in early 1980, a lump appeared high on the right side of his forehead, and he recalls thinking, "Not again Lord, not again!" He went back and it turned out to be a little piece they had forgotten. They excised it and it was a minor surgery, but it put a little bigger dent in the side of his head. "They couldn't radiate because they had already radiated around the area. I was in the hospital a couple of days and then I flew back to Florida."

During the three-year bout, cancer had been discovered in his jaw and it had spread into much of his facial nerves on the right side. Part of the jaw and some of the nerves had to be removed. "The reason I can't smile today is that most of my facial nerves on the right side have been removed. These removals have resulted in the entire right side of my face being frozen," he explains.

### *The Cancer-Free Years*

George went from 1980 until 2003 relatively cancer free. The latest bout, which caused him to lose the entire right eye, was not related to his earlier ones. This time it was basal cell cancer, different than the squamous cell carcinoma that he conquered in the late 1970s.

The situation leading up to his 2003 surgery was quite similar to his earlier clues that something was awry. "I noticed a small growth starting to grow in the inner corner of my right eye and I kept flicking it away but it started growing back larger each time." He went to a local dermatologist who recommended that he get it cut out quickly.

In late spring 2003, he went to a dermatologist surgeon for a procedure called Mohs Surgery, where one layer of skin is taken off at a time and examined in an effort not to over cut. She cut it out and then he had a bit of reconstructive surgery done by Dr. Charles Stephenson and was quite happy with it. Everything was fine, or so he thought. There had been no pain following that minor surgery and his eye looked "better than it ever did. It used to be droopy and it now looked much better."

He became concerned again a few months later when the droop came back. He paid another visit to Dr. Stephenson who told him that he didn't like the looks of the eye and ordered a biopsy. He called three days later and asked George to come back in for a talk.

That was the day Anne and George had planned to go to San Francisco on vacation with their daughter and two of their granddaughters. George stopped at the doctor on their way out of town. "I went in there and my family was waiting for me in the car. I came back out and said the cancer is back, but the doctor said go ahead, go on vacation." He wanted to see George "as soon as possible" when he got back.

When he returned, George visited Dr. Alan Greenway, a prominent head surgeon in San Diego, who started to perform another surgical removal of the cancer, but stopped within 15 minutes. When George awoke, he was told that the only way for him to gain full access to the cancerous area would be to permanently remove the eye.

***Won an Award, Lost an Eye***

George was to be honored with the Lifetime Achievement Award from the Themed Entertainment Association (TEA) in a few weeks, so he set up surgery for two days after that award ceremony.

On October 6, Dr. Steven Pratt, the renowned San Diego eye surgeon, removed both the eye and the cancer.

All the tests came back negative after surgery, but doctors recommended radiation, something that George did not want, remembering how weak radiation had made him during his first major bout with cancer.

Prior to surgery, George and Schultz had a heart-to-heart talk. "He told me that he was prepared to lose his eye, but he was concerned how deep the cancer had grown into his face." He told Schultz that if it has gone deeper than the doctors think, "then I'm probably a dead man, and Jan, I don't want to go yet."

During his recovery, immediately after surgery, Schultz sat by George's bedside. At one point, George had to urinate and asked for a bedpan. He wasn't able to use it, so he tried to stand up and became quite wobbly. "Jan, would you hold me?" George innocently asked. Schultz stared at George and finally figured out that George just wanted him for balance. "George my old buddy," Schultz recalls saying. "I've known you for 34 years and I'll hold you up, but that's all I'm holding."

***The Guy is Tough!***

Schultz called him two or three days after the eye operation and if he hadn't brought it up, "I don't think he would have said anything about the operation. He said he was in a little pain, but nothing he couldn't handle. He's one tough guy, physically tough and mentally tough."

George postponed radiation until January 2004 for several reasons. First, less than a month after having his eye removed, he was to be on a panel at the convention of the International Assn. of Amusement Parks & Attractions (IAAPA) in Orlando. Following that, were the holidays, so he waited until January. "The radiation was a cakewalk this time around," George said. "It was brutal the first time around, but this time, I had no problem whatsoever. They have drastically improved the process."

Today, George wears a patch or dark goggles over the

cavity that was once his right eye. Surgery removed so much of the muscle and skeletal structure that a glass eye would not work. He jokes that he might get patches with classic paintings on them. Following his first operation, George had some vision in his right eye, but it was somewhat blurry. He thinks those 20-plus years of depending mostly on his left eye prepared him to have no vision at all on that side. Therefore, he says he has adjusted well.

The surgeries have left him quite disfigured on the right side, but George doesn't think it has changed his personality or his self-esteem. "I kind of get a kick out of little kids looking at me on the elevator. They yank their mother's arm and say something like, 'Look mom, a pirate.' No, it really doesn't bother me. I never made a living with my face anyway."

Ron Harper doesn't remember George ever feeling sorry for himself during any of the bouts with cancer. "He's not vain, that's for sure." When he had the radical surgery in 1979 that left him disfigured, his comment to Harper was, "Oh well, I didn't look like Tyrone Power to start with." After the surgery that took out his eye, his only comment was, "It does make it harder to drive." Harper is more impressed with George, the man, today than he has ever been. "What a healthy, great way to accept things you can't control. I'm very proud of him."

- CHAPTER 33 -

# Big Time Success in the Big Arena

After losing approximately $400,000 the first year, Wet'n Wild Orlando was off to the races. The tour operators, who sell packages a year in advance, began to catch up and brought a great deal of business to the park. Several new rides, including the unique Kamikaze, created quite a sensation and attracted a great deal of business during the third season. For the first four years, George kept building and building, just barely keeping capacity ahead of the crowds.

Attendance was creeping up by 100,000 to 150,000 a year and by the mid-1980s, it had topped the one million mark. Until Walt Disney World built its first major waterpark, Typhoon Lagoon in 1989, Wet'n Wild Orlando was the most visited water-park in the world. It remains the third most visited today, behind Typhoon Lagoon and Disney's other waterpark, Blizzard Beach, which opened in 1995.

### *Positioning against Competition*

The building of Universal Studios Florida across the I-4 interstate gave George some misgivings at first, but all Universal did was bring more tourists and hotels to the area and Wet'n Wild sailed along in their wake. Aggressive marketing, new and exciting rides, strong group sales, and strict safety codes were where management concentrated most of its efforts. Early on, marketing VP John Seeker, based on the in-depth analysis provided by then consultant Jan Schultz, was able to capitalize on the park's unique niche and build strong marketing programs to support it.

Rick Faber joined Wet'n Wild in the fourth year of operation as director of development. He had an extensive background in recreation before he ever heard of SeaWorld or Wet'n Wild. He had worked as a kid at Cedar Point and he had worked for Truman Woodward at Great America, Marriott's Santa Clara, California park.

"Academically, Rick's credentials are probably the best in the entire industry," George said. "I met him and immediately hired him. I needed someone more organized than I was. He came in as director of development and he served us very, very well. Rick brought a different background to the Wet'n Wild experience, giving us a little broader look at things, as well as an investigative type of approach to a job that wasn't present in our organization. He was one of the few people I'd actually listen to when it came to show and ride concepts," noted George.

Wet'n Wild
—ADULT—
Est. Price 3.60
State Tax .15
TOTAL $3.75
WET'n WILD SPECIAL TICKET
This Ticket Good For One Admission
NO REFUNDS — NO RAIN CHECKS
—ADULT—
Est. Price 3.60
State Tax .15
TOTAL $3.75
1977
Wet'n Wild
Nº 00527


Faber and George worked well together and Faber was a big help to him during the creation of several of the ride innovations, especially the Black Hole and the Corkscrew. Faber transferred to Texas and was responsible for what George calls "a fairly orderly construction" at Wet'n Wild Arlington. "I had a great deal of respect for Rick's abilities, and he rose pretty quickly, becoming general manager within three years. He was a major reason we were able to grow the Wet'n Wild brand as we did."

***Black's Magic***

In his first year out of college, Mike Black, an accountant, went to work for a CPA firm. His first assignment was to oversee one of their accounts, Wet'n Wild Orlando. He met George during his first week on the job.

"Before I'd even met the guy I was hearing all sorts of wild tales. I heard all the stories about him getting in fights when he was drunk, about haranguing everyone in the office, of him being a genius, all of them. I heard these stories from the vice presidents, the managers, the front-line employees out in the park, and the secretaries," says Black. "I've got to say I was a little bit nervous about meeting him because I pictured this guy as just a major Irish hard-tempered, hard-drinking sort of guy. The first time I met him; he was very polite, very gracious. He was a perfect gentleman."

Black stayed on the account, but didn't have too many face-to-face meetings with George for several years. Wet'n Wild brought Black in-house in 1984 and appointed him director of finance at the new Las Vegas waterpark. In 1988, he was sent back to Orlando as director of finance for that park and in 1993, he was named general manager.

He was offered the GM spot on a Saturday in September on his daughter's birthday. Fred Brooks was the general manager at the time. Unbeknownst to the staff, Brooks had resigned as general manager, wanting to return to his first love, design. George flew to Orlando without anyone knowing it in an attempt to talk Brooks out of his decision, which he wasn't able to do. He then called Black at home, something that he had never done before. "I was quite surprised and had no idea what it was about. He said I needed to come into the office right then, so I left my daughter's birthday party and drove in and when I got there, he was sitting in my office," Black recalls.

Knowing George's record of firing people, Black naturally

*Early Wet'n Wild management team, 1986. From left, are Rick Faber, John Seeker, in front, Dave Milhausen, Billy Getz, George Millay, John Shawen, Gary Daning, and Walt Hawrylak.*

thought he was a goner. "Our attendance was static and I had been on a couple conference calls where he was going through tirades with Fred (Brooks), Linda Orgara, the sales manager, and me telling us we had to restore growth to our attendance."

Black walked into his office, sat down, and George was sitting there staring out into space. "Well, son, you've got the job," says George and Black had no idea what he was talking about. "Although I had worked for him for nine years, this was really the beginning of when I got to really know him well. I talked to him darn near every day for those next five years until he sold the company in 1998."

He said George had made it clear to him that he was expected to be at work six days a week and he would often call on Saturdays to make sure he was there. "He would always say that a good general manager should be in the park until at least three on a Saturday afternoon, and I was accommodating."

***Getting to Know George***

One of the first things George did that impressed Black occurred about a month after he had taken the GM position. They were walking the park after closing one night and climbed one of the slide towers. A miniature golf course abuts the property and they were overlooking the course. George suddenly said, "I wonder what they would charge us to be able to provide Wet'n Wild guests access to the golf course."

**A Slight Increase!**

*It cost an adult $3.75 to spend the day at Wet'n Wild Orlando when it first opened its gates in 1977. Ten years later, in 1987, it cost an adult $13.50. Eleven years later when the park was sold to Universal, adult admission was $25.95. In 2004, an all-day adult admission was $32.95. Prices are all plus tax.*

Black asked why he wanted to provide guests access to the golf course when they could just walk next door and pay for their own game. "Because I want to provide it to the guests for free," he told Black.

A couple days later, Black went next door and negotiated a deal with the owner of the miniature golf course. For $75,000 a year, Wet'n Wild guests would have free access to play golf. It was like adding a new attraction to the park.

It was a great idea and worked too well, especially at first. The guest's perception that they were getting something of value was good, but the problem was the course couldn't handle the number of waterpark guests who wanted to play, resulting in huge lines. The course was so overrun with waterpark guests, that on most days, it was hard for the owner to sell to the general public. As a result, Black renegotiated the deal, allowing Wet'n Wild guests access to only nine holes, allowing the owner to sell the other nine. It worked out fine and everyone was happy, until George found out.

On one Sunday, Black's day off, George made a surprise visit to the park, walked over to the golf course, found that only nine holes were available and became quite irritated. "He flew out of town but called me the following day and chewed my ass out big time. He threatened to fire me if I didn't get the 18 holes back." Black got them back and kept his job.

***The Mouse Counter-Attacks!***

In late 1987, George had gotten word that Disney was about to begin construction on Typhoon Lagoon, a highly themed waterpark at Walt Disney World, just a few miles away. George once again hired his trusted marketing guru, Jan Schultz. This time as a consultant to come up with aggressive proactive measures against the new Disney park, 12 months before it was to open. Schultz presented his report and thus was born the popular Summer Nights promotion.

During Summer Nights, the park would stay open later and provide a live band in a party atmosphere. It proved to be a success in Orlando as well as the other Wet'n Wild parks.

After Typhoon Lagoon opened, Wet'n Wild attendance went from growing every year to one of stability, with an occasional downturn. Long gone were the days when people were wrapped around the corner waiting to get in. Attendance stabilized in the million, million-one range, where it still lingers today.

By the mid-1990s, George fully realized that Wet'n Wild Orlando was just one of the small fish in the big pond known as Orlando. It didn't take long for him to discover that those other fish were all big sharks.

MR. & MRS. GEORGE MILLAY,

THE BOARD OF WET 'N WILD, INC.,
MR. & MRS. JOHN BUCHANAN,
MR. & MRS. LARRY CASEY
MR. & MRS. S. FALCK NIELSEN,
MR. & MRS. JOHN E. SHAWEN,

THE SLAVIK FAMILY,
AND
MR. & MRS. ED HOGAN

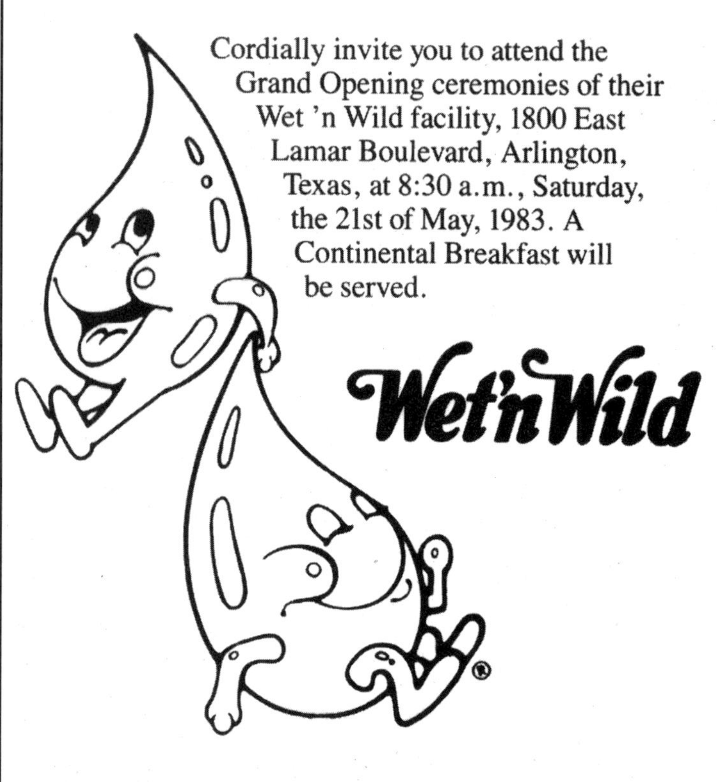

Cordially invite you to attend the Grand Opening ceremonies of their Wet 'n Wild facility, 1800 East Lamar Boulevard, Arlington, Texas, at 8:30 a.m., Saturday, the 21st of May, 1983. A Continental Breakfast will be served.
Wet'n Wild

- CHAPTER 34 -

# Building Wet'n Wild in Texas

Hot on the prospect of building the second Wet'n Wild in the Dallas-Fort Worth area, George called former Six Flags executive Cleveland Smith for help in finding a good location.

In 1981, Smith found a location that George liked very much. It was in Grapevine, Texas next to the dam on Lake Grapevine, on property owned by the US Army Corps of Engineers.

The Mayor of Grapevine, along with the city manager and the city council were solidly in George's corner and liked the idea of having a Wet'n Wild in their city. George worked for several months on the project with the city to prepare for a hearing with the Corps of Engineers. The land was located on a 100-year flood plane (The level flood water is expected to achieve nominally once every 100 years), but George specified he could work around any potential flooding by building the filtration units with special flood protection. He knew he was taking another risk, but was ready to gamble.

***Where's the Ark?***

Following a great deal of effort and cost, Wet'n Wild's plans were turned down, despite impassioned pleas from the mayor. Ironically, two out of the three following years, the area had 100-year floods and the park would have been underneath 20 feet of water both years resulting in countless dollars of damage. "Thank God we didn't get that location," George notes.

To cover his bases should that first site be turned down, George had already been in contact with his long-time friend, Tommy Vandergriff, the former mayor of Arlington, and for whom George ran the Seven Seas marine park.

George asked, "Tommy, we want to come to Dallas, can you find us some property?" Within a week of being turned down in Grapevine, Vandergriff introduced George to Bob Rogers, the chairman of the board of Texas Industries, a New York Stock Exchange member and the biggest cement maker in Texas.

The company owned all the land across I-30 from where the baseball stadium now stands and across from Seven Seas and Six Flags. Following their initial meeting, the chairman of Texas Industries flew down to see Wet'n Wild in Orlando. The next day, he called the head of his real estate division and told them to "sell these guys as much acreage as they want."

It was a tough negotiation process for George and John Shawen, but within five months, Wet'n Wild owned 47 acres on Lamar Boulevard. Part of the deal in acquiring the land was that George would buy all his cement from Texas Industries.

The $22 million waterpark, including the land, was three times larger than the Orlando park and opened with 13 major water attractions. The ownership structure in Arlington was different than that of the first Wet'n Wild. Al Slavik stepped in again, purchased the land, and put in $4 million cash, for which he received 40% of the stock. Wet'n Wild contributed $4 million and was also a 40% owner. West coast tour and travel operator Ed Hogan put in $3 million for a 20% share. In addition, Slavik guaranteed $5 million of debt from Union Bank. Wet'n Wild received a 5% management fee and had total operational control.

At Slavik's death in late 1989, Wet'n Wild Arlington went through a major reorganization with Hogan selling his interests and the land under the Arlington and the Garland parks were sold to Slavik interests.

### *Designing & Building*

Once again, George Walsh was called upon to head up the park's design. "By this time we really knew what we were doing. Rick Faber was with us and he and Gary Daning were very instrumental in coordinating the construction. This freed me up from the hour-to-hour, day-to-day duties I had performed on every project up to this point," said George.

Wet'n Wild brought Butch Von Weller, its contractor from Florida, to Texas to build the park. Von Weller was originally hired by Harper in Orlando as the swimming pool contractor, and in the ensuing years, had become a big-time contractor. Construction and the opening went well. "It was really an easy opening. We were all professionals at what we did best and it went very smoothly," noted George.

***Chamber Music, Please***

Despite the age of the people he saw in his park, George thought Beethoven and other classical music should be played over the park's speaker system. "He didn't like the cultural changes that were happening among the youth," said Marketing Director John Seeker. "However, when it comes to marketing your park to that youth and young adult segment, there were certain liberties, certain music, certain types of things that needed to be done."

Seeker noted that he was also required to advertise in Dallas on WRRR, the classical music station. "They played classical music and broadcast the city council meetings. That didn't matter to George, Wet'n Wild was buying commercial time with that station no matter what. I think the demographics were 70 and over."

Seeker admitted something for this book that he has never said to anyone else, ever. "Since he can't fire me now, I have to admit I bought advertising on several of the stations that he told me not to buy, including MTV, knowing that George probably wouldn't find out. I knew he wasn't going to watch MTV and unless someone ratted me out I wouldn't get caught. I did what was best for attendance."

***Unique Change of Pace***

Wet'n Wild Texas was the first waterpark to put bungee jump towers onto the main deck around the wave pool and used it not only as an additional revenue source, but for professional bungee jumping shows as well. The park would sell rides on the tower all day and evening, but at 2, 4, 6, 8 and 10 p.m., professional bungee jumping shows would be presented. It was successful for several years and when its popularity played out, the tower came down and a Skycoaster was put up in its place.

Another company had an exclusive on Skycoasters and on bungee towers in Orange County Florida, keeping Wet'n Wild from being able to acquire them for their Orlando park. The Skycoaster in Wet'n Wild Las Vegas did well.

Famed water-ski producer Dick Rowe created the first Jet Ski wave pool show and introduced them at all three Wet'n Wild locations. The parks also presented skateboard and roller blades shows, in 1993, long before TV picked up on the sport.

For many years, the evening festival known as Summer

*Dick Rowe produced the world's first waterpark Jet Ski show at Wet'n Wild Arlington, 1993.*

Nights would account for 20% to 25% of summer business, both in Texas and in Florida. It worked especially well in Texas because that park catered more to the local market than to tourists. Mom would come out with the kids in the afternoon, find good seats and play for a while until dad got off work and joined them. Special shows, bands, and other activities, as well as fireworks were featured during Summer Nights, in addition to the regular lineup of rides and slides.

### Meet the Competition

Jack Herschend whose family owns the Silver Dollar City theme park in Branson, Missouri, had contacted George in the late 1970s asking how to build a waterpark. He was interested in building one in Branson. Shawen remembers meeting with Herschend and recalls that both he and George were "quite open" with him.

Herschend had his eye on the Dallas Fort Worth area and in the early 1980s, got wind that George was looking at the market as well. So he moved quickly and began construction of a White Water waterpark in nearby Grand Prairie about a year before George broke ground in Arlington.

George confronted Herschend and told him that he would bury him. "I said dammit Jack, you knew we wanted that

Dallas area and you jumped in there, and you built this cheap-ass park in Grand Prairie just to be first in the market." Herschend replied, "Don't go in there, George, we'll kill each other off." George felt confident because he knew he had a better location than Herschend and he figured he could build a better park.

In 1982, Herschend offered George a deal if he would get out of the Metroplex and go home. He would pay off all the construction bills that had occurred up to that point and would give Wet'n Wild $500,000 in cash. George said no to that offer, and countered by telling Herschend that Wet'n Wild would stay out of the market for $5 million, an offer that Herschend didn't consider even for one second. White Water opened in 1982, a year before Wet'n Wild. Shawen recalls that he encouraged George "very strongly" to take the half a million and "run like a damn gazelle," but it was not to be.

Herschend wasn't finished. Once White Water in Grand Prairie opened and while Wet'n Wild was under construction, he quickly built and opened another White Water in Garland, located in North Dallas. The park was literally surrounded by its competition and had huge crowds right from the beginning "We just buried him, but he was still a thorn in our side," George claims.

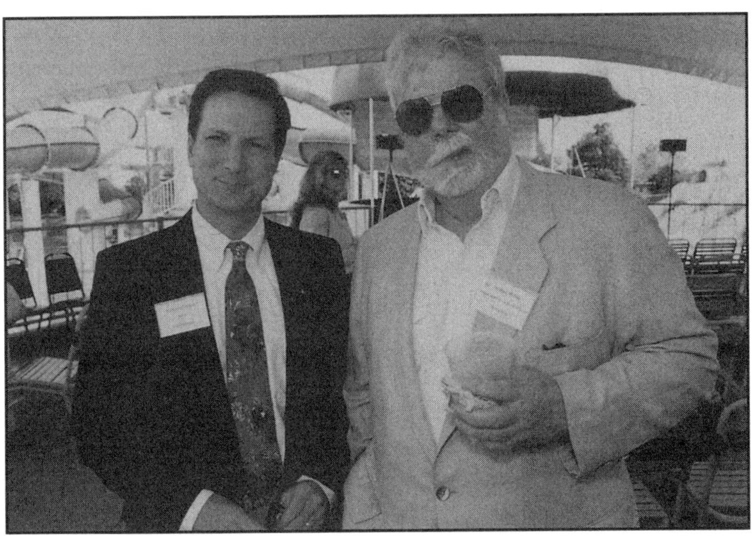

*George Millay shows Arlington, Texas, Mayor Richard Greene around the park, 1994.*

### *The Waterpark Wars*

Errol McKoy, now president of the State Fair of Texas, in Dallas, was the president of White Water waterparks for the Herschend family during what he calls the Waterpark Wars of the early 1980s. White Water was the largest waterpark operator in the country, with parks in Marietta, Ga., Oklahoma City, Branson, Mo., and the two in Dallas.

McKoy said it was inevitable that only one, either Wet'n Wild or White Water would be standing once the competition got underway. "It was a situation where you knew either they would buy us out or we had to take them out but something had to finally happen. Thankfully, we were able to work all that out amicably," McKoy said, adding that the competition never got down and dirty. "During that whole time, even though we were at each other's throat from a marketing standpoint, we always maintained a decent rapport and respect for each other.

Wet'n Wild was the dominant player in the market from the time its front gate opened in 1983. Herschend finally had enough and sold out to Bill Waugh, his partner in the White Water parks in that market.

"We were making money but we figured if that park closed in Grand Prairie, we could add 150,000 people a year to our Arlington attendance," said George. He went to Waugh, who was then the sole owner of the two Whie Water parks and told him he wanted to buy him out. Waugh wanted out, but said he would only sell both parks, not just one.

A deal was made and within two years of coming into the market, Wet'n Wild had bought out its competition for $10 million. The price included the equipment in both parks and the 22-acres of land in Garland. Waugh retained the land in Grand Prairie on which the park was located. George didn't care about the Garland park remaining in business, because it was out of the primary market of the Arlington waterpark.

However, the Grand Prairie location was closed immediately because of its closeness to Arlington. Wet'n Wild had purchased the assets, but not the land in Grand Prairie and had a limited time in which to remove those assets. Waugh could redevelop the acreage as he wanted after Wet'n Wild had taken what they wanted and vacated the land.

During January 1986, Wet'n Wild officials rendered the Grand Prairie waterpark unusable for another waterpark. They dismantled and sold the slides and concrete was dumped into all the pipes, pools, filters and water systems. "We wanted to make sure that after we took what we wanted, he couldn't turn around and lease it out to another waterpark operator who could come in and have the park already half built for him," George said of the bold move.

### *@#%! Hits the Fan*

The morning after the big concrete dump, "Shit hit the fan in Grand Prairie," laughs George. "There were lawsuits threatened and the *Dallas Morning News* jumped in on the city and the land owner's side. That paper's major competition, the *Fort Worth Star-Telegram* jumped in on Wet'n Wild's side. Tommy Vandergriff called up with encouraging words for George and urged him to continue to "give those bastards hell." It seems the two cities were also in competition.

McKoy said George was a serious foe during the waterpark war. "Just as he was a good operator, he was a fierce competitor. We operated there for two to three years just fighting it out for market share. George was constantly adding new, innovative things into his park and we knew from the start that would be his tactic," McKoy said. "It was always tough competing with an entrepreneur and with someone with as much creativity as George. You just never knew what was going to be coming on line in his parks. And by not knowing, we couldn't plan to offset it. He really kept us on our toes."

Who won the waterpark war? "I don't know that anybody won," McKoy thinks back. "Wet'n Wild bought out the White Water parks and I suspect we felt like we had won at the time, but I think George felt like he won because he was able to buy us out."

### *Alone in the Market*

Wet'n Wild decided to keep the 22-acre Garland waterpark open, and invested a great deal of money in that property and operated it until 1995. The park was far enough away that officials didn't think it would hurt attendance at the Arlington gate. However, in later research they found the Arlington park was probably losing 50,000 people a year by keeping the other park open. Garland never made much money but it never lost money, and corporate invested to make it a first class park, worthy of the Wet'n Wild moniker.

When George's oldest son, Pat Millay, decided to join the company after graduate school, George had him overseeing several construction projects in Garland, including a large children's playground that turned out to be quite popular. In 1995, Wet'n Wild Arlington was sold to Six Flags and the Garland park was closed, with all of its ride equipment being sold off. The Garland land was sold two years later for $6 million.

Wet'n Wild never made the money in Arlington that it made in Florida. George says the most Arlington ever made in any one year was a $1 million profit on a $15 million gross. The average profit ranged from $500,000 to $800,000 annually. Florida made four or five times more money and had a longer season.

"One of the reasons we sold Arlington was the short season we had to contend with and the school systems would not work with us or any other attraction on changing school start dates. When Wet'n Wild Arlington opened in 1983, Texas schools didn't go back into session until early September and within eight years they were going back by mid-August creating a very short summer season."

Wet'n Wild Texas was over-built initially, costing too much money for that marketplace. "That was done," Shawen said, "Because of the existing competition right down the road. The park was big and beautiful, but much larger than it should have been."

- Chapter 35 -

# George Builds a Family Entertainment Center

In the early 1990s, George built what he considers the "most fantastic, most expensive, fun-loving family entertainment center in the United States" next to Wet'n Wild Arlington and called it FunSphere.

Originally, George had planned to put a tsunami type wave pool on the land where FunSphere was built, but decided the attraction would not produce the attendance needed in order to dedicate that much space. About the same time he had decided against a tsunami, he got high on the concept of family entertainment centers and started looking at building a major facility on that land.

The $7 million park was beautiful and it was relatively successful, but did far less than what George had expected. On a good day, it's average gross was in the $40,000 to $50,000 range.

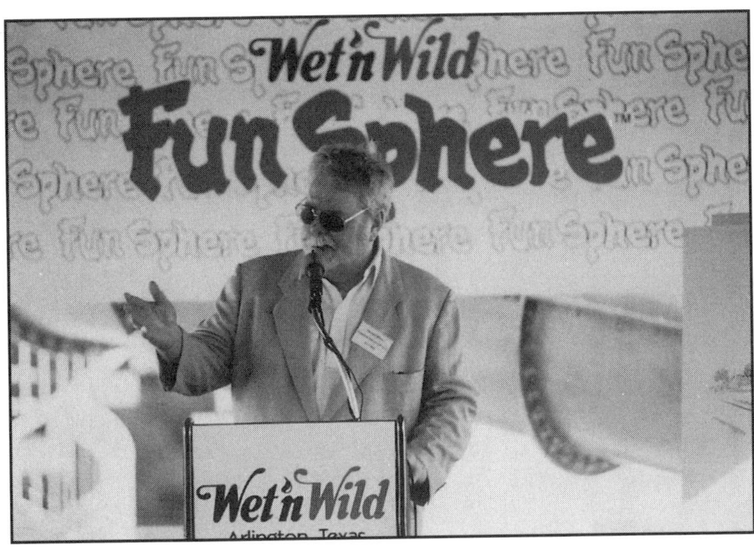


*George Millay at the groundbreaking of FunSphere, fall 1991.*

That's extremely good revenue for a family entertainment center, but not for one that cost $7 million to build.

"We know what we did wrong, and if we did it again we'd make changes and it would be very successful," George predicts. "First of all, we should have put either an ice rink or roller skating rink inside a large multi-purpose building. That would have been something that could have operated 365 days a year in all weather, and we could have used it for all sorts of other revenue-producing activities. That one big structure would have been the core."

Building the two miniature golf courses was the second major mistake, according to George. "Miniature golf only goes well where you have a huge amount of foot traffic, not in a location such as ours."

The maintenance and insurance costs were out of line as well. The park had a total of five go-kart tracks - three regular kart tracks, one of the first slick tracks in the country, and a track for smaller children. They bought the wrong cars, according to George, and it took them a year to learn which cars would work best for them. "We had a maintenance nightmare on our hands, and we had three or four guys at $20 an hour going 24 hours a day keeping those damn cars in running order."

Another mistake they made was going to a pay-one-price

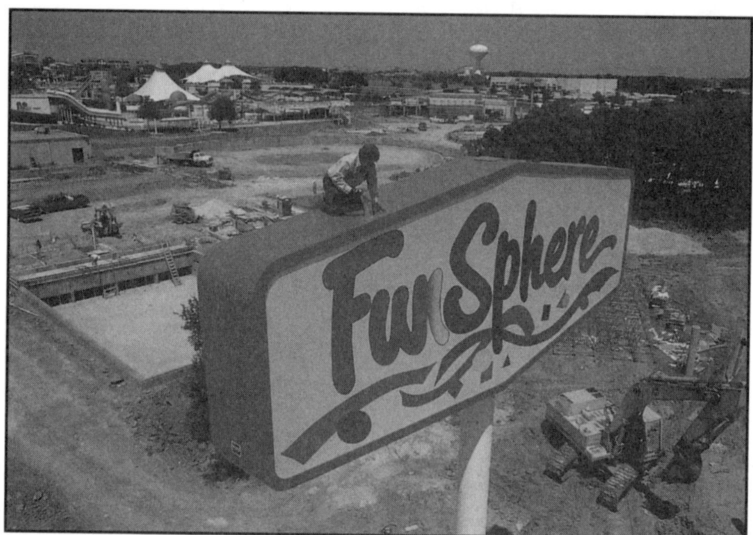


*Worker adding final touches to the FunSphere sign in 1993, with Wet'n Wild Arlington seen in the background.*

gate. It didn't start out that way, but after seeing an attendance slowdown after the initial surge of visitors, park officials started to panic and thought going to a one-price ticket would be the answer. What killed them on the pay-one-price policy was the local high school kids would hit the park after school in the afternoon and they'd drive the go-karts continually until closing time.

To this day, George says FunSphere was the most beautiful family fun center ever built, and admits that while it didn't work financially, it wasn't a disaster.

Shortly after they purchased Wet'n Wild and FunSphere in 1995, Six Flags shut down the family entertainment center, saying it hurt spring and fall business at Six Flags Over Texas, located across the expressway.

- CHAPTER 36 -

# Selling Texas For Big Bucks

John Shawen, from the very beginning, said he was not happy with the pre-tax profits of less than a million in Arlington. Each year he would go to George and say, "Why are we messing around here?" In early 1995, George listened seriously for the first time to Shawen when he expressed that feeling. "O.K., what do you want to do, sell the damn place?" George queried. "He got to me that time and he made it sound very convincing, and in a weak moment I said, all right, let's sell it."

George had always known, even before he built the waterpark, that Six Flags, located across the interstate, would buy if he were ever ready to sell. Once the decision was made, George called Bob Pittman, then president of the Six Flags chain of parks, and offered him first opportunity to buy the park before it was officially put on the market. Pittman said, "Yes, let's talk. I'll be there tomorrow at the Sheraton Hotel and I'll call you when I get in."

It was then that Pittman asked George the big question. "How much you want for the park?" George told him $40 million and Pittman said he would think it over and get back to him. Two weeks later Pittman had still not responded, so George called him again.

"Bob, aren't we going to talk? I thought you were interested." Pittman said the price was too high, George said the $40 million was just a starting point and that it was negotiable. Pittman asked how much George would really take. George said $30 million, but he would keep the six acres of land across from the Arlington park and all the land in Garland and would close down the Garland park.

Pittman offered $29 million and the deal was sealed. Including the $6 million received when they later sold the parcels of land, Wet'n Wild pocketed $35 million out of their Texas properties. "It was a real sweet deal," George now says. "We would have taken $22 million for everything."

After the Texas parks were sold, George decided to keep the Wet'n Wild main offices in Arlington. They were close to the airport and the company was getting deeply involved in international expansion in Brazil and Mexico. It made sense to be close to a large international airport that easily served South America.

- CHAPTER 37 -

# The Las Vegas Experience

Thanks to long-time friend, partner and traveling buddy, Gary Zuercher, George got an opportunity in Las Vegas to create what turned out to be his last domestic Wet'n Wild.

In mid-1983, Zuercher received a call from the Howard Hughes Development Corporation in Las Vegas. This was after Howard Hughes had passed away and John Goolsby was running the company. He told Zuercher he wanted to build a waterpark in Las Vegas and wanted to know with whom he should contract to build it. The Hughes Corporation owned land on the strip that was prime casino land, but Goolsby didn't think it was time to build another casino. He wanted something for the land to make it productive until the time was right to build another gambling palace.

"I told him he really had only one logical choice and that was to go with a company that was already doing what he wanted done, George Millay and his Wet'n Wild company," Zuercher notes. Goolsby's people contacted George and a deal was struck with George knowing all along that it was Zuercher to whom he owed the deal.

### *Thanks for Thinking of Me, George*

Zuercher was thanked personally by George, but was totally surprised a couple of months later when he received a check for $25,000 from George. It was a personal check to Zuercher for getting Wet'n Wild the deal. "I thought that was a pretty nice thing, and it was totally unexpected. I think that's a good example of how generous the man really is."

Wet'n Wild Arlington had been open for less than a year and George hadn't expected to build another park so quickly, but when the opportunity presented itself, he jumped right in. He recalls meeting Goolsby for the first time.

"I felt like I was meeting God. He was a big white-haired guy in a big office and he was smooth as silk. We started talking and it wasn't long before we had a deal," George said. The deal was that Wet'n Wild would own 20% of the company and operate the park for 4% of gross. Wet'n Wild was to design, build and market the park and the Howard Hughes Corporation would put up nearly all the money. Wet'n Wild put in $1 million, the Hughes group put in $15 million. If any additional capital were needed for expansion or new attractions, it would be available for the asking.

Goolsby wanted a first class park and George thinks he delivered "acre for acre" the most beautiful waterpark in the country. "Originally, we had a $900,000 landscaping budget for those 10 acres, which turns out to be nearly $100,000 an acre to landscape, and much of that is concrete and pools." Goolsby saw that budget, crossed it out, and added $600,000, making the total landscaping budget nearly $1.5 million.

### *Designing from San Diego*

Once again, George called in George Walsh to head up the design team. Walsh and John Deflumerie, the in-house architect for Wet'n Wild, set up an office with a local architectural firm in San Diego to crank out the designs from Southern California. One of the reasons George set it up this way was to accommodate Ron Harper, whom he wanted to build the park.

By then, Harper had a thriving construction business in San Diego and couldn't spend a great deal of time in Las Vegas. When the plans were shown to Goolsby, he said, "Who's this guy, Harper? I want a big-time contractor to build this park." Harper, who was sitting in that meeting queried, "If I brought in Morrison-Knudsen, would that satisfy you, Mr. Goolsby." He was assured it would.

Many years before, Harper had worked for Morrison-Knudsen in Boise, Idaho, and had no trouble lining them up for a joint venture in Las Vegas. Harper says he thinks George might have also been a bit concerned whether he could handle it. "I was a small contractor and the question really was could I build the Las Vegas park without committing 100% of my time to it," Harper points out. "By getting Morrison-Knudson in on the project, it made more sense to have me involved."

### *Oh, Say, is that Robert?*

Robert Goulet sang the "Star Spangled Banner" at the opening in spring, 1985, and in true Vegas fashion, there was an

*George Millay thanks Robert Goulet for singing the National Anthem at the opening of Wet'n Wild Las Vegas, 1985.*

Elvis impersonator present. With the Hughes organization as a partner, things were much easier in Las Vegas than they would have been if Wet'n Wild had tried to build the park on their own. "They just snapped their fingers and things got done. They were the big power," Harper noted.

George and Anne enjoyed their years in Las Vegas and George joined the Las Vegas Country Club as an out-of-state member. There were only three members in that category at the time: Bob Hope, Dean Martin, and George Millay. The three never played golf or drank together, reports a disappointed George.

The business at Wet'n Wild Las Vegas never reached projections. Even though it was a beautiful park with great rides, the market proved to be a tough one to crack. From the second year on, between 50% and 60% of the local market visited the park at least once a year, but officials found that tourists who came to the city were more interested in "gambling, shows, booze and sin" than they were in going to a waterpark.

"Most of the casinos never really cooperated with us, except of course for the Hughes Casinos and hotels - Desert Inn and Frontier. The Riviera and Hilton hotels were also good salesmen for us," George points out.

This was the first time George built an attraction where most of the other local businesses seemed disinterested. "Everybody wanted to help Wet'n Wild in Texas and Florida, and wherever we built SeaWorld parks, the local hotels and businesses wanted to jump aboard and be a part of the excitement we created. It wasn't like that in Las Vegas and that surprised us," George said.

***The Locals Loved Us!***

The locals knocked the doors down and the park had its share of tourists, but not in the quantity expected. George remembers pouring good money after bad into marketing. "We had billboards, the usual tourist-oriented rack cards, and we used radio all over the place but nothing brought in the tourists," George said.

While not hitting projections, the park still made good money, but a change of corporate plans within the Hughes Development Corporation soon made it harder for Wet'n Wild to show a profit. "They decided to liquidate everything and get out of business. They sold the hotels and they told us they wanted out of our deal. They still wanted us to run it and they wanted us to own it, but they wanted to be the landlord, not a stockholder in the park. We had to rearrange our deal."

**A Risk-Taker's Motto**

*George's favorite motto: "Our doubts are our traitors and make us lose the good we oft might win by fearing to attempt."*

*- Shakespeare*

When they sat down to renegotiate, George was a nice guy and wanted to be fair with them. The proposed deal by Hughes was that Wet'n Wild would pay 4.5% of the first $12 million in rent, then 8% of the gross over that amount. George, wanting to keep the landlord happy, went along with it. "We thought the $12 million figure was a good one, never expecting to go over it," said George. "We were not even at $9 million at the time, so wanting to be fair to everyone, I went with those figures. I thought it would be a safe bet."

***Don't Be a Nice Guy!***

George looks back now and says it's one of the most stupid things he ever did. "Business got better and we busted through $12 million dollars in no time and then climbed quickly to $18 million. "These guys ended up making three times more money than we were making, just sitting there, collecting the rent." George said it was a bad deal, but he lived up to it. "Of course Goolsby loved it. I made up my mind at that time that I would never again be soft on a deal or start negotiating a deal thinking I would be easy because these were nice guys."

He never forgot that lesson. Fifteen years later at the 2003 International Assn. of Amusement Parks & Attractions' convention in Orlando, George was on a panel. He told the group of budding parks and attractions entrepreneurs, "Never, never, never give the landlord a break or feel sorry for him, because you're going to be at odds with him sooner or later in life."

Wet'n Wild took over the park and continued to show a positive cash flow, netting a profit of $400,000 to $500,000 year, on a gross of $16 million to $18 million. Attendance stayed in the 550,000 to 600,000 range and George would okay a capital expenditure of $500,000 every two or three years.

- CHAPTER 38 -

# George Deals Happily With the Japanese

In the late 1980s, nearly 50 years after vowing he would never deal or befriend the Japanese because of what he had witnessed at Pearl Harbor, George entered into a business venture that changed his attitude.

It all started one day when he received a call from Dr. Choule Sonu, president of Tekmarine, a marine engineering firm in Pasadena, California. Sonu represented Nippon Tetrapod, a huge Japanese company owned by Nippon Steel. He told George the company was "very interested in getting into the waterpark business" in Japan, and "naturally, we want to work with the best." Following a few visits between the companies, Dr. Shirachi, the president of the company, was ready to sign a contract, a very favorable one at that, George relates.

Tetrapod was going to pay all the franchise rights, architecture, travel and all related expenses tied to creating a waterpark, plus $20,000 a month. Additional commissions and bonuses were built in if and when a park would be built. Wet'n Wild was not going to get a management contract, the Japanese wanted to run their parks.

George recalls an entourage from Japan coming to the states on several occasions, and they always wanted to meet in Las Vegas. "They loved Las Vegas and our Las Vegas park," he recalls.

### *Double Decker Waterparks*

Land in Tokyo is quite expensive and for that reason, George came up with the idea of a two-story park. He looked at building that two-story concept on top of office buildings and over parking structures. A considerable amount of time was spent on it, according to John Shawen, Wet'n Wild's top finance guy at the time.

When the Tokyo project proved not to be feasible from a

financial perspective, George and Tetrapod officials started looking elsewhere. "We looked at three or four other sites around Japan," George recalls. One of the most promising of the new sites was on Kobe Island, next to a proposed theme park.

*George Millay, second from left, goes swimming with the Nippon Tetrapod management team. They are seen in front of the Black Hole at Wet'n Wild Las Vegas, 1993.*

George and Eiichi Matsuura, who was his liaison with the Tetrapod company, attended a meeting in Kobe. As they walked in, Matsuura looked at George and told him "Watch, now I show you, George, how we make the deal in Japan."

George didn't learn much. "We went in and he put on the crappiest presentation you ever saw. Matsuura was leading it and it was obvious he was not a salesman. No one spoke English so I was just a showpiece, as it turned out, I guess not a very good one, since they basically threw us out because we didn't offer them enough rent for the expensive land," George said. "Our Japanese partners had spent nearly $50,000 on preliminary plans, concepts and studies for that land, and we didn't get far at all."

The next attempt was in Okinawa on land adjacent to a big hotel owned by Japan Airlines. Again, a great deal of time and money went into preliminary concepts, feasibility studies and design before the meeting with airline officials. "They weren't interested in us at all," George said.

By this time, Wet'n Wild and Nippon Tetrapod had been

planning and pitching waterpark projects for nearly three years and not getting anywhere. However, Matsuura and his team were learning the business and had realized the short waterpark season in Japan combined with the high cost of land, was not going to make for a profitable venture. Plus, the summers are hot and rainy, especially in July and August.

### *Doubling Dimensions*

The Japanese had fallen in love with the FunSphere family fun center at Wet'n Wild Arlington and they came up with the idea that they wanted a waterpark and a family entertainment combined into one park.

They also liked George's idea of a winter park that he had designed, but never incorporated into the plan while creating SeaWorld Ohio. In the winter park concept, the marine park or waterpark would be converted into a wintertime skating and sledding venue, utilizing many of the summer-time slides and pools in a snowy and cold environment. It would lengthen the season of any seasonal park. The Japanese loved the idea and decided to combine the waterpark, family entertainment park and the winter park all together into one year-round family mega-park.

With George's input, Pat Millay and Billy Getz, the VP of development for Wet'n Wild, started working on a design and came up with what George calls a "damn convoluted mess." The Japanese "absolutely loved it" and were ready to move on it when the country's real estate market collapsed and most leisure projects nationwide were put on hold. By this time, Nippon Tetrapod had paid Wet'n Wild $1 million or so in design work and more than $2 million in additional fees.

### *The Honorable Bow Out*

Matsuura called George to tell him the company was not going to renew its deal but would pay the fees for the remaining seven months on the contract. "I was amazed how honorable they were. They knew they weren't going to pursue a waterpark, but they had a signed deal with us and honored it right down to the end," said George. "Most other companies would have walked and ignored the contract."

George didn't get to build a park in Japan, but working as closely with them as he did for several years, he overcame his life-long prejudice toward the Japanese. "I saw first-hand what happened at Pearl Harbor and I carried quite a bit of resentment for the Japanese all my life. This experience really opened my eyes in many ways. They were great and honorable partners. I was always treated with the utmost respect and I was very much impressed with their business acumen."

- CHAPTER 39 -

# Expanding South of the Border

George's oldest son, Pat, graduated from UCLA and received an MBA from the University of Southern California. Following college, he took a job with Chadwick and Buchanan construction company for two years until his dad convinced him to ply his skills in the waterpark industry.

George went to Pat and said, "Hey, we're on this expansion plan domestically, and we're looking to hire a guy like you. Would you consider it?" Pat told him no for about a year but finally decided to join in the family business. "I was getting married at the time and decided to just do it. I told my wife-to-be, Maria, that we were going to move to Texas to start a new chapter in our young lives." They not only moved, but Pat jumped into the waterpark business with both feet.

Pat and Maria reached Texas in early 1991 and he went to work for Billy Getz on domestic capital expansion projects. Pat's beat was Texas and Florida, where he helped build several rides in the early 90's, including the Bubba Tubs and the Mammoth Rivers.

### *Politicking Conquistadors*

At that time, a good deal of attention was starting to be paid to international expansion, specifically into Brazil. Alain Baldacci, a Brazilian promoter with little knowledge of the waterpark industry, who later became South America's only chairman of the International Assn. of Amusement Parks & Attractions, first piqued Cleveland Smith's and Pat Millay's interest in expanding to South America. To help create that interest, Baldacci escorted several Brazilian businessmen to Florida to show off the Wet'n Wild park in Orlando. They were all intrigued and felt that similar parks in Brazil would work well.

"Baldacci's initial pursuit to get a Wet'n Wild in Brazil was the genesis of our expansion to South America," Pat Millay said.

**Annie Meets Arnie**

*Early one summer evening in the mid-80's, Anne and I went shopping at the Bay Hill Country Club Pro Shop, which is owned by Arnold Palmer. We went our separate ways as we entered. Arnie, always a man attracted to a trim ankle, spotted Anne. His hunting instincts told him to engage, and he went over. "Hello Mr. Palmer," Anne said in her phony shy manner. "Who are you?" Arnie asked. "I belong to him," Anne said and pointed to me across the room. "Oh George, I know George," Arnie said. (We had hired and fired his daughter at Wet'n Wild a month or so earlier.)*

*"Do you play golf?" Palmer asked. "No Mr. Palmer," Anne replied ever that timid little bird. "He won't let me," Anne said and pointed to me once again. "That's terrible, that's shocking," Arnie exclaimed. "Mrs. Millay, if you want to learn to play let me know, will you?" "Yes, Mr. Palmer," Anne meekly replied. Palmer turned and walked over to me with a huge grin on his face. Quietly and under his breath he mumbled, "George, I want to shake your hand. Golf needs more men like you." The fact that I never broke 100 in my life made no difference.*

*- George Millay*

Cleveland Smith was, at the time, spearheading the southerly expansion for Wet'n Wild.

Smith had worked closely with Angus Wynne, founder of Six Flags, for years, but when Wynne died, he made contact with George. "I was anxious to associate with George. I had known him for years, and knew he was a very complex and interesting individual. I had worked for Angus who was a visionary and I wanted the opportunity to work for another," said Smith. George hired him as the vice president of international operations in 1991.

"When the possibility of international operations arose we began looking around for a man to head it up," George said. "Cleveland, a Spanish speaking Texan was a natural. Cleveland went to work developing a franchise policy and screening potential partners. His charm, demeanor and appearance all contributed to the skills he possessed. His job was to interest, sell and maintain a confidence with potential and existing franchisees that was solid and genuine. Our Japanese, Brazilian, and Mexican investors had full trust and confidence in Cleveland which made for smooth sailing in the early stages of negotiations, development and construction."

***On to Rio***

With Baldacci's help and Smith's direction, Wet'n Wild went after Brazilian, and to a lesser degree, Mexican business. "We negotiated for five Wet 'n Wild water parks in Brazil, three of which were actually built, and we had two negotiated in Mexico, of which one was built," Smith said, adding there was no shortage of potential partners south of the border.

"There were many good potential partners, and others we ruled out as soon as we met them," Smith said. "After talking with several groups, we began thinking there really might be something down there for us."

George acquired his first taste of being courted by the international market in the early 1990s by the Japanese, but the overwhelming reaction he received from the Brazilians was a total ego-boost. It was also further validation that the Wet'n Wild park was a universal concept, not just American.

***An Exciting Challenge***

Taking the concept international and having the potential to build a park from the ground up with all the accumulated knowledge and experience of the staff, was an exciting challenge for the senior executives at the company.

"We couldn't afford to completely renovate one of our existing parks all at once in order to utilize our new ideas, so we had to be content to add one new ride or attraction at a time," Pat said. "That was frustrating to some degree, because we had all these new ride and entertainment concepts that were better than were being offered, even at our own parks."

The potential to create a new park from scratch, using other people's money was a good feeling, Pat recalls. "Working internationally, we got to use our knowledge to design and build modern, state-of-the-art waterparks with virtually no capital investment of our own."

***First Franchise is Sold***

As legitimate, potential investors were identified, the Wet'n Wild design crew went to their drawing boards, and following George's lead and vision, produced concept after concept. They then refined those concepts until George felt the package was the best he could offer. About that time, they got their first partner, the Cavalcanti family of Rio de Janeiro, Brazil.

"They were the first ones who stepped up with real money and wanted to do a deal, and that led to our first franchise agreement," Pat said. "We decided the best way to pursue international business was to sell our system, our way of doing things, along with our design concept and vision."

> **George the Teacher**
> *George taught me the fundamentals, the basics of the theme park business. His ethics are strong and he has a heart as big as Texas. He has always cared very much about people and he wants those around him to succeed. Under that rough exterior is a guy with a heart of gold.*
> *- Bob Gault, president, Universal Orlando*

Wet'n Wild would design and build the parks and then collect royalties for the use of the name and the system. The franchise holders would provide the financing and once the park was built, would operate it. Design went forward and 90% of the design work on the Rio park had been completed when the patriarch of the Cavalcanti family died in 1996. Following his death, financial problems within the family business surfaced. That first deal never progressed beyond the drawing boards.

***The Suarez Deal***

As the Cavalcanti deal was dying, the Suarez family deal gained momentum. Mario Suarez and his brother Manuel, of Salvador, Brazil were big developers. Among other major holdings, they owned the Pizza Hut franchise for the Brazilian state of Bahia. The brothers had a strong, growing enterprise and were hot to build a waterpark. Wet'n Wild Salvador opened in 1996.

Shortly after the Suarez family opened its Salvador park, Mario Suarez went to Pat Millay and offered to take over the franchise

*George Millay, center, and Mario Suarez, left, with Orlando Amari, at the Wet'n Wild construction site in Salvador, Bahia, Brazil, 1994.*

for Rio from the Cavalcanti family. Officials had no problem with that idea, and sold the franchise to Suarez for $750,000 cash, plus 4% of the gross and a substantial fee for the architectural drawings. The Rio de Janeiro Wet'n Wild finally opened in 1999 after George had sold the business.

As the potential of the Brazil market unfolded, Pat and Billy Getz were relieved of most of their domestic duties to concentrate on South America. "We told George that if he wanted this to happen, we needed to spend more time there. We needed to hire some good people so we could really watch the store," Pat noted.

### *Creating the System*

After tangible investors started putting cash on the table for the Wet'n Wild "system," it became apparent to Pat that a "system" should be created. "We were selling it, but there really was no system. The system was in our heads, it wasn't quantified, it wasn't tangible, and yet we'd sold one to the Japanese, one to the

Cavalcanti group, and now, one to the Suarez group."

Pat thought this would be a good time to put his high priced education to work. "Being the good MBA that I was, I saw things that needed to be done. I wrote a detailed business plan for my dad, and I marked it, 'Confidential, I don't think anybody else needs to see this.' It was quite critical of our operation and frankly, critical of the directions that a couple senior executives were taking us." Pat used his position as son as well a senior executive to call attention to several things that he thought could be done better.

"I found that within three days, dad had made 10 copies of it and called an all hands meeting. I figured at that point, I was dead. We all attended the meeting and to my surprise; everybody had their eyes wide open." At the end of the meeting, George turned to Pat and said, "OK, dummy, make it happen."

With that response from his strong-willed father, Pat was taken aback. "When I created the business system and designed the organizational plan, I had not even thought about me being in a position to take the thing on," Pat confessed. "I agreed to give it a shot. I told him I needed to have the ability to be a decision-maker. If I went down to Brazil and they sensed that I would need to run home to dad to get approval on things, it wasn't going to work, they would eat me alive."

While not giving Pat total carte blanche for Brazil, George had enough confidence in his son to allow him to make many of the major decisions.

Pat knew the company "could go hog wild" on the international scene if they wanted, but the big question was, "How do we do it?" Many decisions had been made before this juncture, some of them good, some of them not so good, but Pat and his team went headfirst into the Brazilian market.

### *Work at Home, Build in Brazil*

One of Pat's first major decisions was that the design work should be done at company headquarters in Arlington, Texas, not in Brazil. During their early work in that country, the company's architect, Mark Hatchell was sent to Rio where he had worked in the Brazilian architect's office. It soon became clear that idea wouldn't work on a permanent basis.

It was tough on Hatchell being away from home for that length of a time, it made communications and planning cumbersome, and it was quite expensive flying Hatchell, or whoever, back and forth to Texas.

So, instead of sending theirs to Brazil, they decided to bring Brazil's to them. "We decided to bring Brazilian intern architects up to our Texas office," Pat said. By 1995, the international team was in place. It consisted of Hatchell as senior architect, head designer Billy Getz, and four intern architects from Brazil. Pat headed up the team and was the dealmaker.

Cleveland Smith, with other interests growing in priority, had left the company in 1994 and Pat had taken over as head of the international division.

As work progressed on the completed deals, Pat continued looking for more partners and was busy sending packages to pension funds and big banks. At one time they were producing plans in three languages and the company was making a great deal of money on design.

***Must be in Sao Paulo***

If you're a company doing business in Brazil, you've got to be in Sao Paulo. Knowing that, Pat worked hard getting a deal for that city, the world's second largest metropolitan area with more than 22 million people. He succeeded, and the company's third Brazilian partner was Metado, a large construction and development company based in Sao Paulo.

"We found that in Brazil, to make money, you've got to be both a contractor and a developer. It's the way the system works. You overcharge for the construction so that you make your development profits before the turnstile ever turns," said Pat. "We didn't understand that at first, so when they'd come in with an estimate of $50 million for a park that could be built in the U.S. for $25 million, we started asking questions. They told us that we didn't understand and that's the way it had to be done. 'Just be quiet

**Dad's Quite the Guy**

*He's an over-achiever. Whenever he enters a room, he is usually the most intelligent man in there. My dad's extremely intelligent, but he also has the guts to pursue things in life. He acts on what he wants and has been an amazing risk taker.*

*- Gavin Millay, son*

and we'll give you a taste,' they said. We said, okay, great."

According to Pat, Metado had perfected this angle and had worked the Brazilian pension funds and financing sources for years. "They had a crack finance team and a combination of young journeymen and old pros, all brilliant," said Pat. It was also easy for Metado to sell the deal, which they did in less than a year. By the time Hatchell and his team had designed the Sao Paulo park, financing was in place.

Construction began and was on schedule until an unforeseen problem slowed down the final process. "Just as we approached the finish line, our partner was hit with some sort of an environmental permit problem. In Brazil a building permit at that time was like a manila envelope full of cash. That's how you got approval. As it turned out, some mayor or city manager of a small city adjacent to the park hadn't received his share."

The developers were accused of discharging sewer waste into the river, while in reality, Wet'n Wild's tests showed that they were treating the sewer affluent to a level higher than required. The water was actually cleaner than the river into which it flowed. However, the situation pushed the project back 10 months and it eventually ended up getting solved by having the right person get a thick envelope. That park opened in November 1997.

### *Hola, Señor Millay*

A great deal of industry publicity was generated during the building of the Wet'n Wilds in Brazil. That publicity helped create further opportunities and partners, one of which was Bernardo Zambrano, whose family controlled Cemex, a giant cement company with offices in Monterey, Mexico. He called George saying he had done his research and wanted to build a water park in Cancun and that Wet'n Wild was his first and only choice. Perfecto!

George and his group were delighted not only with their new partner, but with the location as well. According to George, the site was nearly perfect for a waterpark. It had good year-round weather and a strong base of American tourists.

Pat was assigned the project and he, along with Getz, designer Billy Watts, and George jumped into the design. As part of the deal, Wet'n Wild agreed to provide experienced operations people, but otherwise Zambrano would run the operation.

"It turned out to be a disaster," George remembers. "Zambrano did nothing right. First he alienated the ever-important hotel, tour and bus operators in the state of Qunitana Roo. It was a constant battle during construction to make sure the franchisee and his contractor were using the right materials." A Wet'n Wild, American-style waterpark meant that only quality materials were installed with top-notch workmanship. After all, "It was our name on the door," George added.

Wet'n Wild always specified in its contracts that the franchisee be required to use top quality U.S. and Canadian suppliers, including but not limited to ProSlide, SCS, Anchor Industries, Sevylor, and Taylor & Associates, whom Wet'n Wild had the sole discretion to select.

"To that culture, sole discretion obviously meant that we were on the take with these suppliers," said Pat. "They couldn't figure out why we would spend $65 for a safe, comfortable, durable, aluminum beach chair when they could get a crappy plastic one locally for $12."

He said they spent half their time convincing franchisees that they must buy only the best products and that Wet'n Wild wasn't getting kickbacks. When the franchisees finally realized the officials of Wet'n Wild weren't crooks, "we spent the other half of our time convincing them we weren't crazy for not taking advantage of that potential," laughed Pat.

**Saint George?**

*I am a Roman Catholic and I go to church regularly. The church is really for sinners not saints and I fit unfortunately right into that unsavory category. The story of my life in book form might sell far better if it included a few episodes of the early stages of my 75 years. You can't hang around worldly, lovable scoundrels like Al Slavik, Gary Zuercher, Jan Schultz, John Seeker, Clint McKinnon, Bill Evans, Harris Rosen, Burt Arnds, and David Tallichet and acquire sainthood. Lovable rogue maybe.*

*- George Millay*

Zambrano appointed one of his buddies as general manager, who, George points out, showed up at 10 and left at noon each day. He also allowed construction equipment to remain on the property for months after opening making it look as if the park was still under construction.

"Neither Zambrano nor his people would listen to anything we said," George notes. "Our royalties began accruing from opening day and we never received a cent. It's so sad. Here's a magnificent waterpark in a great location like Cancun and it went to the dogs. It is still not performing as it should and it is badly maintained." Wet'n Wild Cancun opened during spring 1996.

### *Productive Times*

The International team had been busy. Within 13 months, they had opened three international waterparks that were all the size and scope of the biggest facilities in operation in the United States. They were state-of-the-art parks in terms of the rides and had very innovative designs for the time.

Wet'n Wild officials in the states were "borrowing" pictures out of the brochures of the Brazilian Wet'n Wild parks to put in their own brochures because they showed a fresh, contemporary approach to the industry.

The move into Mexico and Brazil was a profitable three and a half year period for the company. "We took in a couple million dollars' worth of design fees and then the franchise fee stream started to come in. Things were looking pretty good," Pat said.

### *George Gets into Trouble in Brazil*

During that time, George himself would travel to Brazil to search out additional potential waterpark sites, much as he had done in the states. On one trip in 1996, while looking for a waterpark location in the south of Brazil, George and his entourage stopped off at the famous Iquazu Falls on the Brazil-Paraguay border.

George, notorious for always being cold, couldn't get warm that afternoon and being in Brazil, the rooms didn't have any heaters. He checked in to the area's best hotel, a four-star establishment owned by Varig Brasil Airlines. He went to his room, and as the story goes, he turned on the shower as hot as he could make it, searching for a way to get warm.

As the room started filling with steam, he left to go to lunch and then to tour an area that he was told would be perfect for a Wet'n Wild. Over the course of the next five hours the steam saturated the room. The draperies got so heavy they fell, yanking the brackets out of the wall. The water logged plaster ceiling collapsed into the room.

Upon his return to the hotel, George saw a fire truck in front and the hotel's management was in a near-panic mode hunting for him. He showed up, they started screaming at him and then proceeded to throw him out of the hotel yelling after him to never show up there again. Of course he felt terrible about the mess and paid for all the repairs, but they still won't let him come back, so the legend goes.

***Tough Business Down There***

The company had made a great deal of money in the international arena by designing and building parks, but the promised royalties from the franchised parks proved to be merely a pipe dream. "We got snookered because we just couldn't keep the royalties coming, and as a small company, we couldn't work through the court system. It seemed our partners quit paying as soon as they didn't need us anymore," Pat added.

The biggest success of Wet'n Wild International, according to Pat, was that "the old man got to create again and what he created was phenomenal stuff. It was the classic George Millay formula. It was taking what he already knew, combining it with the expertise of incredible consultants and suppliers and making it all happen, against all odds."

The South American and Mexican businesses also postured the company for the creation of new U.S. parks, based on those new designs. "We conducted new research and development work on those international parks. At the time of that work, we also had incredible, state-of-the-art attractions designed for new parks in San Diego and in South Florida," Pat said.

George looks back and becomes somewhat frustrated that the Mexican and Brazilian ventures didn't pay off better for everyone.

"Anyone who invests a nickel south of the border is in my estimation, nuts! We always got good money upfront and were well paid for the architectural costs, but royalties were kaput," George alleged. "Once they didn't need you south of the border, forget it. Contracts mean nothing and courts are an illusion."

- CHAPTER 40 -

# Searching for Sites: Santee & Nashville

In the early 1990s, with the burgeoning success of Wet'n Wild Orlando, Texas, and Las Vegas, the company turned its collective eye to potential sites within the U.S. Locations, ranging from Fort Lauderdale to Nashville to San Diego, were considered.

In addition to its climate, San Diego was ideal for a waterpark. It had a large local population, 15 million tourists visited the area each year and it was the proud home of the world famous San Diego Zoo and of course, the original SeaWorld.

An even more compelling reason to build in the San Diego area was George's desire to return to his hometown and "show them all," both friends and foes, that George Millay had returned with yet another unique and successful recreational concept.

It would show "them" that SeaWorld was no flash in the pan and that George had once again proven that he was the star of the imagination, drive and talent behind most of SeaWorld and its success. "It was a personal thing with me and I had a strong urge to show them," he admits.

**Watching Those Stats!**

*George's son Gar played minor league baseball in the Texas Rangers system and spent most of his playing time in Triple-A ball, something of which George was quite proud of. Part of my job during baseball season was to call over to the Rangers' office each morning and get Gar's statistics from the night before and have them waiting for George when he got to work. If Gar went zero for four I'd leave the report on George's chair. At first I'd give it to him, but if Gar had a bad night, George would get pissed off and yell and cuss. Of course if he went 3 for 4 and had a good game, I'd personally hand it to him.*

*- John Seeker, VP, MARC USA*

In their analysis of the area, George and his son Pat, had determined that a waterpark needed to be located north of I-8 and east of I-15. They retained Joe Bonin, an East County real estate agent, to help locate possible sites.

Santee Center was identified as a possibility and they began to further study the location. It gets hot in Santee and daytime summer temperatures are in the high 90's to low 100's. The site was situated at the terminus of I-56, an east-west freeway that connected to all the north-south freeways serving the San Diego area. It was within a 20 minute drive of 80% of the local population and accessible to tourists.

### *Go Home, We Don't Want You!*

The site consisted of more than 30 acres located on a two-square mile section of city property that at that time was completely undeveloped. Wet'n Wild's proposal generated significant approval from local businessmen but local residents opposed the creation of the park right from the start.

"We wrestled with this site and spent a considerable amount of money trying to convince the mayor and council of the benefits we would bring to the community, all sorely needed by this backwater community; a community of trailer parks and pre-fabricated houses," George said.

"At an open session of the council we were humiliated, vilified and excoriated by the council members. Even though we were from San Diego we were painted as a bunch of out of town jaspers wanting to wreck this community. This is typical of a trend firmly established now in California. We struck out. Forget about family fun, investment in the community, jobs, and taxes - get lost!"

### *Finding Discord in Music City*

Licking his wounds from the Santee disappointment, George started looking around at other domestic markets that were in need of a Wet'n Wild waterpark. With its long hot summers, Nashville, Tennessee was a potential market. George had become familiar with the city because several of his friends lived there, including Tom Powell, then editor of *Amusement Business* magazine, Johnny Hobbs, owner of the famous Nashville Palace restaurant, and Larry Schmittou, the owner of the Nashville Sounds Triple-A baseball club.

"I was very familiar with the city and went up there a couple of times. I liked the whole layout and it had a good strong tourist base. We started investigating and did a few of our own quick studies and liked the potential, but never had success in finding the right piece of ground," George recalls.

He talked with Opryland USA Themepark executives and they weren't interested in having a Wet'n Wild moving into town. He looked at some land owned by Johnny Hobbs and decided against any of those locations. George then went out to Johnny Cash's House of Cash Museum and sat down with Cash, who was very interested in Wet'n Wild building on his land about 20 miles outside Nashville, but George felt he needed to be closer to the city center.

About a year after he started looking in Nashville, a city-owned wave pool opened a mile and a half south of Opryland, on what George calls a beautiful piece of property. There was plenty of room around it for parking and a great deal of room for expansion.

George fell in love with the site but his quest to be a part of that development became a political football game. Even with two local, influential partners, George didn't have any luck with that location or in finding another site. It was the same old story: The locals didn't want more traffic, didn't want more cars parked along their streets, and didn't want more noise.

The project was turned down by the Parks Department even before it got to the council. The Wet'n Wild Nashville was never built, but definitely, it wasn't the first or the last family-oriented attraction to get the cold shoulder from the city.

- CHAPTER 41 -

# Back to San Diego, Finally

The most successful and most profitable waterpark George never built was in Poway, California. However, that profit didn't come easy and there were many heartbreaks and fiascos along the way.

In 1994, following many fruitless attempts at trying to find a site for a Wet'n Wild in Southern California, George found available land in Poway, a city in North County, San Diego, three miles east of I-15. George was able to buy 55 acres of land, with an option to buy nine more, for approximately $20,000 an acre.

### *Ambassador Pat*

George had his development team, still in Arlington, Texas, start designing the park and construction was set to begin in 1997. Pat Millay, president of Wet'n Wild International and assistant director of development, and Billy Getz were put in charge of the project.

Pat served as company ambassador and represented it well during the approval process. He spoke with the various Chambers of Commerce and neighborhood groups, many of which were against the project, even before they had heard all the facts. "Pat was the smooth, fair-haired young man with the big college education so we used him. He's smooth and sophisticated, not like his old man," George laughed. Once approvals were granted to proceed, George entered the picture and returned to San Diego from corporate headquarters in Texas.

Over one long weekend, he was able to raise $4 million in equity. The business plan for Poway was to acquire as much equity as possible by bringing in a partner. That would free up more of the Wet'n Wild capital so it could proceed with another park, near Ft. Lauderdale.

"I raised all the money for the Poway park in one weekend, and I went back to Arlington just walking on air. I thought I was the biggest wheeler-dealer in the world," George said. Originally, he thought he might have to bring in 15 or 20 different people to get the capital he needed, as he had to do at SeaWorld.

### *Raising the Money*

George had met John Gillette, a successful sports investment counselor, through his second oldest son, Gar, a professional baseball player. "I sat down with him, went through a song and dance explaining the capitalization. I told him we would put up our $4 million, he and his players would put up $4 million and Wet'n Wild would be responsible for getting the mortgage." Gillette said he would do it. On top of owning half, Wet'n Wild was going to get a 5% management fee.

**George on Praying**

*I pray first for the Lord to have mercy on my soul. Then I pray for the Lord to have mercy on other people's souls, my mother and father, all my relatives and all of my deceased friends. Then I pray for peace in the church and in the world. I thank Him for all the things He has given me – health, money, fame and being an American. I have a wonderful wife and wonderful children and grandchildren. God has blessed me with everything.*

*- George Millay*

George explained that he would need the money in eight months, no later than January 1, 1996 and was assured by Gillette that it would be waiting.

The day after George got the commitment for $4 million, he received a verbal agreement for an $11 million first mortgage from San Diego-based Golden Eagle Insurance, which was owned and controlled by his old friend John Mabee.

In late 1995, George received a letter from Gillette saying he had his money tied up in Mexico, but that it would be available by March 1, 1996. He closed his letter with, "It will be here for sure, don't worry." By this time, Wet'n Wild had purchased the land and footed the bill for all the engineering and the preliminary stages of grading. Jan Schultz, who at that point was COO of Ogden Entertainment of Florida, at Silver Springs, had been tagged to run the park.

March went by, no money. George wrote Gillette a letter

pointing out that he was under contract and that money now. About that time Gillette was arrested ly would serve several years in jail for misar client's money. George's dream partner ended up

***Doing it on their Own***

With that deal kaput and with his contract with Pow on the table, George went to his board and got approval to raise Wet'n Wild's commitment to $7 million, up from the original $4 million, and to look for a bigger mortgage. No partners would be needed in the new business plan.

George received a one-year grace period on the building permits. Then another huge setback occurred. Golden Eagle Insurance, the company that promised George $11 million in first mortgage loans, was taken over by the state and John Mabee and his team were relieved of duty.

The insurance company immediately returned to Wet'n Wild the $150,000 it had deposited at the time of the loan commitment and proceeded to cancel the $11 million mortgage. George once again had to go shopping for money and landed a promise for a $12 million mortgage from a major San Diego bank. With that money and the $7 million from Wet'n Wild coffers, the project seemed ready to get started in earnest. Grading of the site had been completed and the wave pool hole had already been dug.

It wasn't to be; but don't feel sorry for the players.

By that time, Lincoln Properties wanted the Wet'n Wild property and made George an offer of $6.50 per square foot for the land that George had purchased for 59-cents a square foot. With the additional costs and work already completed, the company had a total of $2 invested in each square foot, meaning if they sold, it would be a capital gain of $4.50 per square foot.

***Deciding not to Build***

What did they do? George had finally found the perfect location for his San Diego park. Did he sell out for a huge profit?

"You bet I did. That was $14 million and we couldn't turn it down. It would have taken us more than 12 years of very successful waterpark operation to make that kind of profit," George pointed out.

The story doesn't end there, however. For the sale to be

completed, zoning of the land had to be changed to industrial and the city, upset that they weren't getting a waterpark, initially refused to change the zoning. However, with the help of two law firms and $80,000 in legal fees, it was clear to most that the city had no choice but to change the permit.

The city refused and it looked like a long, costly court battle loomed ahead. The lawyers suggested George settle with the city. He did, paying $1 million to the city coffers. Shortly thereafter, the zoning was changed and the sale went through.

At that point, John Shawen and George decided they needed to take a serious look at assessing the future for Wet'n Wild. "Maybe we should sell the whole shooting match," Shawen suggested to George.

- CHAPTER 42 -

# The Last Good Waterpark Site in the U.S.

In 1995, the Parks and Recreation Department of Broward County, Florida sent out a request for proposals asking for ideas to develop a waterpark on 40 acres of land. The site was near the Florida Turnpike and Sample Road outside of a small city called Coconut Creek, a neighbor of Ft. Lauderdale.

George and Mike Black, general manager of Wet'n Wild Orlando, along with Kelly Smith, the company's attorney, made a trip to see the parcel and meet with officials. George retained a local attorney who was well connected with Broward County to serve as the company's voice. Wet'n Wild submitted the RFP and was awarded the contract to start working through the hurdles of negotiating with the county.

Progress on the Florida park was slow. Being closer to George's home in San Diego, the Poway project which was still active at the time, received most of his focus. Secondly, raising funds for the proposed $30 million Coconut Creek waterpark was running into difficulty. Negotiations were also getting bogged down on several issues with the county, including rental and development costs.

It was during those negotiations and the search for financing that George decided to sell the entire Wet'n Wild company. The development rights for the Coconut Creek property went to Universal, the new owners of the company. Universal later sold the rights to the Ogden Corp., which let the options lapse for that property.

"We were going down to Coconut Creek quite a bit for awhile and George was always very passionate and very animated and just wonderful to be with," Black recalls, noting that in early 1998, during one of those trips, George was uncharacteristically quiet.

Black said it was then that he first sensed that George might be thinking about selling the entire Wet'n Wild company.

- CHAPTER 43 -

# The Sale to Universal

Three years after selling Wet'n Wild Arlington to Six Flags in 1995, the rest of the company, including all international franchises and development rights, was sold to Universal Studios. What led up to the decision to do so involved countless hours of discussion and analysis.

In late 1996, Shawen and George began to realistically look at the company's long-term potential, both domestically and internationally. By that time, they knew their efforts in Brazil and Mexico were not going to be as fruitful as they had hoped.

The company also started to assess its long-term viability in Florida. The lease payments were favorable at the time for Wet'n Wild Orlando, but they knew that in approximately 10 years, it would become a very unfavorable lease, tripling in price. Also, the Florida Flex Ticket, which accounted for a great deal of predictable income for Wet'n Wild, looked like it was about to change.

## *Another Reason to Sell*

For several years Wet'n Wild had partnered with Universal Studios and SeaWorld on a multi-park, multi-day ticket sold throughout Orlando. The Flex Ticket, which is still sold today, gives the buyer unlimited access to Universal, SeaWorld, and Wet'n Wild.

The ticket was doing very well for Wet'n Wild and was profitable for the park. There was constant pressure on Wet'n Wild to take less money for their part of the ticket. On a $75 ticket, the park would get 20% and SeaWorld and Universal would each get 40%. In 1997, 40% of Wet'n Wild's business came from the Flex Ticket.

"Universal was building a second park, Islands of Adventure. SeaWorld was building the $100 million Discovery Cove and Busch Gardens in Tampa was trying to get into Flex Ticket package as well," said George. "That meant the pie was going to be cut into smaller pieces and we would get an even smaller percentage."

**Dear Stockholders**

*I am now well into the seventh decade of my life, and as the poetess wrote, teetering toward the tomb. Perhaps some of you are wondering what Ole Red wants to do with the few years he might have left on this planet. Well, life is still exciting and all my vital organs are functioning as well as can be expected. I pray a lot nowadays and wonder more about where the final destination will be for my black soul. Our waterpark industry is becoming more sophisticated and professional, and I'd like to participate and lead a further evolution of the industry and make all of us some money while leading the pack. Que sera, sera.*

*- George Millay in his 1990 year-end report to his Wet'n Wild Board of Directors.*

Wet'n Wild Orlando was also running out of room for expansion and would have no space to build big new and exciting attractions in the future, making it less competitive. George was concerned that either SeaWorld or Universal, both with ample space, would build their own waterparks and overwhelm Wet'n Wild with strong attractions and deep pockets.

The combination of all those factors, suggested to both George and Shawen that business was going to get more difficult and the potential to make money corporate wide was going to be tougher.

### *The Big Decision*

However, it was far from doom and gloom and by the mid-1990s, Wet'n Wild had a great story to tell. George Millay, the innovator and "father" of the waterpark industry was still at the company's helm and the Florida and Las Vegas waterparks were producing a mid-seven figure cash flow. Six Flags had paid top dollar to purchase and were now running the Texas park, and three of the four International franchises were up and running. The Wet'n Wild banner was never flying higher.

Pat Millay is quick to point out that if Wet'n Wild had chosen the acquisition route for expansion as many other park companies did in the early 1990s, it would have been a much larger and a much stronger company. "No, George wouldn't let that happen in our company," Pat said. "He didn't want to go into a second generation park. He wanted to design and build from the ground. That's where he was the strongest and where he excelled."

Being in such a strong position poised the company for a buy-out offer, according to Pat. The executives felt it was inevitable that the company would sell sooner than later, and they knew it wouldn't be hard to find a buyer. The time was right. Wet'n Wild had the right story to tell.

### *Who's Interested?*

In spring 1998, Shawen, Pat and George made the decision to put the company up for sale. They went to the board and told them of their decision. "Atta Boy, George," his board members told him. "Go for it."

George didn't officially put the parks on the market. Instead, thinking SeaWorld would scoop them up immediately, he went to them first. "I called John Roberts, president of Busch Entertainment, which owned SeaWorld. To my frustration and surprise, I found I was mistaken. Roberts immediately said no. I was flabbergasted because I knew SeaWorld needed Wet'n Wild very badly to stay competitive with Universal and Disney."

Once Roberts declined the offer, George called Tom Williams, the top guy at Universal Studios Florida. He responded favorably, saying he wanted it, and told George to get over to his office as soon as possible and meet Cathy Nichol, then Universal Recreation's president.

Within a week, a letter of intent was drafted. There was nothing concrete, but the two parties agreed not to discuss it with anyone and the sale process began in a very secretive, quiet and polite way. They shook hands on a deal in April 1998. It was originally set to close on June 15, but it took longer than anyone anticipated. Shawen signed the final papers on September 30, 1998 at 10 a.m.

"The deal closed for $41 million dollars and many people say we didn't get enough. It was paid off over a two-year period, a third down in cash, a third the following year, and a third the next year. Shawen and I had extended consulting contracts for 10 additional years," George said. "It's now great mailbox money."

### *You Could Have Gotten More*

While some said he should have gotten another $5 million to $10 million for the sale, George said that in the long run, "it was the smartest move we ever made. We made millionaires out of many of our stockholders. John Shawen became a millionaire, Seeker walked away with a half million and all of our top executives walked away with $400,000 to $500,000. Everyone came out very well financially," said George.

In a way, George removed himself from the final stages, allowing Shawen to finalize the negotiations. During the summer of 1998, George took a six-week trip to Europe with his youngest son Gavin. "We were right in the throes of finalizing negotiations and George gave me the go-ahead to do what I could to take care of things. He dealt with the things that he needed to, and we consulted as needed on the difficult and tough issues," Shawen said. Following the signing of the papers, Shawen left a note on George's desk simply stating, "The eagle has landed."

### *Post-Mortem Blues*

Shawen remembers the sale. "I think George's most difficult period during the entire time I knew him probably occurred about 30 days after we sold the parks. Wet'n Wild was much more than a business to George. It was his hobby. It was his life and it was what he did. After we sold the parks there was nothing there. He had lost his best friend, if you will, the waterpark was gone."

Over the years, George was so devoted to his parks that he never developed many close friends that were non-business associates. He didn't have a hobby. He couldn't play golf because his mind couldn't stay on it for more than about four holes, after which he'd start thinking about what he was going to build next.

Mike Black thinks a little bit of George Millay was sold along with the parks. "I remember clearly the last day he was here after the company had been sold. He had always been full of energy, very verbal and very passionate. I stood at the window and watched him walk out to his car and he was just kind of shuffling out and looking very sullen and depressed. I think from the get-go he was depressed that he had sold it."

Black remembers George telling him a month or so later that people didn't call him anymore and that he was wandering the halls of his office alone. "He was half joking but it was clear that he was a lost soul. He had been the captain of Wet'n Wild and now he was a man without a position."

George said he was laden with heavy nostalgia at the time, but doesn't think he was depressed. "I was full of mixed emotions," he recalls. "After more than 40 years of problems and victories and parks to run, it was certainly a let-down to be out of the excitement, to be out of the loop. But I knew it was the best thing to do for the company's stockholders, and that helped me through it."

Universal took over the entire Wet'n Wild organization through a cash buyout and Black kept his job as general manager, which he holds to this day. Universal was especially keen on the Orlando property, and saw the park as not only the flagship and most successful Wet'n Wild, but also as the golden goose. They quickly carved Orlando out of the fold and sold off the rest of the parks, including the international rights and Wet'n Wild Las Vegas to the Ogden Corporation.

Within a year Alfa-Alfa Smart Parks purchased the parks from Ogden, and when Alfa-Alfa declared bankruptcy, Palace Entertainment took over the Wet'n Wild brand. Larry Cochran, former Six Flags President and George's long-time friend, now heads Palace Entertainment and the Wet'n Wild parks.

## Pay Up & Come On In!

*As pioneers, George and his team learned waterpark business the hard way. They spent millions, gained skills through trial and error, and made many mistakes along the way. George was adamant about sharing that hard-learned information with his potential competitors.*

*"We had learned the hard way and we weren't handing out free advice. In fact, we weren't handing out any advice," Gary Daning, one of the four originals at Wet'n Wild, said. During those years, George wouldn't even let his colleagues into the parks for free, he made them pay. People would come in, walk around and take thousands of dollars worth of pictures of what they were doing and go home and copy it. George figured the least they should do for all that information was pay to get in.*

*"If he saw people shooting photos through the fence, he would chase them off the property. We could always get into other parks free," said Daning. "But we were't allowed to comp those colleagues when they came to our park. Sometimes it became embarrassing."*

### How it All Started

*George said he never felt bad about charging his colleagues. "I always paid my way when I visited another park, unless of course, I was personally invited. I never asked for a free ticket in my life."*

*He said he started objecting to free guest passes back in the early-1970s when a group of 40 from Six Flags, led by Luther Clark, asked to get into SeaWorld San Diego free to take pictures and look around for ideas so they could build their own marine park in Arlington, Texas. "No way was I going to let them in," he recalled.*

*Then in the late 1970s, when Wet'n Wild Orlando opened as the world's first waterpark, ride builder Gary Zuercher and feasibility expert Bill Haralson, both friends of George, would ask to get in free and bring clients in with them. They would then show them around and get the newcomers excited about the waterpark concept. "They would get psyched by looking at what I was doing and end up building a park and becoming my competition," George said. "That's when I started the policy that no one got in free."*

*In the early 1990s, George's attitude about freebies created quite a stir within segments of the industry. Nearly 18,000 industry leaders were in Dallas attending the International Assn. Of Amusement Parks & Attractions convention and many wanted to go out and see George's Wet'n Wild Arlington and tour the new FunSphere family entertainment center.*

*Many showed up at the gate, expecting to be allowed free access, as is customary at most parks, especially during this particular convention. "He made them all pay," Daning laughed. The word got out that George needed money so badly, that he was charging his industry friends to get in. In reality, of course, George was proud of what he had there and he didn't want potential competitors to get in free to steal ideas. If they were going to steal, they must pay, was his attitude.*

- CHAPTER 44 -

# A Few Final Words on Wet'n Wild

The idea that if you can make one waterpark profitable you can run one anywhere is not quite accurate, according to George. Any market worth investing in has its own characteristics, both positive and negative.

Except for the "devious and duplicitous" East Coast tour and trade operators and wholesalers, George said Florida, from the late 1970s until the early 1990s was an ideal location for an attraction. The state had a strong reputation as a national as well as an international destination and supported the industry with abundant marketing funds. The behemoth Disney organization sailed along setting attendance records year after year with little advertising effort of their own.

To a point, SeaWorld was aggressive and it too was setting records each season. Wet'n Wild came along in 1977 and after a year of struggles, fit into the market as the number three attraction, sharing in what George calls "the benevolent monies of this amusement Shangri-La known as Orlando."

Then things began to change. "Into this tranquil setting of the early 1990s jumped the wily and aggressive Jay Stein and his pack of Hollywood hucksters from Universal Studios," said George. "The tidal wave they precipitated bounced around Central Florida with disruptive force for a decade. Nothing was the same after Universal dealt themselves in." The only good thing, according to George, was Universal hated Disney and therefore benignly "ignored us little guys."

Universal immediately jumped big time into outdoor billboard and TV advertising. The cost of the billboards on the Bee Line Expressway and I-4 skyrocketed, as did local TV rates. The annual Wet'n Wild marketing budget went from $1.3 million to $3 million in three years.

### *Different in Dallas*

The Dallas-Fort Worth, Texas market, of which Arlington is in the middle, is a totally different story. It had a big local population and good regional tourist visitation. Wet'n Wild had hot Texas weather in summer and the popular Six Flags Over Texas amusement park next door. Sounds nearly ideal.

"Well, it was and it wasn't. First of all a great many Texans don't swim and when they do, the water has to be real warm," said George. "I remember Texans staring at me swimming in late May in 72-degree water, thinking I was absolutely nuts."

Also, the "Hollywood reputation" of Texans as big spenders is way off, according to George, noting that the average Texan watches his money and spends it only when he finds a bargain. "When they do spend it, they get their money's worth, often staying in the parks for eight hours or more causing congestion. Ironically, those who stay the longest are the ones who usually got in on a highly discounted promotional ticket," adds George.

Operating a waterpark, the world's largest at the time, in Texas was no small endeavor. The biggest problem turned out to be the surprisingly short summer school holidays. "You can't count on good weather in May and June. July and August were the months in which you had to make it," George said. "Fortunately, the evenings are balmy and humid and our Summer Nights promotions proved successful. We did as much as 25% of our attendance after 5 p.m." The shortening of the Texas school vacation period is what killed the goose, he notes.

"That sad development, plus the fact that other cities in the DFW area were developing their own municipal waterparks - today there are 10 in operation - left me no alternative but to sell our Texas parks to Six Flags. Our timing was perfect," George reflects.

### *Rolling the Dice in Vegas*

Contrary to popular belief, the desert is no panacea for a water park. The dry, low humidity accelerates cooling of wet bodies and pools. Ninety-degree weather is cold when you visit a desert waterpark. Wet'n Wild easily penetrated the local Clark County population. Nearly 60% of the locals visited the park, when counting repeat visitation, versus 20% in Orlando and Texas.

The Las Vegas problem, despite its claims, is not a family destination. "People come to Vegas to drink, gamble, and sin.

Casinos are protective of their guests' activities and discourage anyone trying to go out of their domain," said George. "Outside of the Hughes properties, we got little cooperation from the majors. We owned outdoor billboards in northern Arizona, eastern California and the I-15 corridor in the summer and it was exciting. The one radio channel across the California Highway to Vegas got the greatest percentage of our radio budget."

Despite an "exciting, beautiful, well-run and efficient park" on the strip, "we never achieved attendance of more than 600,000, but we were always in the black." The Vegas venture never produced the profits the Hughes Development Corporation people or Wet'n Wild had expected.

- CHAPTER 45 -

# The George Stories

Many of the stories written in this book as well as told elsewhere about George Millay depict him as egocentric, bigoted, crude, hasty, belligerent, and gruff. Most who know him or have dealt with him in the past would agree that one or more of those adjectives does in fact, describe him at one time or another in his life.

Interestingly, many of these same stories also illustrate his positive attributes as well, including being a creative genius, being loyal to a fault, being overly generous, and being a good friend and mentor to many who he gave breaks to along the way. He truly was a career maker for dozens who started with him.

"Out of context, many of these stories sound like he was a real jerk," John Seeker said. "He absolutely was at times, but we always knew he cared for us and we always knew where we stood with him."

### *A Little Fear is Good*

Seeker worked for George longer than any other person and has seen him at his very best and his very worst. "It was a long but very interesting run. It was never boring with George," Seeker laughs, noting that he didn't stop fearing George until he went to work for him at Seven Seas, in Arlington, Texas in 1975, five years after originally being hired at SeaWorld San Diego.

"A little fear is good. I still subscribe to that. When I was very young and working at SeaWorld I was truly afraid of the man, but after awhile the fear turned to respect," he said. George would ask him what he thought about this or about that and Seeker couldn't figure out why George would ask him those sort of questions that were totally out of his field of expertise. "I later discovered he would ask them because he knew I would tell him the truth, not tell him what I thought he wanted to hear," Seeker notes.

Speaking of fear, Larry Cochran, now president of Palace Entertainment and former president of the Six Flags chain of

**Made in the Shade**

*I hate this so-called retirement. I feel useless not accomplishing much. I badly miss the action, the sweet smell of success. One good aspect is that I pray more, read the Bible, and attend mass two times during the work week in addition to my Sunday obligations. Nobody should ever say they have it made, if they do they're not too bright.*

*- George Millay*

parks, remembers the first time he met George. Cochran had been sent in 1966 on an information gathering tour to Southern California by his boss, Angus Wynne, founder and then president of Six Flags, and was told to stop by and say hello to George.

He visited the park office and asked to see George and after waiting for about 15 minutes, went into his office and was greeted with a, "What the hell are you doing here," by George. "He started asking me all kinds of questions about Angus and raised his voice at me several times. I was sitting there scared to death. I got up to leave thinking it had been a bad idea to meet with him. I thought it was quite clear he didn't like me or want me there," Cochran recalls.

"But he wouldn't let me leave, bought my lunch and we talked for three more hours. I walked out of there still a little scared, but totally impressed with that man. Sure he was one of the meanest SOB's I had ever met, but it was his career-long style and he got a thrill from chewing out people's butts!"

Cochran calls George a creative genius and "the only man I know who birthed two major genres of parks. Walt Disney only birthed one."

Gary Daning, who worked for George for 22 years and was one of the original four at Wet'n Wild said having the reputation of an "irate maniac" was part of the mystique of George, but doesn't truly feel that image was justified. "Those who hear the stories and who don't know him, take things out of context and think everything they hear is true. Anyone who has worked for him for any length of time, knows what a loving, warm, generous person he really is," Daning adds.

### *His Management Style*

His style has been called crude, rude and anarchist, but

according to his wife Anne, George knew exactly what he was doing. "His general style in life is charging ahead, being aggressive with a kind of anger and determination. Those are his natural tendencies," explained Anne.

"After consideration he put that all together and concluded that was the way he had to lead. That was the way he got results. I've always said he ruled by intimidation and I think people learned that pretty fast," Anne said. "As a man of 30, he was set in his ways and opinions. Many thought he was narrow-minded and they had to be convinced otherwise. George has what I call earthy finesse."

George always felt he could learn more by asking questions. He is by nature, very inquisitive. Sometimes the question asked was one for which he thought he already knew the answer. He loved to go out in the park and ask guests questions and would store the information he learned from those conversations in his memory bank. He always appreciated another view and another thought. In most instances, George made quick decisions with a minimum amount of analysis and had a great success rate.

***Never Lie to George***

He also seeks truth in everything he does. "I've always said that if you ever lied to George, you were dead. Sometimes it wasn't easy to tell him the truth or what you thought was the truth but we all knew never to lie to the man," Seeker notes.

George's management style was a balance of butt chewing and praise, Seeker remembers. "Everyone got chewed out, and most everyone got praised. He would compliment privately and would compliment publicly as well."

Daning adds that George is an emotional leader and that passion drove him to his demand for excellence. "Nine out of 10 times he would talk before he would think and once he got started yelling, it was hard for him to stop," Daning notes. "I would just stand there, wait for him to finish and then explain the situation to him. He would say, 'Oh, why didn't you tell me that

**George on New Ventures**

*Too many new ventures in our field fit the description of the classic American business failure: they are under-financed, underbuilt and mismanaged.*

*- George Millay*

to begin with.' Yeah, like we had a chance."

Jumping the gun and reacting before he knows all the facts is George's style, Daning notes, adding that George's yelling and screaming "was never hateful. It was just that he demanded excellence in his product and excellence in his people."

### *Generous to a Fault*

Seeker said George proved many times that he was overly generous. "George was a true pigeon. We'd be over at his condo sitting and having a drink and some con man would call up selling light bulbs or raising money for the police from one of those back-room operations and George would always buy something," Seeker said.

One morning in the parking lot of Wet'n Wild Orlando, a disheveled man who fed him a line about his misfortunes and how he needed money approached George. He offered to sell his "Rolex" for $60. George bit and went parading into the office wearing his new Rolex watch. "I knew right away it wasn't a Rolex and that he had been had, but I didn't want the day to get off to a bad start, so I went back to my office and didn't say anything," recalls Seeker.

Shawen wasn't as considerate and told George he had been sold a fake. George ran out to the parking lot, but the guy had already high-tailed it for the woods. Ironically, George never wore a watch.

During the first couple of years at Wet'n Wild Orlando, groups were given discounts of 25-cents a ticket, and Seeker, Shawen and the rest of them watched the process of discounting very closely, not wanting to give out too many or too big of a discount. After all, they were struggling to make it. However, the military and the clergy were always admitted free or at a large discount.

### *Bless Me George, I Goofed*

Seeker recalls one instance where he was a little too tight. "We had this priest, Father Sierra visiting from Massachusetts with a bunch of kids. I kind of forgot my place when he ended up asking for another nickel off the ticket. We're standing there talking and George walks up, hears what's going on and tells me to give him another nickel discount. After the priest and the kids went in, I looked at George and said something like, oh, screw,

Father Sierra why does he think he should get a better discount? I found out quickly that wasn't the right thing to say to George, a good Irish Catholic. I paid for that one for a month or so."

George is a pigeon because it's his nature to believe what he is told and to believe in the best of everyone. He was always very generous to his employees and would often lend them money. It didn't matter whether the person was a vice president or a manager or a filter washer, he would lend a hand to nearly anyone who would ask for help. As could be expected, he got burned on several occasions, but he never dwelled on it or got angry.

"Through the years, numerous employees got into health-related situations that prevented them from working and collecting a paycheck," Daning said. "When he heard about it, he would tell me to keep the person on the payroll while they were off work sick. It didn't matter if they were a lifeguard or a top executive, George made sure he took care of the people who did a good job for him."

### *Forgive Me George, for I Screwed Up*

It's surprising to many that George, the big gruff Irishman who demands the best out of the people around him, has always been a very forgiving person. He knew others, as well as himself, would make mistakes. It was only natural that mistakes were going to be made while creating and pioneering in totally new genres of business. He allowed employees to make mistakes once, but he couldn't tolerate those who made the same mistake twice.

When someone let George down, it was normally because they let themselves down and that bothered him. When people failed he would try to help and push them along and work with them. When they gave up, that was a real disappointment because he thought everyone, no matter what, should believe in himself.

Kym Murphy was raised without a father and he appreciated George's strong-armed guidance. "He was tough, but he was also wonderful at encouraging me to do all kinds of things. He pushed me and gave me many opportunities." Murphy said he would go to George with an idea and request funding. George would question him, sometimes argue with him but most often, would look at him and say, "OK Murphy, if this doesn't work, I'm going to kick your butt. Here's the money."

Murphy said George's "rambles, snorts and fumes" encouraged his entire staff to be creative and imaginative. "He encouraged us all in different ways because we were all different. He was astute enough to know how to motivate each one of us individually," Murphy said.

**Not Welcomed in Canada**

*In 1993 George traveled to Canada to inspect and make a large payment on a new ride he had ordered. Since it was not required, he didn't take along his passport. Upon debarking the plane and walking with dozens of others to baggage claim, he was randomly selected for a security check and taken into a small room.*

*One of the questions asked was, Have you ever been arrested? Millay answered yes and listed the various offenses committed in his youth especially his Navy days. They ran a computer check and up popped a DUI in Arlington, Texas that he received the year before. The charge had been dropped, exclaimed Millay, but a customs officer told him, "We don't want people like you in Canada. I am denying your entrance!"*

*Millay was livid. The officer was an Athabaskan Indian and George said he showed contempt for "this red-headed Irishmen." Millay demanded to see his supervisor who entered the fray, polite and understanding. George told him he was on his way to spend hundreds of thousands of dollars on Canadian goods and that his company had spent millions in Canada during the past two decades. What kind of treatment was this?*

*The senior officer agreed and said the examiner had been overly aggressive in this case but he was sorry, the decision was in the computer and nothing could be done. The denied status had to stand. The officer gave George permission to spend 48 hours in Canada and he had to check in with authorities upon his departure. If he ever intended to return, he would have to file a formal application and have it approved by Ontario officials. As a point, George refuses to do that.*

*To this day George still can't legally travel in Canada. "A thousand terrorists a week can get in but not Ole Red. They can have the damn place as far as I'm concerned," George notes.*

***On Being a Chauvinist and a Bigot***

George has left the impression with many during his life that he is a male chauvinist, a racist and a bigot. "I don't think he is or ever was a racist or a bigot, but he certainly was a chauvinist. He would poke fun and say things just to get a reaction at times," said Seeker.

"Oh yes, he's every bit a chauvinist," said Anne. "As an example, he never had a woman on any of his boards throughout his career."

Daning agrees with Anne about George's chauvinistic attitude, but defends George by saying it was much more acceptable, and sometimes totally expected, during most of George's career. As he was growing up, the general attitude was simple. Women were homemakers and men were business makers. Daning says George is "only a product of his time" and no different than hundreds of other executives of that era.

According to Ron Harper, George has always been intellectually honest. He never tried to fool people and he could never be accused of saying one thing and meaning something else. He surprised friends and colleagues alike through the years by saying outrageous things, many of which were read incorrectly by others.

On one occasion, Harper was interviewing architects for SeaWorld Ohio and George sat in on one of the interviews. Harper was talking with a man who had a beard and fuzzy hair, "A rather strange looking person, as most architects are," notes Harper. George was in his sweat suit, as he had just returned from jogging. He sat there, put his feet up on the table and started scratching himself. Harper said he was taken aback and sat there trying to figure out what George was thinking and doing.

The architect notes to Harper that he had created the master plan for the Tel Aviv Zoo, and George looks over at him and asks him if he was a Jew. "I couldn't figure where he was going with this and why he would even ask," recalls Harper. "I got real embarrassed, but the architect looked at him, said no, and went on with his presentation. In hindsight, I don't think it would have made one iota of a difference if the guy had said he was Jewish because I never once saw George discriminate. He talks a great deal and isn't socially correct most of the time, but when it gets right down to it, he's the fairest person I've ever known."

### *Pardon Me, Lady*

Doug Stewart, who runs Economic Consulting Services with his father Don, was contracted to do several studies for George's parks through the years. On one occasion, he was meeting with George in an office tower in San Diego. As they were coming down the elevator after the meeting, a well-endowed young lady was standing there with her hands crossed in front of her showing off a very large diamond ring.

George looked over at her and said what sounded to all, including the young lady, as "that's quite a rack." She looked shocked and exited on the next floor. After she left, Stewart asked George about his comment. He was quite embarrassed. "I didn't say rack, I said rock, referring to her diamond," he noted. Stewart laughed but wasn't real sure. "George often says what most people think but are too inhibited to say," he added.

On the wall behind George's desk for years was a three-dimensional soapstone sculpture of the great warrior Genghis Khan and two of his sidemen. Anyone sitting across from George had the feeling that the warriors were overseeing all activity. "It especially upset the Brazilians when they were here working on their franchised waterparks," said Harper.

George always kept an emery board in his desk drawer and during discussions, he would sometimes pull it out and start filing his finger nails, acting as if he wasn't paying a bit of attention. "He wouldn't even look at them and it would infuriate and really piss them off. It was a game. It was his way of disarming these guys."

Another way George liked to disarm guests in his office was with the clothes he wore. He would go running three or four days a week and often would jog from his house to the office in the morning. Jan Schultz recalls the "odor related" problem surfaced many times. He would work up a sweat while he ran, and when he got to his office he would immediately start working, sitting at his desk in his sweat suit. He conducted meetings and sometimes didn't take a shower until noon. "We all tried to avoid meeting with George prior to noon. Whew! I don't think he ever saw anything wrong with that," Schultz recalls.

### *Keeping the Boss in the Loop*

"George was the greatest boss from the standpoint of giving you the money and the tools to do your job. He always

*George earned a reputation for jogging to work, as portrayed in this July 8, 1971 cartoon. Published with permission from* The San Diego Union-Tribune.

expected you to defend and to justify what you were doing, which we always did. We met with him and made it a point to keep him well informed. Sometimes he would give us too much direction that we didn't need or ask for, but he didn't tinker too much with the day-to-day stuff," notes Seeker.

Playing people against one another to encourage dialogue and reaction was another game George enjoyed. He called Seeker one afternoon and told him that Daning had mentioned that Seeker made a specific comment that George didn't like. "That's not true," Seeker said. "I'll deal with Daning on my own." George had made it all up and he started to get nervous when it appeared that Seeker was going to confront Daning. "He had to admit that he was just bullshitting me because he knew all kinds of problems would have resulted. Why did he do that kind of stuff? I don't know. George is a complex person to say the least," Seeker chuckled.

### *Politically Incorrect George*

Is George politically incorrect? Seeker is quick to answer that. "About as far as you can get. You never knew what the heck he was going to say or do. But I truly believe that no matter what he said or did, he always thought he was right. He still marches to his own drummer."

Although he got into screaming matches, George would always think, look and listen more than people realized. It was his way of communicating back then and it didn't bother him to argue. In fact, he often judged a meeting by how many "good" arguments took place. He was also smart enough to know when to stop. He knew he needed good people working for him and was savvy enough not to push too far those he really cared for.

"The younger guys in particular were quite scared of him. He could be vicious when he was mad, but even then, he practiced a very fair management style," said Harper. "He wanted ideas and he wanted people to communicate."

John Shawen said he never had any doubt that George respected his top employees. "Yeah, he would argue with us and it would get ugly sometimes, but nobody took it personally because it was the nature of the man, and it became the territory. You knew it early on. You knew at times he was going to fly off the handle and scream at you, and you either dealt with it and accepted it or went somewhere else," Shawen noted.

Seeker adds. "We would argue to great lengths and he was right 90% of the time, but his approach most often sucked."

"I speak for many people from the past, especially the Wet'n Wild ones, when I say we all cared for and respected each other very much because we were all on this amazing journey together," Seeker said. "There was a tremendous amount of camaraderie, especially within the management ranks. We laughed together and cried together and many, many times we drank together."

"He trusted us to do what he paid us to do," adds Daning. "A good quarterback knows which team member he can trust with the ball and that's to whom he throws the passes. George was like that with those he knew and trusted. He had his favorite receivers and he knew he could trust us and we would do whatever we could to catch the pass and run with it."

***Greed and Scandal***

"I try to avoid what I think are the most serious of offensives against God. One is greed and the other is scandal," George professes, adding that his mother used to pray, "Lord, save my sons from sin, shame and blame."

In regard to greed, George said while he has always tried to make money, he never felt as if he was greedy. "I think this country, in general, has this excessive desire to get and to have. It's a tragedy and excessive greed is the thing that's most negatively affecting our country right now. It's more prevalent and it's more pervasive than people think."

He doesn't think greed stops "with a couple of guys" from Enron. "It's much deeper and it goes right down into the community. I see it as the main reason for the lack of confidence the average person has in the economy today."

The other fault George says he has always tried to avoid is scandal. He defines scandal as the corrupting of the young or virtuous, the encouragement of an activity or way of life that is criminal, corrupt or mean-spirited, reconciling an action that breaks a moral law. "Clinton's actions in the Lewinsky episode gave great scandal, and some movie stars lead scandalous lives and flaunt it in front of everyone, thus scandalizing the young," he said.

The world knows the United States, George says, through our media. "I think our movies and our television are full of filth. I call it scandal. The Muslims who have an entirely different philosophy than we have really have a point when they call the United States the Great Satan because all most know about us is what they see in movies and on television."

### *Always on Duty*

Seeker remembers that no matter what your job was for George, you were always at his beck and call.

"One day at about 6 p.m., DeEtta Sharp came in to my office and asked me if I would go pick George up at his house, which was about a mile from SeaWorld," said Seeker.

That day, George had driven to work and had jogged home and Seeker was to take George's car, pick him up and bring him back to work so he could have his car. "I was a young kid and scared to death of George because of his history," Seeker said, noting that he was wearing his regulation shirt, tie and jacket. He got in George's car, turned on the air conditioner, switched the radio off the classical music station and drove over to the condo, pulled in the driveway and honked the horn, as he was instructed to do.

It was a warm summer evening, but George came out in a full sweat suit, with the hood pulled up tight, showing only his face. He got in the car with Seeker and immediately turned the radio back to the classical station, turned the air conditioner off and the heater on. "I want to sweat," he told Seeker. "I found that very inconsiderate of him, but of course I didn't say anything. All the way back to the office he kept saying how great it felt and he's just sweating up a storm. Well, I was sweating up a storm too, but I was in a coat and tie."

### *George Could be Frustrating*

Gary Zuercher traveled quite a bit with George and his stories on how frustrating and absent-minded the guy could be would fill another book in and of itself. Here's one of the best:

"One time in Seville, Spain he said he wanted to get an early start the next morning. I said I couldn't agree more. We were headed to Cordoba and then to Cadiz and then to Algeciras. We were going to spend the night at Gibraltar and then take the boat over to Tangier, Morocco and spend some time in Morocco. We had a car and had driven from Madrid.

"We agreed that we would get started no later than 8:30 the next morning. My wife was with me and George's daughter Chrislyn, was with him. That night he got absolutely shit-faced. The next morning we're all up and ready to go at 8:30, and no George. At 9:15, I called his room and he asks what time is it? I said it's 9:15, George; it's 45 minutes after we're leaving.

"He told me to call him back in about 45 minutes

because he hadn't slept well. I called him back about 10 and he's just getting out of bed and said he wanted to take a shower, and then he would be down. By that time I'm really boiling, and my wife is kicking the shit out of me for getting her ready so early. We had checked out and we're sitting in the hotel lobby twiddling our thumbs.

"About 10:45, George comes down in his bathing trunks and says he was going to take a quick dip and then have a little breakfast before we left. We got into an argument there in the lobby and we were all pissed-off at each other. Finally, we left about 1 that afternoon," Zuercher recalls. "We barely spoke for the rest of the trip and my wife and I got our own rental car and went off on our own."

**Zoo Friends**

*Within a month of the opening of SeaWorld in 1964, Dr. Charlie Schroeder, the legendary director of the San Diego Zoo, who George calls one of the most extraordinary men he ever met, visited SeaWorld. The two became fast friends, a friendship that lasted until the end of Schroeder's life in March 1991. He wanted SeaWorld to be successful for San Diego's benefit and knew that two world-class animal-based attractions was a good draw for the community. George said that through the years, he stole a couple of Schroeder's employees and that Schroeder stole a couple of his, but they remained friends and helped each other when asked. "We always had a great relationship with the zoo, which is fortunate for all of us!" George recalls.*

- CHAPTER 46 -

# The Absent Minded Genius

George has a reputation for losing things and for being non-technical. He still doesn't know how to run a computer or return an email. He does own a computer and makes sure his secretaries know how to work everything.

Gary Zuercher and George took a three-week trip to Jakarta, Singapore, Hong Kong and Tokyo. "I think he lost his airline ticket in every city. He bought a very expensive leather coat in Germany and when we arrived in Jakarta, he said, 'Oh my God, I lost my coat.' Thankfully, another person with us had picked it up but hadn't said anything. He just loses everything, and I've decided it's because he has his mind on other things. Think about it, if you don't have to keep track of belongings, that clears your mind to be creative."

### *Ticket Please*

Seeker remembers flying from San Diego to Los Angeles with George to meet with an advertising agency. DeEtta Sharp, George's secretary knew Seeker was going with George and briefed him before they left. She told him to take George's wallet and airline ticket from him as soon as they joined up. "I said, ma'am, why should I do that and she said if I didn't he would lose them."

They got to the airport and Seeker asked, "Sir, may I have your wallet?" and George mumbles, "Yeah, yeah, here," and gives Seeker his wallet. "I said I also need your return airline ticket after we get on. He asked why, and I said Ms. Sharp said you'd lose it. He said, 'bullshit. I'm not giving you my airline ticket.' He was just as defiant as hell."

They arrived in L.A., got their work done and on their way back to the airport George looks over at Seeker and asks, "Do you have my airline ticket?" Seeker says, "No, sir, you wouldn't give it to me." George looks around and says, "Damn, I've lost my ticket, why didn't you take my airline ticket?"

As he proved many times, George didn't only lose leather jackets and airline tickets. In the early 1970s during his SeaWorld days in San Diego, George had three cars and a Bertram 31 boat. It wasn't uncommon for all four to be missing at one time, according to Jan Schultz.

**The Pioneer**

*No one else in this business can lay claim to the invention of two major types of theme parks, the sea life park and the waterpark, each a major industry in itself. George Millay is brilliant. He's one of a kind and a true pioneer.*
*- Harrison "Buzz" Price, semi-retired legend*

They were always in the greater San Diego area but George usually had no idea where they were. He would meet one or more of the guys at a restaurant and they would have dinner and more than likely, numerous drinks. George would then take a taxi home, leaving the car or the boat at the restaurant. Maybe he'd do that again the next night or the next several nights, and not realize it until he ran out of transportation.

At that point he would go to Art Ashcraft, the head of security at SeaWorld and ask him to find his vehicles. Ashcraft had an extra set of keys specifically for situations such as this. "I don't know whether he forgot that he arrived by boat or car, but he'd just leave it there and take a cab home. It got to be pretty funny," Schultz said.

Seeker went to work one Saturday morning and walked into the kitchen to get coffee only to find water all over the floor and counter tops. As he was cleaning it up, George came in. "Hey, do you know anything about making coffee? I think I've made a big damn mess here. Could you make a pot for us?"

He still laughs at that morning. "You have a brilliant man here who has built all these restaurants and parks but he still doesn't know how to make coffee."

- CHAPTER 47 -

# George As Husband, Father & Grandfather

"How can you live with a man like that?" That's the most-asked question of Anne Millay, the loving and devoted wife of George since 1963. "It's like living with a moving storm, thunder and lightning included," is her stock reply.

That was her answer in 1963 "and it's still appropriate today," Anne laughs, noting that she has never, as most wives have at some time or another in their marriage, had to kick her husband in the butt to get out and do something. "Can you imagine? I couldn't be in the same room with a man like that. I could never have put up with that. Life is short and there are things to do," she said.

During the early years of their marriage, George was seldom gone for more than a few days at a time. As the business grew to other cities, he would set up an apartment or condo in that city. He had condos in Orlando and Arlington, Texas, and would commute from San Diego.

How could she put up with her husband being gone so much is another question asked of Anne. "What most people don't realize, is that he was rarely gone for more than two weeks at a time. He would buzz back here for a long weekend or even a week at a time," she said, adding that they talked at least once every day. "He called every single evening from wherever he was - Orlando, Singapore, Brazil, to talk with me and whatever children were around."

Through those phone calls, George stayed in touch and was always aware of what was happening at home. He could never stand to be away for too long at a time. When he was busy and couldn't fly home, he would ask Anne to join him. "I can't tell you how many times I was on a plane with any of the kids I could pull together at the last minute and off we'd go."

Gavin, the youngest of Anne and George's children, says many people think of his mother as weak because of his dad's

*The Millay's at Chrislyn's Baptism, Aug. 3, 1967. With Anne and George, from left, are Pat, Chrislyn, and Gar.*

strong presence and openly chauvinistic attitude. However, he is quick to point out that, "My mom has always been a very strong figure and I never witnessed one thing that made me think she was submissive to him. She knows how to handle him and that's what she did. She is a highly intelligent woman, well-educated, and has wonderfully profound views on all matters."

### *George as the Father*

Anne, totally aware of George's "management through intimidation" policies at the office, would try to intercept him at the door when he came home from work, especially during the early days. "I would meet him at the door with a fond embrace, and I could immediately tell when he was full of himself and still on the power trip of being the big boss," Anne explained.

"I would lead him inside and we would sit and talk, maybe have a drink, whatever it would take for him to decompress. It was like a cooling-off period until he realized that I wasn't his secretary and his children didn't work for him. That we were wife, we were children, and guess what? You're home. Most of the time he came down quickly and we could get on with our family life."

George was also deeply involved with the raising of their

children. "He was king of the discipline for all the children," Anne notes.

### *Along Comes their First*

Pat Millay, George and Anne's oldest, was born in December 1963, a year before SeaWorld was born. Pat doesn't remember life without the marine park or without Shamu. "They were always a part of everything," he said.

His first memories come from 1968 when the Richfield Hydrofoils would come over from the park and pick up George to take him to work. Pat also remembers the helicopter landing on the beach in front of the house to pick up or deliver his dad. "He'd wave to everyone, get in, and take off for the one mile journey to the park," Pat laughs.

Garrick was born 16 months after Pat and the two shared a close childhood. "You know, we didn't really understand what we had. We were definitely advantaged and we had a lot of material things as well as wonderful opportunities. I don't think we were spoiled because he made sure we weren't. We didn't realize what we had was special, until he pointed it out to us," said Gar, as Garrick is called.

George constantly made sure the boys knew they had a

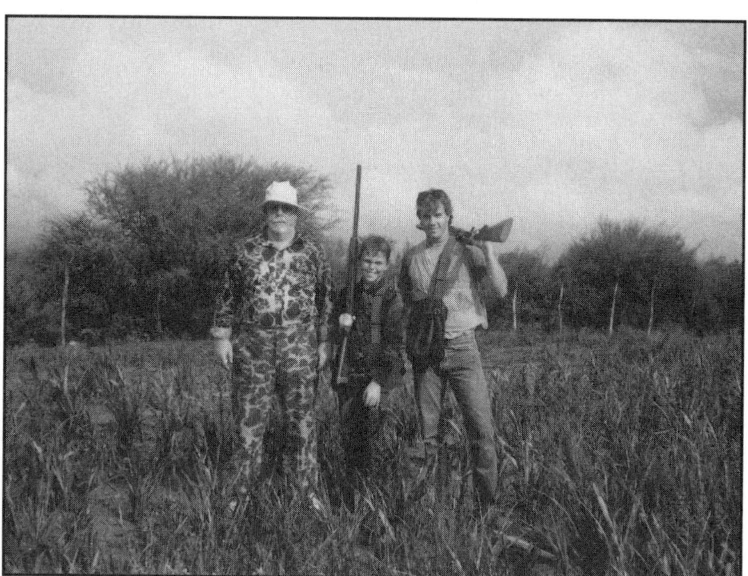

*George, Gavin and Pat Millay, on a 1981 dove hunting trip to Lago Guerrero, Mexico.*

good life, by pointing out to them those who didn't have the same luxuries. When the two boys were in their early teens, he took them on trips to South and Central American Third World countries where they would hunt, but also where they would get a close-up look at how people lived.

"Dad took us on those trips to demonstrate just how fortunate we were. We'd come back to sunny San Diego and he would tell us to get down on our knees and thank God for what we had," Gar recalls. "He's a tremendous leader by example and always knows how to get a point across."

Gavin, the youngest of the family, also has the same perspective. "He taught us, mostly by example, how not to act like we came from wealth. He wanted us to act more blue collar and be more appreciative and respectful," Gavin notes.

### *The Boss' Son*

George also taught that being the boss' sons wouldn't take them far in this world, especially in his organization. When Gar was a sophomore in high school, the Millay family spent the summer in Arlington, Texas at Seven Seas, the park George ran for one season. "He gave me the crappiest jobs in the park, just to teach me. I'm sure he told the supervisor, 'Hey, put my son to work, and I want him doing the shittiest, hardest things so he will learn what he has.'"

Pat said they all had a normal childhood and grew up in what he calls "a kind of male chauvinist pig household." Chrislyn, the only female offspring, had to deal with that, living with a bunch of macho guys, plus ex-jock George.

"When George Millay left his office and strolled through the park you had better have had your act together if you worked for him," adds Pat. "Your hair length better fit the standards of the company. Your shirt had better be tucked in because he wasn't going to miss one detail. Your area had better be picked up. I would walk with him through the park and I remember people cowering when he walked through their area. That made quite an impression on me."

Gar has a similar story that made a big impact on how he remembers his dad as boss man. "I was seven years old and I remember walking through SeaWorld holding dad's hand. He sees a guy about 50 yards away, a teenaged employee, and he goes, 'Son, get over here.' The kid sprints over. My dad goes into his wallet, whips out a $20 bill, grabs the (already) short hair by the kid's temple and tells him if he doesn't have a shorter haircut by Monday, he's fired. Dad gave the kid $20, and haircuts were only $2. He was intimidating on one hand, but at the same time very generous."

***The Physically Fit Sons***

"We kids feared him for many of the same reasons as his employees did," said Pat. He wanted things to be his way. He would jog home and we were supposed to be waiting for him. He had a checklist of military physical training activities for us to do: running, pull-ups, sit-ups, and pushups. We had an hour of physical training and then we had to run."

Gar remembers those runs with a smile. "He would make us run to what used to be called Vacation Village and we'd have to get a brochure from the rack in the lobby to prove we'd been there. That was after we had already done all the pushups and sit-ups. We thought we got smart one day and took a bunch of different brochures and stashed them under a bridge right around the corner from our house," Gar recalled.

*The Millay Clan gathers for a picture following the opening of Wet'n Wild Orlando, 1977. From left, are Gar, George, Chrislyn, Gavin, Anne, and Pat.*

The two would run around the corner and then walk to the bridge, sit for a while, take a brochure from their stash, walk a few blocks and then run the rest of the way home. They found quickly that their dad knew all the tricks. "He must have been timing us one day, or maybe it was just fatherly intuition, but he knew something was up. We were walking home, he drove by and we were caught, big time."

Pat said all the physical workouts actually proved worthwhile and gave him and Gar an advantage. "While the other kids were struggling to do pull-ups in physical education classes at school, we were knocking out 15 at a time. Dad pushed us ahead of the curve," Pat said, acknowledging that a person could look back on those days with a great deal of negativism, but he has none. "I have nothing but good, funny memories about those days."

Gar said he was in great shape, even though he ate a bowl of Captain Crunch every night after school. "During the President's Physical Fitness at All Hallow's School, in the fourth grade, I did 46 chin-ups, which was probably the national record at the time. No one else could do more than 10," Gar remembers.

George oversaw physical training for Gavin as well. "From what my brothers say, he was tougher on them and eased up a little on me." Daughter Chrislyn didn't face the daily regime.

***Playing Hard Ball***

Gar went to the University of Arizona on a baseball scholarship and played right field when his team won the College World Series in 1986. Gar was one of the heroes of that final game with Florida State going 3 for 4 with a home run, double, and four RBIs. At age 21, he was drafted by the Texas Rangers baseball club and ended up playing professional baseball for eight years. First he played in the Texas League, spent two and a half years in Triple-A for the Rangers, and then spent a year in Taiwan and a year in Italy playing pro ball. During those last two years, he rarely saw his father.

He said some of his happiest memories are when he played in the Texas League and his dad would travel to watch him play. Afterward the two would go out to dinner together and talk for hours. "It felt very good and I knew he was proud of me. He had a son who was a professional ball player. It was a wonderful time of life for him and for me and for us together."

Pat says Gar's baseball career brought many good memories for him as well. "When Gar started playing minor league ball, at first he was in the Texas League, Dad would send me a plane ticket and say, 'Hey, your brother has a three-game series in Little Rock, meet me there.' That was awesome!"

George only found true success when he worked for himself, a positive role model not wasted on Gar. "I now own my own business and it's absolutely because of what I've seen him be able to accomplish. He's always been his own boss and I've never had a boss. His success made me realize I could do the same thing."

In the male-dominated Millay household, two sons were born within two years of each other, then several years later, a daughter, and then five years later, another son.

"Pat and I are really of a different generation than Chrislyn and Gavin because my dad was at SeaWorld then and we grew up with him being home just about every night," said Gar. Chrislyn was on the cusp of George's career change and Gavin grew up when George was at Wet'n Wild, and away from home quite often.

### *The Female Arrives*

Chrislyn could have been doomed, but George adapted to her quite easily, Anne said. "He would be barking commands at the boys one minute and as soon as she walked into the room, his voice would be softer and sweeter. He's a very affectionate person but I didn't see it much with the boys, but certainly with Chrislyn. The boys, of course, noticed their father's voice change and they would eyeball her. The boys felt like second class citizens when she was around."

The lovely daughter was definitely a princess "which was maddening when we were young," recalls Pat. "Hey, how come she's not getting spanked? She was doing the same thing we were doing." She wasn't getting spanked because that's not something George believes you do to girls. He has a deep respect for women, not necessarily a respect for their skills or their equality, but a respect for the gender. "That's something I've always had, and I think it came from him," said Pat.

Surprisingly, Chrislyn was able to fight off the inevitable destiny of being a Tomboy, even with all that testosterone in the house. Anne would take her to the ballpark and explain baseball to her and Chrislyn would stare into space. She turned out to be a first-string Little Leaguer in softball and was a good hitter and a fast pitcher. She went into high school and played on the freshman softball team.

During her sporting years, "there wasn't a hair on her head out of place. She had painted, acrylic nails and she was so well-groomed, Chrislyn's coach once told me she always looked more like she was ready for a photographer than for the shortstop position," Anne laughs. "She eventually became a cheerleader and showed off that side of her skills for three years."

*The Millay Clan in their penthouse home in San Diego, 1987. From left, are Pat, Gar, Chrislyn, Anne (seated), George, and Gavin (seated).*

Chrislyn is now national advertising and marketing manager for Hitachi's Home Product's Division in Southern California.

Then along came offspring number four and everyone had their hands full with Gavin. "He was our only, what I call situationally hyperactive child," Anne said. "He was the only one who consistently talked back to George. Gavin was the one who'd take him on from the beginning, even as a little child, and George loved every minute of it."

George always enjoyed the sport of arguing and combating. "I have spunk and he likes spunk. I think that's why he married me," Anne guessed. "Spunk is what Gavin has. He wasn't intimidated and wouldn't cower or lay down like a doormat. They built an amazing relationship that continues to this day, all because he was strong enough to stand up to George."

"My sister probably had the toughest time growing up in our family," Gavin said. "She had two older brothers who were pretty nice to her, and then me. I wasn't the nicest kid in the world, even to her. Since we were closer in age, it was like Pat and Gar and then Chrislyn and me. We interacted more with each other than we did with the older boys."

***The Father-Son Lessons***

All four children, in one way or another, worked in the parks as youngsters, but only Pat chose to be the prodigal son and come back into the fold as an adult.

Pat wasn't sure his relationship with his father could hold up once he went to work for him at Wet'n Wild in 1991. "I wasn't sure we could translate that father-son thing to a chief executive - junior executive thing, but we really did. I think it started working when I realized I didn't know anything about the business and I found myself going to him for advice. That's when he became a mentor, as well as a father."

Pat said his dad allowed him to think things through and make his own decisions before bringing them to him for a final analysis. "I also benefited from his experience and wisdom and I really mean that word wisdom. There is not an over-abundance of wise people in the world. When it came to the big picture issues I went to him," Pat said.

Sometimes it was just the two of them sitting down and talking for hours in George's office. "We would sit there and talk through things. He would explain why he didn't trust certain people and why he wanted things done a certain way and he schooled me on how to protect myself from being taken advantage of in business deals. I learned what he really wanted in a concept and then I was better able to translate it for the company. I might have been the guy on the airplane going to do the deal, but in my bag I had George Millay's direction and guidance."

When Wet'n Wild was sold in 1998, Pat was able to put his vast knowledge of development and construction to good use. He is now a partner in Del Mar Heritage, a San Diego-based real estate development company.

***Don't be Hokey, Dad!***

Gavin admits he thought much of what his dad told him during his youth seemed "funny or hokey, some old guy trying to impart wisdom on me." He also admits that most of what George told him over the years proved to be true. "I always kidded him that he was right a great deal of the time, and of course, he brings that up every time I appear to doubt him," laughs Gavin. "Looking back, I can say much of the information he has given me through the years has been real useful nuggets."

George pushed Pat and Gar in different ways, just as he always pushed his employees in different ways, realizing each was different. He pushed Gar to work harder at his trade. With Pat, it was his education. "He would tell me to take these classes and prepare for life," Pat said.

"With Gar it was, get yourself prepared for your sports career by doing this. Those are two different mindsets. Dad realized each of us was different, saw early on the direction we were going, and was smart enough to push each one of us in the right direction. For that, I have a profound gratitude." Today, Gar owns United Sports Consultants in San Diego, a marketing and event coordinator for football and baseball athletes. He is the only sibling who runs his own company.

All four children said they benefited greatly and learned much from being around George's entourage of high quality colleagues. "He always surrounded himself with the best people he could find. We grew up in an environment surrounded by people who were the best in their trades - the best marketing people, the best construction people, and the best finance people. That in itself was an amazing education," said Pat.

There was really a fifth child with whom the Millay offspring grew up. "Wet'n Wild was as much a child to him as any of us," said Pat, noting that the waterpark was a sister. "It's the princess. It got dad's tender loving care and most of the attention for awhile."

***Doting after Granddaughters***

One must sense a wonderful case of irony in the fact that George has seven grandchildren, all girls. "There goes the male-oriented Millay clan," kids Anne. "George and I agreed on the rules of a male-dominated household, but now, with these sweet, little thin-boned, frail creatures running around, it's quite a change. One a year for seven straight years, girls just kept popping out."

Anne said all those girls "were a shock to our system," but she got with it very quickly, and George "was right behind me."

She points out that George's biggest achievements were behind him when the granddaughters first started arriving and those cute little things dressed in pink "soon became his second round" of achievements. "I think the girls bring out the warm side of him and today, since he's less focused on business, he has time, and a desire, to let those feelings bubble up," said Anne.

Long-time friend and colleague John Seeker feels the reason George's life has been prolonged this long has been his grandchildren. "I definitely think they have added to his longevity," he supposed. Seeker said he has been quite surprised and very pleased at George's reaction to having granddaughters. "I never thought I'd see George act that way. He looks at them and appears to melt. He makes noises. He's like a new parent," Seeker said.

Youngest son Gavin smiles when he says the life of rough and gruff George now revolves around his granddaughters. Gavin said he saw an almost immediate "radical transformation, from a hard-ass to a softie when his granddaughters started arriving. The entire family pulled closer together and I think mom and dad became closer as a result of all those cute little granddaughters."

George and Anne live within 40 miles of all of their grandkids and Gavin says on average George sees one of the girls five days a week. Gavin, who has seen his share of George's wrath over the years, says he looks at George and sees a totally different person when he is around his grandchildren.

"First of all, it's quite obvious he has a true, profound love for these little girls. The fact that he dotes over these granddaughters makes for an even better story, because we all know that George Millay has always been a man's man," adds Gavin.

- CHAPTER 48 -

# George Turns 70 & Searches for His Next Big Idea

An elegant surprise party was thrown in honor of George's 70th birthday in July 1999. For most mortals, the party with nearly 80 of his closest friends and family would have been the perfect landmark occasion on which to start slowing down. However, within two months of the party, George had his next big idea.

Daughter Chrislyn and her husband Dominique went to Anne with the party idea. There had been a huge beach party 20 years earlier for his 50th, and Chrislyn thought it was time for another.

Chrislyn organized it all and her husband put together a top-notch video salute to George. That was only part of it, according to Anne. The big challenge was to get him there. "He hates these kinds of things," she notes.

It was held at the Torrey Pines Golf Course at what was then a Sheraton Hotel. George and his family were never big at celebrating birthdays or anniversaries, so Anne knew she would have to do "a very good job of lying" if she wanted to surprise him and get him there. She created an elaborate scheme that involved her sister, Pat, and a fictitious chef who allegedly worked at the hotel.

### *George Puts on a Tie*

On the day they were all to visit the chef and have dinner with him at the hotel, George dressed up, which was quite unusual. "George loves to dress casual and it's always hard to get him in a tie," she said.

"We got him there, on time, and all the guests were outside among the palm trees waiting for him. As we walked in at the top of the staircase, he looked out and saw the group of well-wishers," said Anne.

Wise to the scheme at that point, George stopped, looked at Anne and told her he was not going in. Anne looked back and hissed, "You're going to this thing if it kills you." He turned back to the people, made up his mind, and proceeded. There was a pre-party and then a sit-down dinner. A few people, including Dave Tallichet, Jan Schultz, and Ron Harper made remarks before they viewed the video presentation Dominique had put together.

Anne said since George didn't sell tickets to the event, and didn't have any control of what was going to happen, he at first felt very uncomfortable, then emotional, then almost overcome by the outpouring of love shown by those attending.

***Back to the Sea***

In August 1999, a few weeks after that surprise party, Anne and George drove north to Santa Cruz County, California to visit their friends Paul Kilmartin, a friend of George's since high school, and his wife Brigid. On their way home, they stopped at the Monterey Bay Aquarium to visit with Dave Powell, whom George had hired as SeaWorld's aquarist nearly 35 years earlier.

On a quick tour of the aquarium, Powell took George into the California Reef, an exhibit he had designed. "Big Red was impressed," George said of his reaction to the exhibit. "I stood transfixed before this Marine Cathedral in awe at what Dave and his cohorts had created. I resented anyone crowding around me. I wanted to be alone to silently worship this miracle of God and man."

Later that day, as they were heading back to San Diego, George mentioned to Anne that the many distractions he witnessed while viewing Powell's exhibit - school kids, lecturers, open doors to rooms with running motors and noisy pumps, and glare - all had interfered and spoiled the solitude so necessary to enjoy such an exhibit. "There was too much confusion," added George.

For the next several months, his thoughts continued to center "on that fantastic display and how it could be modified or presented in a more quiet and serene environment." Waxing poetic, George said he "wanted the setting of an ancient German Cathedral with just a sprinkling of aged worshippers in silent meditation." That's what that display deserved, "not the ranting of a Coney Island patron and humming motors and pumps!" he added.

As he thought about the necessary silence, he remembered the quiet solitude he experienced inside a diving bell that he would often ride as a boy at the Long Beach Pike and Catalina Embarcadero in the mid-1930s. Air pressure would push the bell four to five feet under water in a circular steel tank. Riders would look through a small porthole at a few hardy fish swimming around in the murky waters. Following a minute or so under water, pneumatic pressure was released and the bell would be catapulted to the surface.

### *Another Water-Based Patent*

His creative juices began to flow. Instead of a tubular acrylic tank holding the fish, he reasoned it might be a good idea to put people in a vertical tubular acrylic tank and let the fish swim around them. Then he took another leap of creativity. He could transport the people in and out of the tube on a revolving elevator - an underwater mini-sky tower.

George brought Dave Powell and Billy Watts, the ex-SeaWorld and Wet'n Wild designer into the deal. Then he brought in Walter Larson and Jeff Novotny, veteran and finan-

*George Millay and Dave Powell viewing Powell's California Reef exhibit at the Monterey Bay Aquarium, 1999.*

cially successful ride manufacturers. Sea Venture, George's next big idea, was born.

A U.S. Patent was granted for Sea Venture in 2001. Full colored architectural drawings and cross-sections were printed, a video created and a brochure was produced. Sales activities commenced. Three different sized capsules were designed, each carrying up to 800 passengers per hour. The installed ride would cost approximately $750,000.

George hit the road with his creation, feeling confident he had hit another home run. "For two years I scoured the industry, crisscrossing the globe pushing the need for our product. Every potential user was identified and visited," said George. "Zip - Nada - Zero. No interest."

The lack of interest in Sea Venture still has George baffled. "Why I haven't sold a Sea Venture is troubling. Is it a lousy concept? I don't think so. Is it too costly? If you are building a 400,000-gallon exhibit for $5 million, adding a Sea Venture to it will cost an additional $2.5 million dollars. Not bad when considering its marketing potential and the word of mouth it will generate," George said.

He has identified one potential problem as to why he hasn't sold any to date. He is quite candid in describing it as he sees it. Few aquariums in today's marketplace are built by the private, risk-taking sector. Most are built with public money, by states or municipalities. "I have tried to market it to an industry where unsupervised architects work for civil servants. The aquariums they design and build are operated by bureaucratic zoologists and financed by political entities."

Except for a Ripley's Aquarium, a Monterey Bay Aquarium, and one or two other creative risk takers, the aquarium industry is "a dull, uninspired collection of poorly attended and financially distressed institutions still being designed, built and operated with a Dark Age mentality," George claims.

Not that he has given up on Sea Venture, but George is currently applying for a second patent on another aquarium type ride that is a little more thrilling and appealing to a younger demographic. George laughs at himself for coming up with yet another idea for an aquarium. "I can't sell my first one, so what do I do? I go out and create a second one."

***Another Try for San Diego***

In early 2003, the Port of San Diego issued a Request for Proposal for a 20-acre site on port property on its embarcadero. George went to Bob Masterson, president of Ripley Entertainment and proposed that Ripley enter the competition with George as a partner, a deal that Masterson readily agreed upon. The development site was extraordinary and included 1,000-feet of bay front.

Only two major entities met the port's deadlines for proposals. The Ripley proposal was innovative, entertainment oriented - a potential gold mine to the port, according to George. It complemented rather than competed with other tenants and would have made a destination area of the entire embarcadero.

The proposed complex contained a 70,000-sq. ft. two-story Ripley aquarium with a 350-seat restaurant featuring a view into a tropical fish tank and splendid bay views. It also included George's Sea Venture as the primary feature of the complex. Accompanying the aquarium was a 30,000-sq. ft. dinner theater, a Ripley's Believe it or Not! museum, a Japanese Pearl Village and various other aquatic participatory activities.

The Ripley group and George threw a bundle of time, energy, innovation and capital into the proposal. "It was by far the finest exploratory effort I have even been associated with," George contends. The competitor's proposal was also impressive but George felt it lacked vision and optimistically overstated potential revenues to the port.

In an unexpected move by one of the commissioners and against the recommendations of staff, the commission decided to reject both proposals - too commercial - not enough open space. "Sorry about that," the commissioners told both entrants. "We changed our minds, and want to go a different route."

George was quite miffed about the entire deal, and feels that the Ripley/Millay proposal was never fully and seriously considered. "The incredible team we had are true professionals and deserved much better treatment from the port than they received," noted George.

Gar is amazed that his dad is still so active. "He has ideas left and right. It's unbelievable. I am amazed at some of his current ideas. He's 75 now and he knows he's running out of time and he wants to do so much more," Gar said. "He's slowing down physically, but his mind is still as sharp and creative as it has ever been."

- CHAPTER 49 -

# Trade Associations, Kudos & Awards

George pioneered two major genres of outdoor entertainment and he learned everything, from ride selection and marketing to development and business planning, the hard way - by trial and error. There was no one for him to turn to for answers and at that time, there was no one out there to copy. He did everything from scratch.

***Don't Tell them our Secrets!***

He didn't want to share his knowledge with those who would be his competitors. He felt they should learn the hard way as well. That's the major reason he never had much to do with any of the industry trade associations for most of his career. The fraternal nature of trade associations encouraged sharing, and that's something he wasn't willing to do.

Attributing it to his conceit and ignorance, George never joined the International Assn. Of Amusement Parks & Attractions during his SeaWorld or his Wet'n Wild days. It wasn't until he was voted into the IAAPA Hall of Fame as a Living Legend in 1994, did he fully endorse and become friendly with the world's largest amusement industry trade organization.

"He was a real tough son-of-a-bitch before he received that award," said Larry Cochran, a former IAAPA president. "I think the significance of the award hit him and he mellowed after that."

After his Hall of Fame award in 1994, George served three years on the IAAPA Board of Directors, a role he immensely enjoyed. "I really did, and I looked forward to the board meetings where I was able to renew and cement many of my older relationships with such people as Larry Cochran, Carl Hughes of Kennywood Park, and the late Geoffrey Thompson of Blackpool Pleasure Beach in England."

### *Lifetime Achievement Award*

As this book was going to press, George learned that he was to receive the Lifetime Achievement Award from the World Waterpark Association (WWA), during that group's Symposium and Trade Show in Fort Lauderdale in October 2004.

The "Father of the Waterpark Industry" was set to be the keynote speaker at the gathering, the third time in which he has accepted that honor. Rick Root, the WWA's executive director, said no one else has ever given the keynote address three times. "It's only appropriate that George gets that distinction," Root notes.

George was to also receive a special proclamation from the WWA board, officially recognizing him as the "Father of the Waterpark Industry," a title he has unofficially held for decades. With this proclamation from the world's leading waterpark association, George will hold that official distinction forever.

Receiving the kudos from the WWA is quite an achievement, especially for a person who shunned the association for many years. While he was constantly courted to join the group during the 1970s and 1980s, he would have nothing to do with the WWA.

Of course he usually went to the group's trade shows to see what new products were out there, but that was where he drew the line. He forbade anyone in his company to serve on boards, committees, or on panel discussions. The meetings and gatherings of the waterpark association in those early years were only "disguised sales pitches by vendors and consultants looking for work," George said.

"I think it was Rick Faber and my son, Pat, who persuaded me to finally join the WWA. In the early days, I wouldn't even allow our guys to attend, because I knew others would want to talk with them about waterparks and I was extremely protective," admits George. "The waterpark industry was relatively new then and I didn't want to share our knowledge and help it grow any faster than it was already spreading. We had paid for our knowledge with our sweat, blood, and losses. Let them do the same thing and find out for themselves."

### *George is Honored*

George said he was "totally surprised" by his IAAPA Hall of Fame induction in 1994. He said many things didn't add up in the days approaching the induction, but he didn't realize what was happening until he walked into the theater at the IAAPA Convention that morning in Miami. Several people came up to him and escorted him to a special seat in front. He then understood that something was happening.

Anne was living in Texas at the time and she doesn't like to travel as much as George does, so he became suspicious when she informed him that she was going to Florida with him. Another clue was when Anne got up early to go to the meeting with George the morning of the ceremony. "For some reason Anne wanted me to go to this opening session which I've never gone to in my life. She's up at 6:30 that morning, and all dressed and ready to go. I said what the hell is going on here because she'd rarely done anything like that."

The week before Seeker and Pat set George up by telling him there was something they really wanted him to check out at that opening session of the convention.

The tough Millay admits that winning the Hall of Fame Award from the world's most prestigious industry organization and his peers, meant a great deal to him. "We all like to be admired and recognized and anyone who says they don't is a liar. You've got to be pretty cold, if you can't be proud to win an award like that, especially when you consider the list of previous winners that included C.V. Wood, Walt Disney, Marty Sklar, Buzz Price, Walter Knott, and Angus Wynne."

### *A Hollywood Award*

On October 4, 2003, two days before he underwent major cancer surgery to remove his right eye, George was honored by the Themed Entertainment Association (TEA), a Los Angeles-based trade group of designers, artists, developers and architects.

He was presented with the association's Lifetime Achievement Award. He says today that award was extra special for him since "I was already yesterday's news and that award was a great shot in the arm for me."

His award reads: "For having been judged to represent the highest standards of excellence and creative achievement in the arts and sciences of the Themed Entertainment Industry."

Ironically, George's designs for SeaWorld and for Wet'n Wild nearly always stayed away from intricate themeing and

**Signs of the Times**

*Every time I visit Orlando I take great satisfaction in seeing the Wet'n Wild and Sea World names plastered upon directional signs, on airport property, on the Bee Line Expressway and along the I-4 interstate. Just think, I muse, two companies I started are right up there with the Universal and Disney signs, being viewed by tens of millions of people annually. It gives this old man a warm and fuzzy feeling.*

*- George Millay*

storytelling. "We did some at SeaWorld, but as far as architecture goes, I don't normally like to theme. I don't mind themeing the show itself, inside the theater or pavilion, but I don't like to theme permanent buildings inside a recreational or amusement park." He adds though, "If you're a theme park you've got a theme, you have to stick with it."

Dressed in black tie and tuxedo, George accepted the award with graciousness and poise. His speech was clever and as unorthodox as most hoped it would be. He closed his short homily with these words:

*"At the offset of the Korean War, McArthur said, "How nice of Mars to send this old soldier just one more war.*

*"In that vein, to my fellow Social Security and Medicare compatriots bored and hating every minute of retirement; knowing we know more now than ever, but are now only the recipients of honey-do-this and honey-do-that - here's a thought. Let's fly to Greece and motor to Olympus to the Temples of Poseidon and Neptune and other gods of antiquity.*

*"At their altars, let's burn incense and on bended knee and in sonorous Gregorian tones of supplication, plead with these gods to send us "just one more deal!"*

The attendees roared with approval and gave George a standing ovation, filled with admiration and love.

- CHAPTER 50 -

# Epilogue, or Living Happily Ever After

*Monday, August 2, 2004*
*Riviera Drive, San Diego, California*

George sleeps late this morning. He walks downstairs and looks out at the sailboats on Mission Bay. He hears the voices of joggers as they tread happily along the walkway in front of the penthouse in which he and Anne live.

He's excited. Today, he will see two of his seven beloved granddaughters. Later this morning, he is to go downtown and meet a few officials to discuss further plans for his new professional dinner theater complex that he's developing in San Diego.

Life goes on. He walks across the hallway to his office, listens to his voice mails, and looks at his computer, only wishing he knew how to retrieve emails. He'll have to wait for his secretary, Jeri Jean to come in and print those out for him.

He calls his biographer to see if it's too late to add a couple more thoughts to the book that he has put so much heart and soul into this summer. It's too late to add anything else, but he's reassured that the book will be delivered to the printer this afternoon. It will be published in time to debut at the 40th SeaWorld Alumni Reunion, set to be held at SeaWorld San Diego on September 18.

On top of one bookshelf is a hard hat with "Tragic Mountain" printed across the front, a dire memory of the chaotic couple of years he spent creating, building and operating Magic Mountain amusement park. His IAAPA Hall of Fame Award and his TEA Lifetime Achievement Award hold down honorable spots on the shelves.

There are piles of notebooks with old presentations bulging from the binders. Piles of manila folders contain evidence of his illustrious career. Video tapes of his project presentations and his TV appearances are piled haphazard on the shelves.

*George Millay, 2003*

He walks across the room, stops to think where he was going, laughs, shakes his head and walks back to the penthouse.

Life goes on, and it's good. He and Anne spend time with their four children, and their grandchildren. They dine out often, and they spend a great deal of time talking to each other and thanking God for this wonderful journey on which they have been. Their 40-year marriage is stronger than it's ever been, and they appreciate each other more than they ever have.

Retirement? Never. Why spoil a good thing?

Section Two

# TRIBUTES AND ACCOLADES

*The following five chapters*
*feature the people who have*
*meant the most to George*
*through the years.*

*Here, he pays homage*
*to those who have helped him,*
*loved him, supported him, challenged him,*
*and helped him maintain his sense of humor*
*through his amazing journey.*

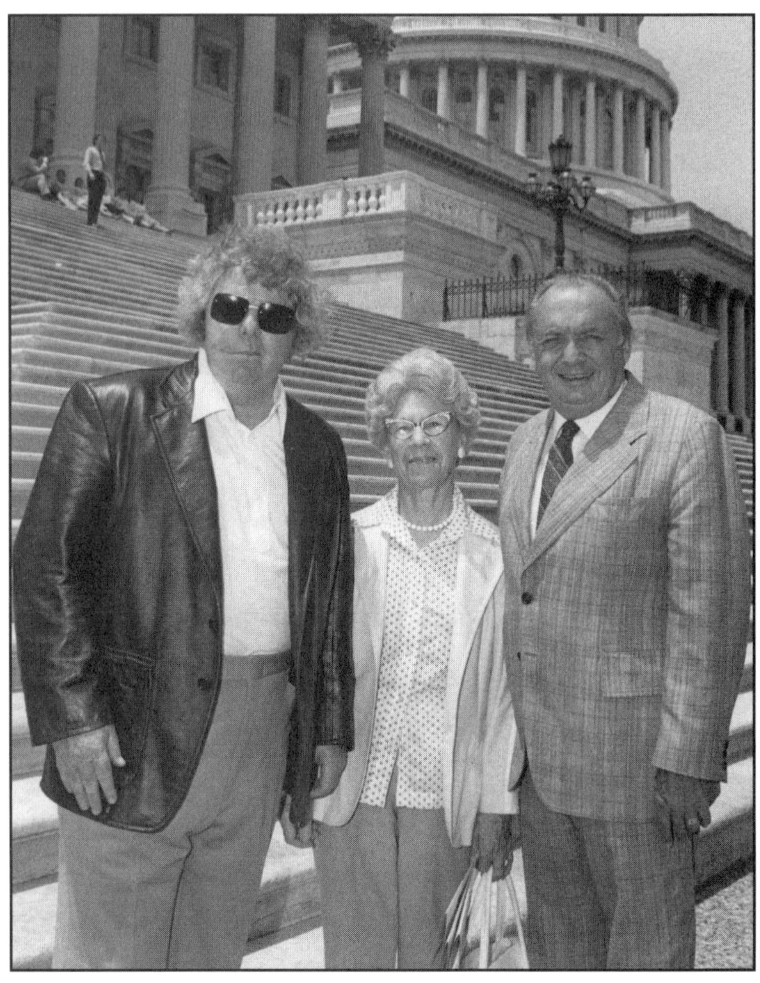

*George Millay, left, and his mother Anna, took a trip together to Washington D.C. in 1982, where they met with Congressman Bob Wilson.*

- CHAPTER 51 -

# Mother and Wife: The Dominant Forces

### *In George's Own Words:*

There is no question that Elizabeth Anna Brannigan and Anne Therese Reul have been the dominant and preeminent forces in my life. Each in her own way and quite differently, they encouraged and pushed me to attempt. Both realized that I wasn't much of an organizational man, didn't take to regimentation or regulation.

A great saint once said, "Peace is the tranquility of order," and both women constantly reminded me that there was little peace in my life. Out of chaos sometimes comes progress, so I like to think.

Both women stood back, held their breath and let their son and husband do this thing called being a "risk taker." A half dozen times in the last 50-plus years, first my mother then my dear pal Anne, have watched me roll the dice. Fortunately I have won more than I have lost. A couple of times in the 1970s and then again in the 1990s things got a little hairy.

Mom was gone, but as always Anne was at the hearth-side. Steady, caring and compassionate as old Red came home sometimes licking his wounds, sometime victorious, sometimes telling her to cut her budget. She never questioned my actions or uttered a reprimand. Just let her maintain her home and raise her children; that was all she asked. If either were jeopardized then I would hear from her.

My mother was married to a very conservative man. Anne's father was the same. Maybe they welcomed a difference in attitude and pursuits in their son and husband. All I know is that I have been blessed by their predominant presence in my life.

- CHAPTER 52 -

# Top 3 Most Influential People in My Life

When a person looks back over a career, he often wonders who were the ones that made the most difference in his life. During the process of reminiscing for this book, George said his choices for those who most influenced his business life are "simple and unequivocal - two friends till death and one a contemptible adversary."

### *In George's Own Words:*

***Milt Shedd, Fraternity Brother***

Milt Shedd, a fraternity brother eight years my senior steered me into a career in the investment-brokerage business upon graduation from UCLA. I never enjoyed the business and it really bored me, but it did present me with the education of how to raise capital.

The Reef Restaurant was the result of that knowledge. Later, Shedd was a 50% contributor to the fund-raising activities leading to the financing of SeaWorld San Diego. Without his help the San Diego Park would not have come about.

His insatiable drive for power and his "bull in a china shop" approach to everything he attempted from fishing to finances led after 12 years of harassment, to my resignation. A couple of years later that approach led to the sale of the company to Harcourt, Brace Jovanovich for peanuts.

Despite my misfortune at his hands I do admit to his making quite a significant positive contribution. However, I blame him for bringing about a most disruptive and destructive financial event that nearly destroyed not only me, but my family as well. He also caused a dire financial loss to all of the SeaWorld stockholders.

***David Tallichet, Mentor***

David Tallichet stands clearly at the top pedestal of George's earthly icons. Dave took me from an unsophisticated stock and bond salesman to a partner in a successful restaurant chain. He showed me by example how to structure and sell a deal. His creativity and his ability to dominate in all business situations became a valuable textbook for me in the following years.

"What would Dave do?" I would always ask myself. Of course the money I made with Dave became the foundation of everything I did thereafter. No Reef, no Castaway, no SeaWorld, no Wet'n Wild. Tallichet has a reputation of being a rough, tough son-of-a-bitch but to me he has been one great teacher and I treasure his friendship.

***Al Slavik, Financier***

In the mid 1970s money was tough to raise, venture capital was scarce, the Vietnam War, Watergate, oil embargos, and a huge jump in interest rates all occurred simultaneously, causing three to four years of great uncertainty.

Al Slavik and I had been partners in the ill-fated Zsa Zsa Gabor Cosmetics deal. He invested in our ABC deal in Arlington, Texas in 1975 at Seven Seas, which fortunately made a moderate profit. Al and I had one good and one bad business venture under our belts together when Wet'n Wild came along. Like SeaWorld earlier, I had most of my financing in place, but just not quite enough to finish the project.

Once he saw the plans and the location of Wet'n Wild Orlando, Al said, "George I'll buy the land and lease it back to you." A smart move by a guy used to making smart moves. All because Big Al had the vision and confidence in his buddy George to stake him on some crazy waterpark venture in central Florida, it became a reality. Al is gone now and they don't make guys like him anymore. He was an open, friendly, gregarious, generous guy, but shrewd from start to finish.

- CHAPTER 53 -

# The SeaWorld Pioneering All-Stars

The history of George's tenure at SeaWorld can easily be sorted into two chronological groups: the Early Years, from 1964 to 1968 and the Growth Years, from 1968 to 1974. During these two periods, a number of men and women joined his ranks and contributed greatly to the success and growth of the parks. They were all pioneers in the modern marine park genre, as George was. Few who went to work at SeaWorld had a roadmap to follow. It was new and they had to be creative, flexible, and maybe most importantly, they had to please George with their results. This group of individuals created, mostly by trial and error, many of the standards still being used in the industry today.

George has singled out a few who he feels contributed the most and brought growth and sophistication to the company. While many are mentioned elsewhere in this book, here are a few additional thoughts on those individuals.

## In George's Own Words:

### The Early Years

**Mike Downs** was with us from the get-go. An ex-Air Force B-47 bombardier, he left a job as VP of marketing for Pacific Southwest Airlines to take a crack at putting a small marine park on the map. Mike built a diversified department that covered advertising, sales and public relations, and he truly got the best out of his staff and consultants.

Mike staffed his various departments with aggressive, young professionals and stayed with us until the beginning of our Ohio venture. He came to me one day and said SeaWorld had been solicited to help build Opryland in Nashville, Tennessee. I said for God's sake Mike our plate is full.

A month later Mike came into my office and told me he had just accepted a job as GM of the proposed Opryland Park. Mike was a close confidant and would be sorely missed. We went through three vice presidents of marketing over a four-year period at SeaWorld and suffered through several years of stormy relationships before Jan Schultz came in and filled Mike's shoes.

**Kent Burgess** and **Dave Powell** ran the guts of our parks and showed their worth by delivering to the stockholders and myself the world's #1 marine park. In my humble opinion, fate could not have delivered two better men than Kent and Dave to propel us to world attention. (Both men are discussed in more detail within the SeaWorld chapters earlier in this book).

**Dave DeMotte**, a fraternity brother from UCLA, labored constantly during our early years developing budgets, advising me when they were off, and dealing with the directors, banks and insurance companies. He was indispensable. We remained an aggressive and competent team into the early 70's. After Magic Mountain, which he had fully endorsed and even suggested as a way for SeaWorld to become more profitable, our relationship began to go south.

According to Milt Shedd, the country was going to the dogs. Tourism was off everywhere and Shedd saw the opportunity to split two men who had made him rich. Foolishly I tolerated Shedd's meddling with Dave and the board thinking they knew Shedd well enough to see through his maneuvering. I was conceited enough to believe I was indispensable to the company's growth and the direction it should take.

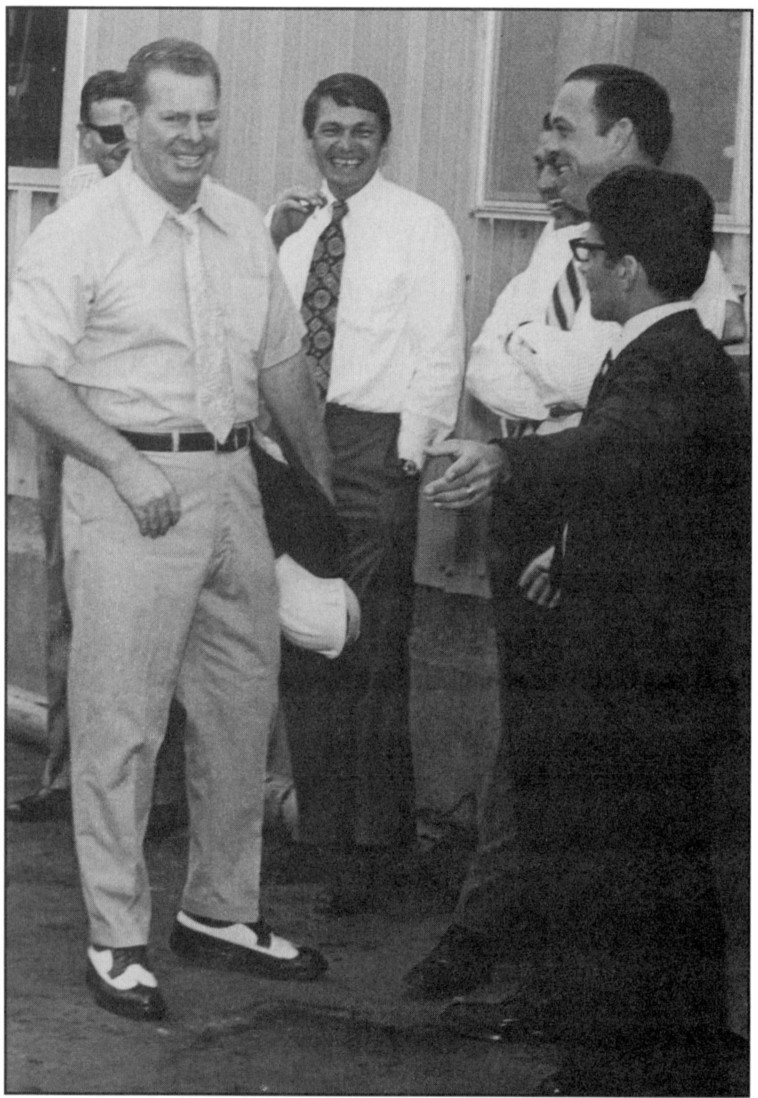

*The boys banter during a break at SeaWorld San Diego. From left, are Jim Eddy, George Millay, Mike Demetrios, Jan Schultz, and Carlo Mosca.*

### *Comparing the Accountants*

During my business career I have surrounded myself with two competent accounting administrators, Dave DeMotte and John Shawen of Wet'n Wild. People ask me who was better. DeMotte was smarter than Shawen, his mind quick and nimble and he had a good memory. Shawen was better organized, tough-minded and he was his own man. He had his ways and nobody was going to change him unless they could prove him wrong. DeMotte and Shawen had one thing in common, they were never satisfied with profits, like most accountants, and their solution was to tighten belts and cut overhead. That's fine but you don't grow a company that way, you regress.

One man who led with a steady, well-organized hand was **Lee Roberts.** Originally our food and beverage manager at SeaWorld, he was thrown into the job as operations director after another poor devil failed. Lee was organized and constant. He brought people into his department like **Bob Gault** and **John Baltes,** both who would be general managers later in their theme park careers. He slowly but surely brought organization and systems to the structure.

Lee (Roberts) and I hired **John Rognlie,** our first professional superintendent of maintenance. For the first time at the park, Rognlie brought focus and direction to a dazed maintenance department plagued with numerous glitches in our state-of-the-art water system. Roberts really never wanted the responsibility and after a few years went back to food and beverage but he was always a man you could count on.

### *Others During the Early Years*

So many others contributed to our early success. It was more than 40 years ago and the memory fades, but a few still are indelibly imprinted on my memory. **Phil Roberts** was announcer and show manager, a real trooper if there ever was one. Phil could take a lousy show and with his exuberance and passion send the audience on their way praising a second-class performance.

**Fred Lowe** was an ex-Marineland merchandise manager. He was invaluable setting up merchandise operations that eventually became worldwide and also guiding us on what Marineland had done under similar circumstances. His commentary on the staff was insightful and accurate.

Two go-getters on our sales staff deserve accolades: **Jay Wilson** and **Judy Byrom**, the core of our early sales staff. They set records month after month. With different styles they filled the park with school groups, church groups, and international travelers. To this day I have not seen the likes of them, considering they started from scratch and created new programs and a great sales department from the ground up.

**What's the Porpoise?**
*The first SeaWorld internal newsletter came out shortly after the park opened in 1964. It was called SeaWords and called itself, "A paragon of publications published periodically on pulpy paper by the personable people at SeaWorld for our personnel's (and porpoises) perusal."*

**Dr. Dave Kenney** was our first veterinarian. He was a smart, self-confidant, and fast-talking kid and while working under Burgess' direction he soon proved invaluable. With better health, the quality of animal behaviors in our shows tripled. He was a saleable commodity, good-looking and well spoken. He was soon given the job as company spokesperson on animal matters. Dave was the first person that we know of, to capture a gray whale. He was instrumental in engineering the Shamu purchase and transport to San Diego in 1965, as well as the first transcontinental flight of an entire collection of park animals, including Shamu, to SeaWorld Ohio.

***The Growth Years***

In 1967, we opened the Atlantis restaurant at SeaWorld San Diego, and the connecting Von Roll sky ride to the park. More than $2 million was spent and fortunately all went together without too many major problems. However, I began to realize that our contemplated growth needed more attention, skill, and organization than anyone currently on board could bring to the table and I began looking for a development director. John Buchanan knew the perfect person for us, and recommended **Ron Harper.**

I called him and we met in late 1967 at the Atlantis. I described our setup as it regarded the development and construction at SeaWorld and told him we needed a fulltime development director. I made an offer on the spot. He called the next day and said OK but he wanted $2,500 more, I accepted and he came to work. The rest is history. He brought a flock of competent architects and engineers to the fold.

Most notably, **George Walsh,** designer of SeaWorld Ohio, SeaWorld Florida, and Wet'n Wilds in Florida, Texas, and Las Vegas. Ron first built the sky tower and then the first big Shamu Stadium, both in San Diego. He then headed up the

SeaWorld Ohio and SeaWorld Florida projects. In late 1974 he left SeaWorld to go out on his own but came back and helped build Wet'n Wild Florida and Wet'n Wild Las Vegas.

Demotte's right hand lady, **Cherry Dimeff,** played a key role in keeping everyone on budget and handling all personnel chores. She probably worked for the company longer than anyone. She was always cheerful and always efficient, as was **Levita Ott,** our merchandise manager. She kept that department on an even keel for decades.

With a couple of in-park improvements under his belt, Harper hired **Farris Wankier,** a talented architect who had worked for Moffatt and Nichol and had worked on the SeaWorld project earlier. Harper was headed to Ohio and knew Farris could do the job for us in San Diego. When Harper left Sea World in 1974 his logical replacement as head of the five-man development staff was Farris Wankier.

Our first marketing director at Magic Mountain was a total disaster and a couple of months after he came aboard we fired him. I hired **Jan Schultz** to take over and he proved to be exactly what we needed. He studied the market, brought in a competent PR and sales staff and got ready for the big time in competition with Knott's Berry Farm, Disneyland and Marineland. After we sold our Magic Mountain equity to Newhall, Jan became marketing director at SeaWorld. Later, he became president of SeaWorld San Diego, under HBJ ownership.

If ever a person lobbied for a job it was **George Becker.** In late 1969 he began pestering me incessantly for a job in marketing. George came highly recommended by my good friend, Clint McKinnon, an ex-congressman and a San Diego newspaper publisher. I finally hired him as assistant director of marketing in San Diego and as part of his duties, Becker was given the responsibility of monitoring and expanding sales and marketing activities in Ohio. Becker became general manager of SeaWorld Ohio in a year after being hired.

**Gil Rigdon,** an ex-Busch Gardens official, ran SeaWorld Ohio the first year. Rigdon was quite the character, likeable and affable, he was popular with all the SeaWorld executives and the instant success of the SeaWorld Ohio park gave him credibility despite his eccentricities. I began receiving alarms from Ohio managers about Gil's antics.

I let Rigdon go following our first season and replaced

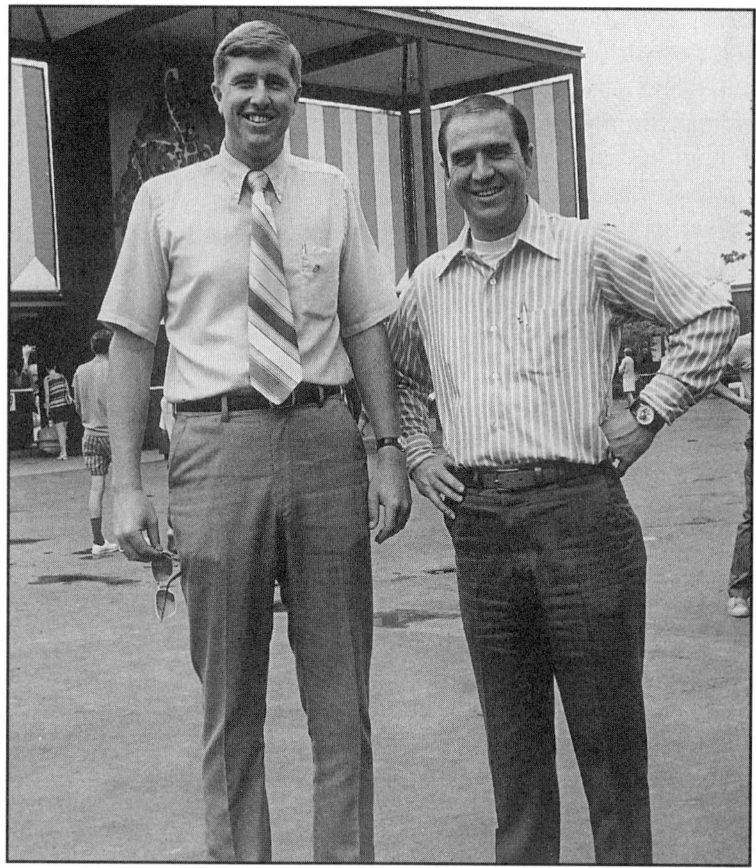

*Bob Gault, left, and Ron Harper take a break at SeaWorld Ohio, July 1971.*

him with George Becker and George never looked back. In 1971, 1972, and 1973, George produced record numbers in Ohio and represented the company in fine fashion. His Ohio organization grew and produced a number of people who would go on to success at SeaWorld and other entertainment companies in the following years.

### *Loyalty Over Brains*

SeaWorld San Diego was indeed fortunate to have been served by many smart and aggressive young men in its formative years. "Loyalty over brains" was their code and maintaining and supporting a safe, orderly park was their sole goal. They worked hard and took the discipline imposed on them for the first time in their lives in a jovial fashion and pressed on. **John Martin, Chris Conyers, Tim Brown, Terry Hanks, John Baltes** and **John Tighe** were but a few pieces of the glue that held the park together during the 1964 - 1968 years.

The standout in this group was Bob Gault. He became operations director, co-engineered the Shamu moves and became Ohio's first director of operations, where in the first year he had to handle 20,000 guests a day, unheard of at the time for a marine park. Several years later, Gault became general manager of SeaWorld Florida and upon the park's acquisition by Anheuser-Busch, Bob moved on to corporate headquarters in St. Louis. Less than a year later, he joined the Universal group of parks, and later became the primary impetus behind Universal Studios Japan. He is now head of the Universal Orlando complex.

During 1968, it became apparent that the San Diego park was having trouble in two vital departments, training and production. Kent Burgess and **Don McQuarry,** his capable replacement, both had resigned and the shows were beginning to appear lackluster. The two departments reported to operations on a day-to-day basis and I began to realize they were being stifled. I sensed an atmosphere of gloom engulfing fish and training, a classic trait of operations people.

One day a gent by the name of **John Campbell** called. He told me George Whitney had told him to call me. I then called Whitney and found out about Campbell. He had just left ABC in a huff and was looking for a job.

Campbell came in and completely mesmerized this small town beach boy. Like most TV executives he was physically impressive, a redhead which did him no harm and he was a storyteller par excellence.

His visit started me thinking. I wasn't happy with the shows and more and more of my attention was being drawn to Ohio and Magic Mountain. We dared not endanger the San Diego park, the goose that was laying the golden egg. We hired John Campbell as VP productions in charge of all shows, trainers, announcers, sound and lighting. It turned out to be a very wise move.

He brought so many qualities that were lacking in the SeaWorld arsenal of expertise. His knowledge and advice of media buying produced savings that more than paid his way annually. His contacts vastly increased the talent available to us, and he knew how to handle people, including me. He brought a breath of fresh air and work ethic to a stagnating department and company. John spent nearly three years working at SeaWorld and left abruptly in late 1972 to return to ABC to run their Silver Springs and Weeki Wachee parks in Florida. In 1975, John Campbell and I got back together and under the ABC umbrella ran Seven Seas marine park in Arlington, Texas.

John Campbell hired **Larry Sands**, a talented Hollywood TV producer. Sands captained the production of our Sparkletts' Water Fantasy Show and he produced the big "Shamu Goes Hollywood" shows in San Diego and Ohio. With his contacts, he was able to bring an illustrious group of Hollywood stars to the gala opening of these shows that paid homage to Shamu - the World's Biggest Showman.

- CHAPTER 54 -

# The Wet'n Wild Pioneering All-Stars

As any good leader does, George gives a great deal of credit for his success to those who worked for him. Many have already been listed, but here are bits and pieces about some of the more positive and more influential characters that worked for him throughout the Wet'n Wild years.

***In George's Own Words:***

Designing, building and operating the Wet'n Wild parks was a cakewalk compared to SeaWorld's opening years. At SeaWorld, we were pioneers. By the time we started building waterparks, we were all professionals and most of us had years of hands-on experience in the industry.

**John Shawen** heads the list of the most influential people who worked for me during the Wet'n Wild years. **John Seeker**, formally of SeaWorld and Seven Seas headed up all marketing and sales efforts and is a true waterpark marketing pioneer. **Fred Brooks**, a former Disney and then Circus World operations manager got us open and running as a safe, clean park with a courteous and well-trained staff.

**Gary Daning**, a former Silver Springs and Seven Seas operations and food and beverage manager was our second general manager. Shawen acted as our first GM from 1977-80. During my recovery from cancer in 1979 and 1980 Shawen, Seeker and Daning held down the fort and produced considerable profit for the shareholders in those years.

As I recovered from my operation with one-half a head and 10% less brains, we started in earnest to expand the Florida park. Gary Daning headed up the creation of the Arlington, Texas venture with **Rick Faber** and then moved on to Las Vegas where he molded that park into a first class operation.

Wet'n Wild®

***Best Manager of them All***

Daning is the best "all-around" waterpark manager in this business. Two other waterpark pioneers, Pat Cartwright, now retired, and Chip Cleary of Long Island's Splish Splash come close.

Maintenance in a water park is centered on safety and preservation of expensive filtration and entertainment equipment. **John Rognlie** brought vast experience and drive to our Florida park and built a top quality department, just like he had done at SeaWorld. From Seven Seas came **Bob Wilke.** With pride and bailing wire he diligently worked at both Wet'n Wild Florida and then Wet'n Wild Arlington. Rognlie and Wilke both had the attitude that we'll get it done now!

When **Joel Manheim** was hired, our food problems were solved. We had better quality along with sharply reduced food and labor costs. His attitude and leadership created an environment where there was almost no employee turnover and he was a master in keeping his staff motivated and happy.

Rick Faber came on board as director of development and brought along a wealth of experience, know-how and organizational skills to the Wet'n Wild organization. He worked on many projects, such as the Bonsai Boggan, the Black Hole, The Corkscrew and the Blue Niagara.

In the 1980s we sent Rick to Texas to head up design and construction of the Arlington park. **Butch Von Weller** of Orlando was our contractor and between those two, the project opened in 1983 with very few of the usual construction catastrophes. Rick then returned to Florida as GM and Daning went to Texas as GM. They both performed with vigor, inspiration and innovation.

I was never a big fan of architects. It's their attitude and demeanor, but there have been exceptions. **Ben Southland** was a giant. He had the vision and flare to create an ambiance in our first SeaWorld that carried us through our rough, formative years. In other words, the joint looked great even if the shows and exhibits were mediocre in the beginning.

The modest and under-publicized **George Walsh** designed the SeaWorld parks in Ohio and Florida, and the Wet'n Wild parks in Florida, Arlington and Las Vegas. He certainly ranks high on my list of competent, patient and practical designers. He deserves belated and heartfelt thanks from the entire water park industry. He was more than just one of the pioneers in designing this industry. He was the first.

The late **Bill Dunn** deserves mention because he was a real engineering pioneer. He designed many of the mechanical engineering features of Wet'n Wild attractions, including the first Lazy River, the first Willy-Willy, the Bomb Bay and the Hydra-fighter. Dunn also served SeaWorld and the San Diego Zoo for decades. He is a real unsung pathfinder of this industry.

After his completion of the Las Vegas Project and many in-park improvements throughout the system, **Billy Getz** proved to be a real and valued asset to my team. He did not have Faber's knowledge of the industry but Getz was far the better man at handling consultants and contractors. Pat, my son, put Getz in charge of designing and administering all construction contracts in the Brazilian and Mexican operations. With **Mark Hatchel**, his design and architectural control manager, they easily guided the Brazilian partners in building some of the worlds most beautiful and functional water parks. Hatchel's work in Rio and Sao Paulo is a hallmark standard that will be copied for years to come.

In 1993, Getz hired another talented designer who had been the chief designer of SeaWorld San Antonio design, **Billy Watts**. Getz instructed Watts to design the Salvador Brazil park, a difficult and daunting task because of the poor configuration and hilly site condition. Nevertheless the park had charm and an excitement about it and Pat and Getz were proud to put the Wet'n Wild name on it. Watts also designed the exciting and innovative Wet'n Wild Cancun.

Our south of the border team of **Pat Millay,** Getz, Hatchel, and Watts proved their worth in all areas - building four of the most beautiful and guest-pleasing waterparks anywhere.

### *Financial Help Given*

As we exploded from coast to coast, my staunch alter-ego, John Shawen, who was also a stockholder and director of Wet'n Wild, needed help and got it from two fine industry-wise accountants, **Dave Milhausen** and **Mike Black**. Milhausen was an enigma to me. He was quick and alert but somewhat flashy and extroverted as accountants go. I used Dave as an accounting checkmate to Shawen from time to time.

In 1993 Mike Black ascended to the top spot as Florida GM. I felt comfortable in making that decision because we were ably staffed with two excellent operations directors, **Ron Satula** and **Pat Finnegan**. Satula, a tough and well organized by-the-book leader, later spent four years in Brazil heading up, staffing and managing the Sao Paulo park and monitoring the parks in Rio and Salvador.

### *The Ladies of Wet'n Wild*

Where are the women? Contrary to what many still believe, I entrusted much during my career to women. The guts of all our marketing in Florida consisted of the wily, aggressive, eye for an eye, tooth for a tooth, sometimes sinister and vindictive efforts of two remarkable and unashamedly aggressive females, **Gail Kohler** and **Linda Orgara**, my marketing and sales ladies.

Gail was always laughing and smiling, but always had an eye on the sale. Linda was reserved and had a teacher's demeanor, but underneath it all, was tough and suspicious. Words cannot describe how these two operated and prospered in the wild, cut-throat, competitive atmosphere created by the existence of so many competing attractions in a 10 square mile area.

With some help from John Seeker and I, they put little Wet'n Wild right up there with the big boys and kept us up there. Of course, I loved every little victory especially if it was at SeaWorld's expense. Gail and Linda belong in the pantheon of "lovable and successful marketing shrews."

### *Going to the Big D*

One day in 1985, I got word that **Walt Hawrylak**, the GM of SeaWorld Florida was not happy. He had been the chief numbers guy at SeaWorld Ohio and had been transferred to Florida by Bob Hillebrecht, the Harcourt Brace Jovanovich big shot. I called Walt, we chatted, we negotiated, and Walt became GM of Wet'n Wild Arlington. He was smart, organized, and fair and always did the work of two managers.

In late 1988, **Bob Gallagher**, one of our rising stars, had been moved to Garland, Texas, to run that park, reporting to Walt Hawrylak. Shawen needed help in the main office in Arlington and we both decided to promote Hawrylak to senior vice president administration, an office job, and move Gallagher into the GM spot for both Texas parks.

### *Don't Under-Estimate Seeker*

The marketing staff soon recognized that when you worked for John Seeker you had to work hard and when you did, you had his complete loyalty in times of crises. Two men who know this well are **Bill Monty** and **Joe Gibbons**. Monty, a scholarly Vietnam Vet, was one of the most well read, best prepared sales and marketing managers with whom I have ever had the pleasure of working. He came to us from the Silver Dollar City organization and we made him our GM in Garland.

We prospered during our first season in Garland and we added 75,000 to 85,000 in attendance but it never climbed to what we wanted or expected. I blamed Monty. Seeker, with Shawen's support took Monty's side saying we weren't reading the market correctly and that the newly built City of Garland wave pool with basketball, volleyball and softball courts, and picnic areas was the real culprit.

Their $4.95 front gate against our $12 was hurting us. I wasn't convinced and wanted to fire Monty. Somehow Seeker convinced me to make Monty director of marketing for all Texas parks and let an operations man be the caretaker of the Garland park.

### *Seeker Won One Occasionally*

It was a good move and Seeker to this day wallows in telling how he saved Monty and the Texas operations by his shrewd personal manipulation. Monty proved to be a well-organized and motivating director of marketing. Always yearning for the scholarly life, he left us in the mid-90's to pursue a career in teaching at prestigious Trinity Prep in Dallas.

I always saw Billy Getz as the Wet'n Wild version of the Ron Harper of SeaWorld. He was the superintendent of the mechanical construction crew that built Wet'n Wild Arlington, which was no small task. That's where he came to our attention. Conscientious and knowledgeable, we hired him to become corporate VP of development. Las Vegas was his baby and teaming up with the obsequious Ron Harper and George Walsh produced the most beautiful 15-acre park in the world.

- CHAPTER 55 -

# The Secretarial All-Stars

*"Go ye guests of SeaWorld and Wet'n Wild to IAAPA and tell; that we have served George nobly and will not tell."*

**In George's Own Words:**

So might go the shibboleth of the dozen or so poor wretched souls who have had the misfortune of being my secretaries over the years. They were fired on Christmas Eve, made to lie, remember where and if Red filed a lost document, worked Saturdays for no money, spent sleepless nights trying to memorize excuses of all sorts for my shortcomings and eccentricities. They would unfold their sad predicament to Anne from time to time but usually suffered in silence.

- DeEtta Sharp, SeaWorld stalwart in the 1960s, early 1970s
- Joy Firby, great sales and marketing secretary
- Carole Angiolette, served Harper, Campbell and Millay adroitly
- Suzy Johnson, post-SeaWorld buffer
- Lee Land, Seven Seas secretary
- Carolyn Stewart, Wet'n Wild stalwart of the 1980s and 1990s
- Wendy Soos, Great post-Wet'n Wild aid in Texas
- Beverly Clark, Post-Wet'n Wild helper
- Jeri Jean, present secretary who has labored long and hard on this book, for which I will buy her and her boyfriend dinner.

Any success or credit or accomplishment I had during the last 40 years has to be shared by these gallant, beautiful and talented ladies who truly epitomize the virtue of patience.

The two gals who took the brunt of those tumultuous years, DeEtta Sharp at SeaWorld and Carolyn Stewart at Wet'n Wild, who coincidentally were both southern ladies, were indispensable. They served as ambassadors, umpires, prefects of discipline and housemothers to the entire organization.

I couldn't begin to count how many times I heard associates say "George doesn't need a secretary, he needs a wet nurse, governess, and a curator all in one." Carolyn in Texas used to say, "George Millay is the most absent minded, disorganized man I have ever met."

We managed to get a great deal done in a few short years. My sincere appreciation and admiration goes out to all of these wonderful women.

# Index